INSPIRATION AND INERRANCY:
GOD HAS SPOKEN

INSPIRATION AND INERRANCY:

GOD
HAS SPOKEN

ISBN: 0–89957–360–6

Unless otherwise noted, Scripture quotations are from the NEW AMERICAN STANDARD BIBLE, © 1960, 1962, 1963, 1968, 1971, 1972, 1973, 1975, 1977, by the Lockman Foundation. Used by permission. (www.Lockman.org)

Jacket Design by Market Street Design, Chattanooga, TN
Interior Design and Typesetting by Warren Baker
Edited and Proofread by Warren Baker, Agnes Lawless, and Patrick Belville

Printed in the United States of America
08 07 06 05 04 03 –P– 7 6 5 4 3 2 1

*To a younger generation moving into the twenty-first century
to remind them that this war still rages
and could grow even stronger under the weight of confusion
over the necessity of strong, evangelical theological studies.
If the church of Jesus Christ downplays the importance of the Word of God
as the basis for all we believe as Christians,
spiritual chaos and darkness will enshroud our congregations.*

Preface

When I set out to be a minister of the gospel, I became intrigued with the controversial theological issue of the inspiration and inerrancy of the Word of God. This is not to say that I was ever tempted to deny these great doctrinal truths; however, I simply wanted to know all that the Scriptures record as to how they came into being. From my early years as a fledgling student, I studied intently the verses that speak both directly and indirectly on these subjects.

My first master's thesis was on inerrancy and its implications in the formation of our Bible. After seminary I translated both Old and New Testament verses on inspiration and became more convinced that the original writings of the Scriptures are the very words of God and are indeed without error.

Early in my education, I acquired a working knowledge of Hebrew and Greek, the languages in which the Scriptures were originally written. They afforded me the opportunity to sense the heart and mind of God in the great hallmark verses that related to these issues. For example, from the Greek text, 1 Peter 1:10–11 might read this way, "The prophets who prophesied of the grace that was in reserve for you, searched out and examined, seeking to know what period or time the Spirit from Christ within them was indicating as He before confirmed the sufferings of Christ and the glories after them [that would follow]."

The first book I read on the subject of inspiration was Edward J. Young's classic, *Thy Word Is Truth* (Eerdmans). With firm conviction, Young wrote, "The Bible is of the utmost importance, for as much as men of the twentieth century seem to dislike the fact, the Bible has been, all along, their teacher."[1]

The next book I studied was *The Inspiration of the Holy Scriptures* (Moody) written by the great scholar Louis Gaussen. With a detailed understanding of the issues involved, Gaussen wrote that the Word of

God establishes "that the Scripture is from God, that the Scripture is throughout from God, and that the Scripture throughout is entirely from God."[2]

It was not simply the writings of great Christian scholars that moved me; the Bible itself touched my heart and soul. Scripture fascinated me with its testimony of God, His mind, and His will. In Genesis and other books, He is marvelously presented as the Author of the universe and all that it contains. The God of Scripture is pictured not simply as a great force but the Lord who loves His creatures and wishes to communicate with them.

In the Word of God, the reader is confronted with the providence of God—His ways of tender mercies but also His execution of fair judgment. Accuracy and detail flood the pages of Scripture. Half of all Bible prophecies already have come to pass just as they were uttered from the mouths of the prophets.

I fell in love with God's message that seemed to speak only to me. From this marvelous Word, I am continually learning to more and more love Him who shares His care with me and tells me of the future glory I will someday experience with Him in heaven.

Mal Couch
General Editor

Contributors

Paul Benware, Th.M., Th.D., author and professor of theology, Philadelphia Biblical University.

Charles Clough, Th.M., Bible teacher, U.S. Army meteorologist. He lives in Bel Air, Maryland.

Mal Couch, Th.M., Ph.D., Th.D., D.D., Author, founder and president of Tyndale Theological Seminary and founder and executive editor of the Conservative Theological Society, Fort Worth, Texas.

Harold D. Foos, Th.M., Th.D., former professor of Bible and theology and chairman of the Department of Theology at Moody Bible Institute, Chicago, Illinois (retired).

Eugene Merrill, Ph.D., M.Phil., Ph.D., professor of Old Testament, Dallas Theological Seminary, Dallas, Texas.

Mike Stallard, S.T.M., Ph.D., director of the doctoral program at Baptist Bible College and Seminary, Clarks Summit, Pennsylvania.

Table of Contents

Foreword

From the beginning of the church, Christians always have believed that the Bible is the Word of God. They followed prominent orthodox Jewish rabbis in proclaiming that the Old Testament Scriptures came from the heart and mind of Jehovah. But the church also realized that the New Testament claimed the same inspiration, authenticity, and accuracy as the older testament. For each generation, the objective scrutiny of the entire Bible has confirmed the truth that its origins were divine.

Though penned by human authors and bearing the stamp of their writing styles, the Scriptures were nevertheless the work of the Holy Spirit. This conception of coauthorship shows the Spirit's superintendence in both the recorded thoughts and words of each book produced. The result is that "among other things, that entire truthfulness [is assured] which is everywhere presupposed in and asserted for Scripture by the Biblical writers."[1]

Our goal here is to set forth the biblical doctrines that need to be restated and reemphasized to a new generation of Christians who are often confronted about their faith in the workplace or on the college campus. This work is also meant to faithfully represent what the Bible clearly tells us about *how* the God of the universe has revealed Himself to a sinful race.

For those desiring to dig deeper into the critical issues regarding the composition of our Bible, many outstanding evangelical and conservative books give solid technical answers to puzzling and complicated questions. Listed below are a few works that have helped us understand both the complexity and clarity of the Bible.

Archer, Gleason L. *A Survey of Old Testament Introduction*. Chicago: Moody, 1994.

Bruce, F. F. *The Canon of Scripture*. Downers Grove, Ill.: InterVarsity, 1988.

Gaussen, Louis. *The Inspiration of the Holy Scriptures*. Chicago: Moody, n.d.

Geisler, Norman L. and William E. Nix. *A General Introduction to the Bible*. Chicago: Moody, 1971.

Harrison, Everett F. *Introduction to the New Testament*. Grand Rapids: Eerdmans, 1974.

McDowell, Josh. *The New Evidence That Demands A Verdict*. Nashville: Thomas Nelson, 1999.

Metzger, Bruce M. *The Text of the New Testament*. New York: Oxford University Press, 1992.

Miller, H. S. *General Biblical Introduction*. Houghton, N.Y.: Word-Bearer, 1960.

Pache, René. *The Inspiration and Authority of Scripture*. Chicago: Moody, 1969.

Thiessen, Henry C. *Introduction to the New Testament*. Grand Rapids: Eerdmans, 1958.

Thomas, Robert L. and F. David Farnell. *The Jesus Crisis*. Grand Rapids: Kregel, 1998.

Unger, Merrill F. *Introductory Guide to the Old Testament*. Grand Rapids: Zondervan, 1981.

Warfield, B. B. *The Inspiration and Authority of the Bible*. Philadelphia: Presbyterian and Reformed, 1948.

Young, Edward J. *Thy Word Is Truth*. Grand Rapids: Eerdmans, 1960.

Part One

THE INSPIRATION
OF SCRIPTURE

Chapter One

The Blessed Book

The Bible is the most remarkable book ever written. It is also one of the most well-known and popular pieces of literature ever produced. It has spawned other writings from the production of theologies and commentaries to literary history and poetry. It can safely be said that the Scriptures became the central theme that dominates the story of Western civilization. Though one wishes that the Bible had more influence over the hearts of humankind and the moral course of nations, still it has had a greater spiritual impact on a larger number of people on earth than any other book in history. Josh McDowell has compiled some fascinating trivia information about the makeup and development of the Bible.[1]

Bible Facts

- *The Bible was written:*
  Over a fifteen-hundred-year period.
  By more than forty authors from every walk of life: kings, military leaders, peasants, philosophers, fishermen, tax collectors, poets, musicians, statesmen, scholars, and shepherds.
  In different places: wilderness, dungeon, hillside, inside prison walls, while traveling, exiled on an island.
  On three continents: Asia, Africa, and Europe.
  In three languages: Hebrew, Aramaic (portions of Jeremiah, Daniel, and Ezra), and Greek.
  On stone, on a wall, parchment, and animal skins.
  In a variety of literary styles:
    Allegory
    Autobiography
    Biography

1

Didactic treatise

Historical narrative

Law

Memoirs

Parable

Personal letters

Poetry

Prophecy

Romance

Song

- The Bible was one of the first major books ever translated, around 250 B.C., from Hebrew to Greek.
- It has been translated into more than 2,200 languages.
- In all translations, it has touched more than 90 percent of the world's population.
- The Bible has been rejected and criticized by kings, peasants, cults, other religions, fanatics, and scholars; yet it remains one of the most trusted and reliable books ever penned.
- About 40 percent of the Bible is prophecy.
- Around 300 of its prophecies were fulfilled through the person of Jesus Christ.
- Past fulfilled predictions and future prophecies that will take place in time and history make the Bible one of the most unique religious books ever written.
- Some of the works of Shakespeare are far more uncertain and corrupt than the New Testament texts.
- In its translation activity, no other book in history compares with the Bible.

What Others Say About the Bible

Nothing has spoken so clearly and forcefully to the problem of "man according to God" as the Bible. – *Puritan William Ames*

Faith, as it points to the thing to be believed, must finally depend on the authority of God or divine revelation. – *William Ames*

I have found in the Bible words for my inmost thoughts, songs for my joy, utterance for my hidden griefs, and pleadings for my shame and feebleness. – *English poet Samuel Taylor*

The textual critic [who tries to destroy] the New Testament, is embarrassed by the wealth of his [manuscript] material. – *Princeton Bible professor Bruce Metzger*

The ancient Jews preserved their ancient writings of the Old Testament like no other manuscript has ever been preserved. – *Bernard Ramm*

Despite attacks upon it, the Bible is still loved by millions, read by millions, and studied by millions. – *Bernard Ramm*

The hammers of infidels have been pecking away at the Bible for ages, but the hammers are worn out, and the anvil of the Word still endures. – *H. L. Hastings*

Other books claim divine inspiration. But none of those books contain predictive prophecy. – *Norman L. Geisler and William E. Nix*

The Bible is not such a book a man would write if he could or could write if he would. – *Lewis S. Chafer*

The Bible as a book focuses on reality, not fantasy. It presents the good and bad, the right and wrong, the best and worst, the hope and despair, the joy and pain of life. – *Josh McDowell*

Western literature has been more influenced by the Bible than any other book. – *Literary critic Northrop Frye*

This Jesus of Nazareth, without money and arms, conquered more millions than Alexander, Caesar, Mohammed, and Napoleon. – *Historian Philip Schaff*

Is it possible that a book [such as the Bible], at once so simple and sublime, should be merely the work of man? – Philosopher *Jean Jacques Rousseau*

The unity and harmony of the book, written during the space of more than 1,500 years, . . . are remarkable, Law, history, poetry, prophecy, doctrine, worship, and practical exhortations, with the character, illustrations, and arguments which they contain all unite in making the story of Redemption the most fascinating and up-to-date story of all literature. – *H. S. Miller*

God, the Maker of the world, is manifested to us in Scripture, and His true character expounded, so as to save us from wandering up and down, as in a labyrinth, in search of some doubtful deity. – *John Calvin*

The human mind, though often brilliant in what it can achieve, suffers limitations and darkening. Human experiences, even religious ones, lack reliability as sources of the true knowledge of God unless they conform to the Word of God. – *Charles C. Ryrie*

FOR DISCUSSION

1. In what languages were the Scriptures originally written?
2. From this brief introductory chapter, what impressed you the most about the nature of the Word of God?

For Further Study

Apologetics

McDowell, Josh. *The New Evidence That Demands a Verdict*. Nashville: Thomas Nelson, 1999.

Chapter Two

God Has Spoken

*T*he Old and New Testaments together form a vital and insepa-
rable collection of writings that stand unique in our world.
Without question, the entire Bible is the book of books, the
incomparable and inestimable singular writing. Abraham Lincoln called
the Bible "the best gift God has given to man."

Even though the Bible is a best-seller, it is the most forgotten piece
of literature in existence. Many Christians own multiple Bibles but generally do not read them with contemplative thoughtfulness. This book
also has faced hatred, fire, and sword and yet has come through as a
lighted beacon for lost humanity. The Scriptures have endured rational
criticism, skepticism, and doubt, while still standing as the greatest revelation of all religions.

False assumptions and unwarranted philosophical attacks have tried
to discredit the Bible's message but to no avail. Time and historical
scrutiny have shown that it is of divine origin and illuminates those who
grope for spiritual truth. The ancient writings of Scripture are indispen-
sable in an age of rationalistic skepticism and New Age mysticism.

The thirty-nine books of the Old Testament and the twenty-seven
books of the New Testament give us a divine library of sixty-six books
forged into one book. Though these sixty-six books are separate volumes,
they constitute a message that flows from eternity past into the future.
Each book has a unity, a distinctive purpose, and a theme contributing
to the whole. Thus, the Word of God is incomparable. It is God revealing Himself to His ancient people and to new generations as well.

Though the Bible is God's own book, the human writers or hagiog-
raphers were guided and wrote as the Holy Spirit gave His divine message. The result is a divine book in its full and infallible accuracy.

The Word of God and History

The Bible is not a mystical book that gives fictional fancy with little or no historical credence. The Scriptures were penned as a product of historic moments of the past. Critics often call the Bible *holy history*, meaning that it is not part of past real events. Instead, they say, it is the mythical cogitations of wide-eyed mystics. But such criticism will not stand the test. Though a divine book and of spiritual origin, it is evident that the events described were part of the historic drama of ages past.

The sacred penmen were prophets in the real sense, receiving the divine Word immediately and then speaking directly to the people before them. The human authors used commanding expressions such as, "Thus says the LORD" (Ex. 4:22), and "Hear the word of the LORD" (Isa. 1:10). God commanded them to write down their oracles (Ex. 17:14; 24:4, 7; Jer. 30:1–2). The evidence shows that their literary accomplishments were accepted as the Word of God. Thus, multitudes have become obedient and faithful to its message.

The course of human history has been dramatically and providentially directed by the sovereign God. Part of the message of the Bible is that the eternal God is indeed the Author of that history. He revealed His divine activities in the pages of Scripture. The Bible tells us how He as the Author has marked out the great chapters of world events. Paul L. Maier writes:

> Of all religious beliefs in the world, past or present, none have more thoroughly based themselves on history than Judaism and Christianity. The divine-human encounter in the biblical faiths always involves claims about *real* people, living in *real* places, who acted in *real* events of the past, many of which are also cited in secular ancient history. Both testaments of the Bible use the past tense of narrative prose—history's medium—more than any other form of language. . . . *Every* religious system before or since Judaism and Christianity has avoided any significant interaction with history and instead has asked its followers to believe, by sheer faith alone, the claimed revelations of its founder(s). This is true of the mythologies of yesterday and the cults of today.[1]

The Foretelling of Future Events

The Bible makes it clear that God controls the nations. They are like a "drop from a bucket" and "regarded as a speck of dust on the scales" (Isa.

40:15). It was the Lord Himself "who spread out the earth and its off-spring, who gives breath to the people on it and spirit to those who walk in it" (42:5). Someday He will establish "justice in the earth" (v. 4). He also is the Master of coming events. He declares, "Behold, the former things have come to pass, now I declare new things; before they spring forth I proclaim them to you" (v. 9).

Only the Bible tells us how history will end. With graphic illustrations the Book of Revelation reveals that the Lord Jesus will smite the nations with a sharp sword coming from His mouth, "and He will rule them with a rod of iron" (Rev. 19:15). Those who trust the Lord Jesus Christ as Savior will experience a glorious eternal future in the new heaven and new earth. In the final chapters of the Book of Revelation, Jesus says about the approaching eternal state, "Behold, I am making all things new" (21:5), and "I will give to the one who thirsts from the spring of the water of life without cost" (v. 6).

The Revelation of a Savior

In both Old and New Testaments, the Scriptures reveal that people are in deep trouble and can only be delivered from judgment and eternal separation from God by the death of the Messiah, the Lord Jesus Christ. The Book of Isaiah graphically prophesied of the Messiah being pierced and scourged (Isa. 53:5) because people are like wayward sheep (v. 6). The Lord would "cause the iniquity of us all to fall on Him [the Messiah]" (v. 6). The New Testament tells us of the fulfillment of His coming and how He would be that offering for sins.

The four Gospels describe the birth, life, death, and resurrection of Jesus the Prophet. As He was ministering to His own Jewish people, He predicted His return to heaven (John 16:28). Acts 1 describes His ascension into heaven and His return back to God the Father (v. 11). The rest of the New Testament shares with its readers that there is no salvation in anyone except the Lord Jesus Christ. To become righteous before God, we must place our faith in Him, "for there is no distinction [between human beings]; for all have sinned and fall short of the glory of God" (Rom. 3:22–23).

No other book in the world gives such good news (the gospel) to sinful human beings. The writer of Hebrews put it succinctly when he wrote a challenging question:

How shall we escape if we neglect so great a salvation? After it was
at the first spoken through the Lord, it was confirmed to us by

those who heard, God also testifying with them, both by signs and
wonders and by various miracles. (Heb. 2:3–4)

The Revelation of a Plan

Only in the Bible is a reliable plan of history revealed. That plan has several facets to it, including a beginning and an ending for the nations of
the world. It tells of the creation of humankind, the entrance of sin into
the earthly realm, and the final judgments that will fall on the world.

Much about the purposes of God is revealed in what is called the
Abrahamic covenant found in Genesis 12:1–3 and many other verses
that follow. This covenant shows how God will bless the Jewish people
and grant mercy to the nations through Jesus, who is a descendent of
Abraham and King David. The master plan of Scripture also reveals a
final world apostasy and the rapture of the Church (1 Thess. 4:13–18).
It includes a description of a terrible period of worldwide tribulation,
the glorious return of Christ, and the millennial reign of Christ in
Jerusalem (Rev. 19:11—20:6). Sadly, those who reject Christ as the
Savior of the world will be cast into the eternal lake of fire (Rev.
20:14–15). The redeemed will enjoy eternity with the Lord Jesus
(22:1–5). Walvoord notes:

> The world is aflame with the raw passions of men ambitious for
> power and desperate to be freed from poverty and frustration. An
> ominous cloud hangs over the hearts of men and nations. . . .
> Whatever the future holds, it is going to be dramatically different
> than the past. In this dark picture only the Scriptures chart a sure
> course and give us an intelligent explanation of world-wide confu-
> sion as it exists today.[2]

Benware adds:

> The very words of Scripture are critical. Contrary to the view of
> some, God did not simply toss out an idea and have a human
> author develop the thought. The very words of all Scripture,
> including those prophetic portions, are significant and worthy of
> our time and attention.[3]

The Revelation of How to Live

Throughout the Bible, great words of correction and encouragement give
spiritual meaning for everyday living. However, it is important that read-

ers of Scripture trust *all* it is telling us. It would be a mistake to look at the Word of God only as an encyclopedia of morals. Morality comes to us from the character and nature of God Himself. And one of the most important purposes of the Bible is to show us who He is. Unless we place our trust in the God of Scripture, simply trying to live a good life is futile.

Many places in the Old Testament instruct us how we ought to live. Meditating on God's Word is central for daily conduct. For example, the psalmist wrote, "Your word is a lamp to my feet and a light to my path" (Ps. 119:105). Solomon wrote the Book of Proverbs so we could "know wisdom and instruction, [and] discern the sayings of understanding" (Prov. 1:2). But again, morality is not enough. Solomon added:

> Trust in the Lord with all your heart and do not lean on your own understanding. In all your ways acknowledge Him, and He will make your paths straight. Do not be wise in your own eyes; fear the Lord and turn away from evil (3:5–6).

In Ecclesiastes, Solomon continued, "The conclusion, when all has been heard, is: fear God and keep His commandments, because this applies to every person" (12:13). Just before His crucifixion, Jesus told His disciples, "If you keep My commandments, you will abide in My love" (John 15:10), and, "This is My commandment, that you love one another, just as I have loved you" (v. 12). At the end of the New Testament, we read the words of the aged apostle John: "Beloved, do not imitate what is evil, but what is good. The one who does good is of God; the one who does evil has not seen God" (3 John 11). Finally, the ancient church father John of Damascus wrote:

> To search the sacred Scripture is very good and most profitable for the soul. For "like a tree which is planted near the running waters," so does the soul watered by sacred Scripture also grow hearty and bear fruit in due season. This is the orthodox faith. It is adorned with its evergreen leaves, with actions pleasing to God.[4]

To learn of the God of the Bible is to attempt to live the words of the Bible!

FOR DISCUSSION

1. Is the Bible history, or is it some kind of "holy" history that has no relationship with actual historical happenings? Explain.

2. Why does Bible prophecy make the Scriptures unique?

3. List some important elements in the plan of history as revealed in the Bible.

4. For a believer in Jesus, in what way is simply being moral not sufficient for living the Christian life? What more is required?

For Further Study

History

Maier, Paul L. *In the Fullness of Time.* Grand Rapids: Kregel, 1997.

Prophecy

Benware, Paul N. *Understanding End Times Prophecy.* Chicago: Moody, 1995.

Walvoord, John F. *The Nations, Israel and the Church in Prophecy.* Grand Rapids: Zondervan, 1988.

Chapter Three

A Look at Important Terms

B efore going on, we want to define the terms that are important in this study. Because the Scriptures claim to be the Word
of God, believers must take its claims seriously. Personal and
eternal issues are at stake. We need to know what the Lord has said
about His revelations and the methods He used to communicate them.

Bibliology

The Greek word *biblos* means "book" or "scroll" and refers to all the
books of the *Bible*. The Greek word *logos* ("word") implies the study of
these books and the truths and doctrines within their pages. *Bibliology*
then is the science of arranging, comparing, and analyzing the historical
and linguistic data of the Scriptures. By examining what the Bible says
of itself, we conclude that:

> *A revelation is certain.* This we have in our wonderful Bible, which
> claims to be a revelation from God and whose claims are fully sub-
> stantiated by its miracles, its fulfilled prophecy, the propagation of
> Christianity, the fruits of Christianity, and the satisfaction it brings
> to the human heart the world over.[1]

Chafer adds:

> The words *The Bible* distinguish the supreme, incomparable Book.
> It does surpass all other books as to authority, antiquity, literature,
> and popularity, yet its peculiar supremacy is seen in the fact that it
> discloses the truth concerning the infinite God, infinite holiness,
> infinite sin, and infinite redemption.[2]

11

...tion ("to breathe within") implies that God by His divine Spirit has breathed into the writers of Scripture what He wished to communicate to human beings, as recorded in both our Old and New Testaments. Inspiration is a mysterious undertaking and divine causality that did not destroy the individual personalities and styles of the human authors. This directing of what was written gives us this holy book.

Second Timothy 3:16 tells us, "All Scripture is inspired by God." Here the Greek word is *theopneustos,* meaning "God-breathed."

Inerrancy

Feinberg writes:

> Inerrancy is the view that when all the facts become known, they will demonstrate that the Bible in its original autographs and correctly interpreted is entirely true and never false in all it affirms, whether that relates to doctrine or ethics or to the social, physical or life sciences.[3]

That the Bible is without error, or inerrant and infallible, follows the fact that it comes from God in the very words (*verbal*) and that the Scriptures are inspired in every part (*plenary*).

> Thus, in believing that the Bible is inspired and inerrant, we hold that God divinely guided the apostles and prophets to write down exactly what He wanted, and that the Scriptures are totally without error and accurate.[4]

Revelation

In the broad sense, we speak about the entire Bible as being a revelation from above because it constitutes the *revealing* from the Spirit of God of all that the Creator wants us to know. However, in the narrow sense, *revelation* refers to those truths of Scripture that people could not find out by their own searching. For example: the nature of God, the Trinity, the deity of Christ, the fall of Satan and the angels that followed him, the nature of redemption, and all the prophecies of Scripture that form a master plan of cosmic history.

The Greek word *apokalupsis* means "to reveal the hidden" and was used quite often in the New Testament. Paul spoke of being led by revelations (Gal. 1:12), of being given "revelations of the Lord" (2 Cor.

12:1), and of how the Lord Jesus someday "will be revealed" (2 Thess. 1:7). The last book of the Bible is called "the Revelation of Jesus Christ" (Rev. 1:1).

The authors of the Bible had a compelling thought in mind. They were not just recording history, they were recording the mind of the Lord, His revelation in and about world history.

Prophecy

The Greek word *prophēteia* comes from two words: *pro* ("before") and *phēmi* ("to say"). The Bible contains thousands of prophecies and was written by men who "told what was coming before it occurred." Biblical prophecy is the miraculous hallmark of our Scripture because it graphically, and often with remarkable detail, tells us what is going to happen in the future. This only reinforces the fact that the Bible is a divine book that originates within the mind of a sovereign God.

The Lord reminded Isaiah, "I am God, and there is no one like Me, declaring the end from the beginning, and from ancient times things which have not been done" (Isa. 46:9b–10). To John the apostle, he said, "Come up here [to heaven], and I will show you what must take place after these things" (Rev. 4:1).

In a general sense, *prophecy* is broad, encompassing the entire scope of the revealed Word of God. But as has already been shown, *prophecy* has a theologically narrow emphasis of *speaking forth* what has not yet taken place.

In a world that seems so chaotic and so completely in the grip of wickedness, we need to remember that our God sovereignly controls it all. The prophet Isaiah declared that the powerful creator of this world is not at all impressed with the supposedly great power of people and nations (Isa. 40:12–26). The prophetic word proclaims the power and sovereignty of God and reminds us that His sure purposes for the future [of history] will indeed come to pass. . . . This great truth brings insight and comfort to the believer living in this hostile world. . . . Prophecy reveals with crystal clarity that the ending of the story is good for the children of God. . . . Bible prophecy is a precious area of doctrine to the people of God who are suffering.[5]

Canon of Scripture

The word *kanōn* is a Greek word that is possibly related to the Hebrew *qāneh,* meaning "a reed." The word *qāneh* is used in the Old Testament in reference to a measuring rod (Ezek. 40:3; 42:16). From this came the idea of establishing a standard or a norm by which a document could be measured, specifically religious writings, as to their authenticity and validity.

Rufinus of Aquileia (345–410) told us that Origin, about one hundred years earlier, used the word *canon* to describe the authentic Scriptures—"canon of scripture." But Athanasius, bishop of Alexandria, "mentions the *Shepherd* of Hermas (a work which else he calls 'a most profitable book') as not belonging to the canon. More often he uses the verb *kanonizo* ("canonize") in the sense 'include in the canon'."[6]

Harrison adds,

> *Canon* is a Greek word denoting a straight rod; it came to be used for a bar or ruler and was variously applied to special objects. Certain metaphorical applications developed out of the literal meaning, such as standard and model. Patristic writers apply it to the rule of faith or the standard of apostolic teaching handed down in the church. . . . By a natural development, the apostolic writings were designated as canonical to indicate their authoritative character and to distinguish them from other Christian literature. . . . The examples of the use of the word in the New Testament do not exhibit this technical sense, but are more general: "rule" is a good translation in Galatians 6:16, whereas in II Corinthians 10:13-16 a carefully delimited sphere is the idea.[7]

Old Testament

In our common understanding, the Old Testament consists of thirty-nine books covering the Hebrew canon of Genesis through Malachi. The oldest book is probably Job, written about the time of Abraham, 2000 B.C. The closing last book of the canon is Malachi, written around 415 B.C. All the books were written in Hebrew, though small sections of Ezra, Jeremiah, and Daniel were written in Aramaic (Ezra 4:8—6:18; 7:12–26; Jer. 10:11; Dan. 2:4—7:28), the language of the diplomatic court of Assyria.

In the overall theological and technical meaning, the *Old Testament* refers to the legal Mosaic *covenant* or *testament*. Moses said he received "the tablets of stone, the tablets of the covenant which the LORD had made with you [Israel]" (Deut. 9:9). The expression *Old Testament*, like an umbrella, covers all the books of the Hebrew Bible. *Testament* is Old English, meaning *contract* or *covenant*.

The Writing of the Old Testament Books

The Law (Pentateuch)

Genesis	1445–1405 B.C.
Exodus	1445–1405 B.C.
Leviticus	1445–1405 B.C.
Numbers	1445–1405 B.C.
Deuteronomy	1445–1405 B.C.

History

Joshua	1405–1390 B.C.
Judges	1050–1000 B.C.
Ruth	1000 B.C.
1 & 2 Samuel	930 B.C. *and later*
1 & 2 Kings	550 B.C.
1 & 2 Chronicles	450–425 B.C.
Ezra	456–444 B.C.
Nehemiah	445–425 B.C.
Esther	465 B.C.

Poetry and Wisdom

Job	2000 B.C.
Psalms	c. 980 B.C.
Proverbs	c. 940 B.C.
Ecclesiastes	c. 940 B.C.
Song of Solomon	c. 940 B.C.

Prophecy

Isaiah	700 B.C.
Jeremiah	580 B.C.
Lamentations	586 B.C.
Ezekiel	560 B.C.
Daniel	536 B.C.
Hosea	715 B.C.
Joel	c. 820 B.C.
Amos	755 B.C.
Obadiah	c. 830 B.C.
Jonah	773 B.C.
Micah	703 B.C.
Nahum	c. 621 B.C.
Habakkuk	830 B.C.
Zephaniah	625 B.C.
Haggai	505 B.C.
Zechariah	488 B.C.
Malachi	415 B.C.

New Testament

The common expression, the *New Testament,* refers to twenty-seven books, Matthew through Revelation. These works were written in common or Koine Greek. The period of events covered about 100 years from the birth of Christ (4 B.C.) to the writing of the Apocalypse (A.D. 90–95).

Theologically, the New Testament is about the *new covenant* predicted in Jeremiah 31:31–37. It contrasted and even replaced the Mosaic covenant of the Law (v. 32). It was mentioned further in Jeremiah 32:40; 33:14; Ezekiel 37:26; and Joel 2. The prophesied new covenant includes 1) moral mandates placed within the heart of a believer, 2) a permanent forgiveness of sins, 3) a new relationship with the Lord, and 4) the indwelling of the Holy Spirit.

The Writing of the New Testament Books

The Gospels

Matthew	*c. A.D. 32–45*
Mark	*c. A.D. 32–45*
Luke	*A.D. 50*
John	*A.D. 90*

Apostolic History

Acts	*A.D. 51*

Epistles of Paul

Galatians	*c. A.D. 49*
1 & 2 Thessalonians	*A.D. 51*
1 & 2 Corinthians	*A.D. 55*
Romans	*A.D. 56*
Ephesians	*A.D. 59*
Colossians	*A.D. 60*
Philemon	*A.D. 60*
Philippians	*A.D. 61*
1 & 2 Timothy	*A.D. 62, 64*
Titus	*A.D. 62*

General Epistles

James	*A.D. 45*
1 & 2 Peter	*A.D. 63–64*
Hebrews	*A.D. 68*
Jude	*A.D. 68*
1–3 John	*A.D. 90–95*

Specifically Prophetic

Revelation	*A.D. 90–95*

Jesus said his death on the cross would sign, seal, and deliver the new covenant to Israel. At the last Passover with his disciples, he prophesied over the symbolism of the cup of wine, "This cup which is poured out for you is the new covenant in My blood" (Luke 22:20). Later, we are told that many aspects of the new covenant benefit the church, that is, the spiritual body of Christ.

Unique Nature of the Word of God

The Word of God is both a divinely inspired and miraculous book, protected and preserved as God's message to men and women. Yet it is no less a human book, speaking to people about real life. Indeed, it is God's book for people.

The Bible shows us the thoughts of God, but in doing so it shows a richness of both universality and omni-temporality.[8] It is for all people and meets their spiritual needs. It speaks to the loneliest cry of the soul and answers the most vexing questions. By its purity of morality, showing the pristine holiness of God, and its profound accuracy of historic information, it stands above all writings as indeed the Word of the Living God.

Beyond the Original Autographs

The question of inspiration and inerrancy is confined to the *autographa* (original writings) of Holy Scripture, both the Old and New Testaments. The later copying and recopying of the biblical manuscripts down through the centuries, however, brings about other issues that need to be addressed. For instance, copying errors are researched and identified under what is called *lower textual criticism*. Contrary to popular opinion, through this intense scientific scrutiny, very few textual transmission errors have been identified that would call a passage into question. And this careful scrutiny continues to reduce the doubts about the few questionable verses that sincere students of the Bible debate over. Unger writes about Old Testament transmission issues:

> If it can be proved that we have the words [the prophets wrote], transmitted substantially in identical form with the autographa, . . . then a charge of error is a charge against God, not against man, except where the supposed "error" may be due to corruption of the text in the course of millennia of transmission. Where the text has unquestionably suffered in transmission, the labors of devoted scholars are directed to its restoration through the study of ancient versions, textual variants and other linguistic and historical evidence

continually being brought to light by [archaeology] and various phases of Oriental research.[9]

Transmission of the Scriptures

Old Testament Texts

Before the invention of the printing press (A.D. 1500), the texts of the Old Testament were meticulously preserved and copied by scholarly rabbis who honored the sacred Scriptures as given to Israel by the Lord. As shown by history, this care and attention has given us accurate and legitimate renderings of the recorded messages of the prophets.

When the Mosaic covenant was renewed with those who had returned from the Babylonian captivity, the people asked Ezra the scribe "to bring the book of the law of Moses which the LORD had given to Israel" (Neh. 8:1), and then "read from it before" the attentive crowd (v. 3). Nehemiah and others obviously read from copies of the original documents Moses penned. Certainly, they were confident of the fact that they had all that was transmitted through the generations.

Even before the time of Christ, the Old Testament writings had been assembled and long accepted as accurate texts of the Old Testament canon. The Lord Jesus, along with all the writers of the New Testament, quoted the older testament with assurance and confidence. As well, they continually gave honor to this completed revelation as without question from God. Christ copiously quoted the Law and the Prophets; and Paul, referring to all the Old Testament, said, "All Scripture is inspired by God" (2 Tim. 3:16). Without differentiating between specific Old Testament books, Peter made a summary statement about the "careful searches" of all "the prophets who prophesied of the grace that would come to you" (1 Pet. 1:10), and later he clearly placed the letters of Paul on the same plane as "the rest of the Scriptures" (2 Pet. 3:16), meaning the Old Testament.

The care and transmission of the Old Testament books providentially fell into the hands of Talmudic scholars who emigrated eastward to Babylon around the second century A.D. They established academies to care for, copy, and edit the collected manuscripts. Though the details of their work did not prevail, they played a vital part in preserving and transmitting the Old Testament.

From around A.D. 500–1000, the Tiberian School of rabbis continued the work of Old Testament preservation. They worked from the earliest scrolls of the early *sopherim* ("wise men") down to the time of the printing press. They became known as the Massoretes or *traditionalists*, who guarded the integrity of the biblical writings. Not only did they copy the manuscripts, but they also added marginal notes and vowel points so that ancient Hebrew could be properly pronounced.

From 1947–1956, the discovery of the Dead Sea Scrolls only confirmed the belief that we have a near-pristine Old Testament text. A great number of biblical manuscripts were found in ancient jars in the Qumran caves that overlook the Dead Sea. The biblical books are believed to be a part of the library of a reactionary Jewish community known as the Essenes.

These scrolls of the Old Testament (and other religious writings) by the archaeological evidence of the jars themselves were proven to have been copied and recorded from around 150 B.C.–A.D. 135. This dates the Dead Sea Scrolls one millennium before the finalizing of the present Masoretic-edited manuscripts.

The Dead Sea Scrolls include portions or complete copies of Genesis, Exodus, Leviticus, Numbers, Deuteronomy, Judges, Ruth, Samuel, Isaiah, Ezekiel, Daniel, Job, and Jeremiah, along with fragments of the Minor Prophets. Extrabiblical books were also represented, such as Enoch, the Book of Noah, the Testament of Levi, Tobit, and the Wisdom of Solomon.

We may safely say that this find is one of the most outstanding archaeological and religious discoveries of all time. Though the Dead Sea Scrolls are still being studied, a general conclusion gives overwhelming evidence of the fidelity of the Masoretic text, the standard text for the publishing of the Hebrew Old Testament. Several examples of accuracy are cited:

> The Isaiah text discovered in Qumran Cave I proved to be almost identical with the Masoretic edition in more than 95% of the text. The 5% of variations were slight spelling errors or probably simply slips of the pen by the copyists. A further example is seen in the 166 words found in Isaiah 53. Ten words had minor spelling errors, four reflected small style changes. Finally, in this chapter of 166 words, there is only one word of three letters in question after "a thousand years of transmission—and this word does not significantly change the meaning of the passage. This sample is typical of the whole Isaiah A manuscript. Thus, the Dead Sea Scrolls lend assurance to the reader of the dependability of the Old Testament text."[10]

The Qumran community also had a great longing for the arrival of the promised Messiah. By what they wrote, we know that our view of the Messiah as described in the Old Testament is correct. And only Jesus properly and accurately matched the portrait painted of that awaited Prophet.

New Testament Texts

History is bereft of manuscript evidence for the great classics of ancient literature. For example, there are only 643 manuscripts of the *Iliad* and ten archival copies of Caesar's *Gallic Wars*. Yet there are some five thousand Greek manuscripts of our New Testament, along with many thousands of small portions of written and abbreviated texts. The *Gallic Wars* document only goes back about nine hundred years later than Caesar, but our oldest New Testament document, a Gospel of Mark fragment, may go back to about A.D. 45, or least to A.D. 117, with a papyrus portion of John 18:31–33, 37–38.

Scholarly monks of the Middle Ages worked diligently to copy our New Testament. Copy errors were made, but because of the great number of manuscripts, lectionaries, minuscules, and early uncial fragments, we have come to an incredible level of certainty as to what was recorded in the New Testament as first written.

A great number of sciences have aided in arriving at this stage of confidence. By analyzing the age of the paper and ink of ancient documents, the style of the penmanship, the location of where the materials were discovered, light is shed on how to categorize manuscript evidence. Scholars work tirelessly in refining manuscript credibility. At present, many authorities claim we now have upwards of 98 percent of our New Testament as it was originally written. "Both the *authenticity* and the *general integrity* of the books of the New Testament may be regarded as finally established."[11]

Besides the discovery and study of so many Greek manuscripts, a wealth of New Testament quotes is found in the commentaries and writings of the early church fathers. Metzger makes an astounding statement about this evidence:

> Indeed, so extensive are these citations that if all other sources for our knowledge of the text of the New Testament were destroyed, they would be sufficient alone for the reconstruction of practically the entire New Testament.[12]

Add to this the evidence of the Koine Greek language in which the New Testament itself was written, and all signs point to the fact that the text we have clearly comes from the period of the first century. This alone is an astounding conclusion. The origin of our New Testament is the colloquial language of that period.

Hermeneutics

The word *hermeneutics* is related to the Greek messenger god Hermes, who aided the pantheon of deities in the transmission of their messages, interpreting and communicating their fortunes or even misfortunes.[13] Hermes was also the god of science, invention, eloquence, speech, writing, and art. Zuck notes that Hermes

> was responsible for transmuting what is beyond human understanding into a form that human intelligence can grasp. He is said to have discovered language and writing and was the god of literature and eloquence, among other things. He was the messenger or interpreter of the gods, and particularly of his father Zeus. Thus the verb *hermeneuō* came to refer to bringing someone to an understanding of something in his language (thus explanation) or in another language (thus translation).[14]

Hermes is mentioned in the New Testament at Lystra after Paul had healed a cripple. The people cried out, "'The gods have become like men and have come down to us.' They began calling Barnabas, Zeus, and Paul, Hermes, because he was the chief speaker" (Acts 14:11–12). Paul and Barnabas were quick to disavow their connection to paganism (vv. 14–20).

The Greek word *hermēneuō,* translated "to interpret, translate, explain," is used frequently in the New Testament.[17] When Jesus met Peter, He said, "'You are Simon the son of John; you shall be called Cephas' (which is *translated* Peter)" (John 1:42). In healing the blind man, the Lord said to him, "'Go, wash in the pool of Siloam' (which *is translated,* Sent)" (9:7). Following His resurrection, Jesus encountered the disciples on the Emmaus road and "*explained* to them the things concerning Himself in all the Scriptures" (Luke 24:27). Melchizedek "to whom also Abraham apportioned a tenth part of all the spoils, was first of all, by *the translation* of his name, king of righteousness, and then also king of Salem, which is king of peace" (Heb. 7:2). [Emphasis added.]

Ramm describes how the concept of hermeneutics developed into a study in itself. Concerning the Old Testament, he says:

> The Hebrew word *pathar* means "to interpret," and *pithron* means an interpretation. Most of the usages in the Old Testament refer to

the interpretation of dreams for they were usually symbolic in form
and their meaning therefore was not obvious.[16]

Illumination

Illumination is

> the light upon and the insight into the Word of God which every
> Christian may have, and should have, from the Holy Spirit. It is not
> inspiration. Neither are spiritual power, divine unction, enthusi-
> asm, religious zeal, preaching in power and demonstration, and the
> like, inspiration.[17]

Because believers begin the Christian walk with limited comprehen-
sion of the things of the Lord, it is necessary for the indwelling Holy
Spirit to illumine scriptural truth so they may understand the things of
God. Chafer writes:

> Language could not more explicitly convey the fact that certain
> aspects of truth—immeasurable indeed—cannot be gained by
> usual didactic methods. These super-mundane revelations must be
> disclosed from the ascended Lord through the mediation of the
> Spirit and only then as the Spirit speaks from His incomparable
> position of nearness—within the heart itself.[18]

Illumination points to the fact that God has prepared certain truths
for those who love him—things which are not gained by the eye, the
ear, or the heart (i.e., reasoning power; cf. Isa. 6:9–10; 52:15; 64:4;
Matt. 13:15).[19]

First Corinthians 2:9—3:4

The central passage on the subject of illumination is 1 Corinthians 2:9—
3:4. Here Paul quoted from Isaiah 64:4 and 65:17: "Things which eye
has not seen and ear has not heard, and which have not entered the heart
of man, all that God has prepared for those who love Him" (1 Cor. 2:9);
and "to us God *revealed* them through the Spirit; for the Spirit *searches* all
things [or, everything], even the depths of God" (v. 10, emphasis added).
Two words are important to the doctrine of illumination: *revealed*
(*apokaluptō*, "to uncover, to unveil, disclose") and *searches* (*eraunaō*). The
apostle Paul then added, "Even so the thoughts of God no one knows
except the Spirit of God" (v. 11), whom we have received "that we may
know the things freely given to us by God" (v. 12).

Paul made it clear that without this ministry of *inner revealing,* the child of God could not grasp the meaning of spiritual truth. Anyone may comprehend factual information in the Bible. The believer in Christ can further understand the words and thoughts of Scripture. But the spiritual connection, the eternal meanings that are the thoughts of God, is imparted only through the inner work of the Spirit.

The word *searches* is an important and often misunderstood concept in the context of 1 Corinthians 2, but it carries a remarkable thought for our subject of illumination. *Eraunaō* can have "the sense of critical examination, to explore."[20] The word may also imply "to investigate, to explore, to trace out, to shed light on." Paul used the present tense of the verb: God reveals spiritual truth that cannot be discovered by natural means, through the Spirit; for the Spirit *is continually searching out* everything, even the depths of God *in order to share them with us.* Chafer further states:

> These "things" are a present reality, and not, as sometimes supposed, an array of future glories to be experienced in heaven. . . . It is not difficult to believe that the Third Person of the Godhead is in possession of all truth; the marvel is that this Third Person indwells the least Christian, and thus places that Christian in a position to receive and understand that transcendent truth which the Spirit knows. Within his own capacity, the child of God can know no more than "the things of a man," which are within the range of "the spirit of man which is in him." Amazing, indeed, is the disclosure that "the Spirit which is of God" has been received, and for the express purpose in view that the children of God "might know the things that are freely given to us of God."[21]

"The depths [*bathe*] of God" is better translated "the *deep things* of God" (v. 10). "The Spirit is ever *active* in fathoming the depths of God."[22] This refers to "the profoundest secrets of God, whether of His acts or of His nature."[23] Hodge adds:

> What was undiscoverable by human reason, God hath revealed by his Spirit. . . . This revelation was made by the Spirit, *for* he alone is competent to make it; for he alone searches the deep things of God. . . . *The deep things,* i.e., depths of God, the inmost recesses, as it were, of his being, perfections and purposes. The Spirit, therefore, is fully competent to reveal that wisdom which had for ages been hid in God. This passage proves at once the personality and the divinity of the Holy Ghost. . . . He knows all that God knows.[24]

Additional Passages on Illumination

Though 1 Corinthians 2 is one of the most important chapters of the Bible on the subject of illumination, other portions of the Word of God also address this idea.

Many passages in the Old Testament showed God would remove His revelation from the Jewish people. Hence, the opposite of illumination is spiritual blindness. "Blindness in part has happened to Israel until the fullness of the Gentiles has come in," Paul wrote (Rom. 11:25, NKJV). Nationally speaking then, God removed spiritual light from the Jewish people because of sin. But when Christ returns to establish His kingdom as the Deliverer, He "will come from Zion, He will remove ungodliness from Jacob" (v. 26). The Jewish people will be illuminated as "the people who walk in darkness will see a great light," for on them a great light of the messianic age will shine (Isa. 9:2). In the Old Testament, King David asked to be illumined by the Lord when he wrote, "Open my eyes, that I may behold wonderful things from Your law" (Ps. 119:18).

Of salvation itself, a new birth and an illumination is required in order to "see the kingdom of God" (John 3:3). With the coming of salvation, the glorious gospel of Christ shines on the one being saved (2 Cor. 4:4). When Peter made his great declaration, "You are the Christ, the Son of the living God" (Matt. 16:16), the Lord responded with, "Flesh and blood did not reveal this to you, but My Father who is in heaven" (v. 17). This certainly would refer to illumination. Following Christ's resurrection, the disciples were to a degree blinded in their recognition of Jesus. On the Emmaus road when Cleopas and another disciple encountered Christ, "their eyes were opened and they recognized Him" (Luke 24:31). And later, when He met other disciples, "He opened their minds to understand the Scriptures" (v. 45). Earlier, Jesus told the disciples that when the Spirit of truth would come, "He will guide you into all the truth; for He will not speak on His own initiative, but whatever He hears, He will speak; and He will disclose to you what is to come" (John 16:13).

We have already seen how carnal Christians in the Corinthian church could not receive the deeper and more vital truths, which Paul described as strong meat (1 Cor. 2:14). Paul then explained that their *fleshliness* or *carnality* hindered the work of the Holy Spirit (3:1–3). While it is true that such carnality will hinder illumination, the apostle John reminded us that all Christians have been given an anointing from Christ to comprehend such depths of spiritual truth. He wrote:

But you have an anointing from the Holy One, and you all know (1 John 2:20).

The anointing which you received from Him abides in you, and you have no need for anyone to teach you; but as His anointing teaches you about all things, and is true and is not a lie, and just as it has taught you, you abide in Him (v. 27).

Every child of God has this blessing in order to comprehend divine spiritual truths. The immediate context however of 1 John and the issue of the anointing have to do with certain facts about the coming antichrist (v. 18), i.e., that the antichrist denies the Father and the Son (v. 22). Whoever makes such denials, particularly of the Son, "does not have the Father" (v. 23).

John described the truth that *all* believers have a "knowledge base" placed within them by the Lord, and therefore, no human teacher can replace that permanent ability to receive spiritual instruction. This should be balanced by the fact that godly instructors do impart knowledge to those in Christ. Gooding seems to strike a balance on John's meaning:

"The anointing which ye have received of him abideth in you [remains in you];" it is not transient; it is permanently dwelling. The fact that they have not followed the teachers of error is proof that the anointing is still abiding in them. Continuance is always the proof of reality. "The same anointing teacheth you"; the Spirit of God has taught them and is continuing to teach them. Against such deceivers we read "that he may abide with you for ever" (John 14:16). There is no suggestion here that these young believers do not need the teachers God has given to His people. There are both general teaching and special teachers in the Church for the purpose of edification (1 Cor. 12–14; Eph. 4:4).[25]

On the doctrine of illumination, Ryrie concludes:

The experience of illumination is not by "direct revelation." The canon is closed. The Spirit illumines the meaning of that closed canon, and He does so through study and meditation. Study employs all the proper tools for ascertaining the meaning of the text. Meditation thinks about the true facts of the text, putting them together into a harmonious whole and applying them to one's own life. The end result of the illumination ministry of the Spirit is to glorify Christ in the life, or to promote healthy doctrine—teaching that brings spiritual health and wholeness to the believer's life. Illumination is not concerned with understanding facts but with using those facts to promote Christlikeness.[26]

FOR DISCUSSION

1. Define the important terms that describe the nature and character of the Bible.

2. What is meant by the *original autographs*?

3. What defines the unique nature of the Word of God?

4. Define and explain what is meant by the *transmission* of the Scriptures?

5. Define and explain the doctrine of *illumination*. Why is it important to the spiritual life of the believer?

For Further Study

Bible Introduction

Geisler, Norman L. and William E. Nix, *A General Introduction to the Bible*. Chicago: Moody, 1971.

Unger, Merrill F. *Introductory Guide to the Old Testament*. Grand Rapids: Zondervan, 1951.

Bibliology Texts

Feinberg, Paul D. "Bible, Inerrancy and Infallibility of," in *The Evangelical Dictionary of Theology*, ed. Walter A. Elwell. Grand Rapids: Baker, 1984.

Miller, H. S. *General Biblical Introduction*. Houghton, N.Y.: Word-Bearer, 1960.

Commentaries

Edwards, Thomas Charles. *A Commentary on the First Epistle to the Corinthians*. Minneapolis: Klock and Klock, 1979.

Hodge, Charles. *An Exposition of the First Epistle to the Corinthians*. Grand Rapids: Eerdmans, 1956.

Stanley, Arthur Penrhyn. *The Epistles of St. Paul to the Corinthians*. Minneapolis: Klock and Klock, 1981.

Wilson, T. and K. Stapley, eds. *What the Bible Teaches*. 11 vols. Kilmarnock, Scotland: John Ritchie, 1987.

Hermeneutics

Bray, Gerald. *Biblical Interpretation Past and Present.* Downers Grove, Ill.: InterVarsity, 1996.

Couch, Mal, ed. *An Introduction to Classical Evangelical Hermeneutics.* Grand Rapids: Kregel, 2000.

Ramm, Bernard. *Protestant Biblical Interpretation.* Grand Rapids: Baker, 1982.

Language Studies

Balz, Horst, and Gerhard Schneider, eds. *Exegetical Dictionary of the New Testament.* 3 vols. Grand Rapids: Eerdmans, 1994.

Textual Criticism

Kenyon, Sir Frederic G. *Handbook to the Textual Criticism of the New Testament.* Grand Rapids: Eerdmans, 1912.

Metzger, Bruce M. *The Text of the New Testament.* New York: Oxford University Press, 1992.

Thomas, Robert L., and F. David Farnell. *The Jesus Crisis.* Grand Rapids: Kregel, 1998.

Theology

Chafer, Lewis S. *Systematic Theology.* 8 vols. Dallas: Dallas Seminary Press, 1947; Grand Rapids: Kregel, 1993.

Ryrie, Charles C. *Basic Theology.* Chicago: Moody, 1999.

Chapter Four

The Bible as Revelation

*T*he word *revelation* intrinsically means the disclosure of what was previously unknown. Hence, the term implies that the Bible is giving to humanity something they cannot find on their own, mainly the knowledge of the true God of creation who is transcendent and unknowable by human means. God is transcendent because He is God but also because of the sinfulness of humanity. Therefore, on one hand, God has hidden Himself from the world, and yet on the other hand, He reveals Himself in a limited way through natural means. In general revelation God communicates through nature, history, and some say through the conscience. Special revelation comes by the supernatural acts of God: miracles, the Scriptures, and the incarnation of His Son.

> In Judeo-Christian theology the term [revelation] is used primarily of God's communication of Himself or of His will. . . . The redemptive events of biblical history do not stand uninterpreted. Their authentic meaning is given in the sacred writings—sometimes after, sometimes before the events. The series of sacred acts therefore includes the divine provision of an authoritative canon of writings—the sacred Scriptures—providing a trustworthy source of knowledge of God and of His plan.[1]

Calvin states succinctly why revelation from God is so important:

> It is necessary to attend to what I lately said, that our faith in doctrine is not established until we have a perfect conviction that God is its [Scriptures'] author. Hence, the highest proof of Scripture is uniformly taken from the character of Him whose word it is. The prophets and apostles boast not their own acuteness, or any qualities which win credit to speakers, nor do they dwell on reasons; but they appeal to the sacred name of God, in order that the whole world may be compelled to submission.[2]

Nevertheless, revelation is not simply meant to be encyclopedic. As Calvin further writes, it is to touch the very soul of humanity:

> For as God alone can properly bear witness to His own words, so these words will not obtain full credit in the hearts of men, until they are sealed by the inward testimony of the Spirit. The same Spirit, therefore, who spoke by the mouth of the prophets, must penetrate our hearts, in order to convince us that they faithfully delivered the message with which they were divinely entrusted.[3]

In the Bible, the Lord often directly gave to His prophets new information or revelation. In addition, He revealed His Word through the Holy Spirit and through His Son. We read, "'My Spirit which is upon you [Isaiah], and My words which I have put in your mouth shall not depart from your mouth, nor from the mouth of your offspring, nor from the mouth of your offspring's offspring,' says the LORD, 'from now and forever'" (Isa. 59:21). Jesus came to explain the Father to humanity, who had to have such revelation in order to understand His care (John 1:18). The writer of Hebrews added that God "spoke long ago to the fathers by the prophets in many portions and in many ways, in these last days has spoken to us in His Son," (1:1–2).

The ultimate message of this revelation is how greatly God cares for people. The Bible reveals His plan of redemption ordained through Christ. It publishes the good tidings that the holy and merciful God promises salvation as a divine gift to people who cannot save themselves (OT), and He has now fulfilled that promise in the gift of His Son in whom all people are called to believe (NT). The gospel is news that the incarnate Logos has borne the sins of doomed men and women, has died in their stead, and has risen for their justification. This is the fixed center of special redemptive revelation.[4]

The Distant Past and the Future

The Scriptures reveal things about the ancient past, such as the story of creation as found in Genesis. They tell about the attributes of the God who made the universe. They reveal the prehistoric existence of angels and how great companies of them were cast out of the presence of the Lord because of their sinful rebellion (Isa. 14:11–17; Ezek. 28:11–19). The Bible describes many things about ancient times that people cannot find out on their own.

Revelation gives to men and women an understanding of the person of Christ, His death, and His resurrection. It tells us why He came and of the love of God that sent Him to die for our sins. The apostle Peter heard directly from the Lord how Christ was to receive honor and glory. The Father, by His Majestic Glory, said, "This is My beloved Son with whom I am well-pleased" (2 Pet. 1:17). Peter heard this utterance from heaven when on the holy mountain (v. 18) and added, "So we have the prophetic word made more sure, to which you do well to pay attention as to a lamp shining in a dark place" (v. 19).

The Book of Revelation stands as the supreme example of the disclosing of future events. The entire book is called "The Revelation of Jesus Christ" (1:1), but it includes an unveiling of things to come (4:1) before His second advent, as well as what will come next, His work of premillennial judgment (19:11–21) and His one-thousand-year kingdom reign (20:1–6).

The Certainty of Revelation

Many markers and indicators in Scripture confirm that what is said is indeed from the Lord. Not only does the nature of the message itself tell us this, but additional evidences also add corroboration. Predictive prophecy is certainly classified as revelation. It is God telling those who will listen about what is coming within the context of human history.

> The comparative importance of predictive prophecy as related to other aspects of Bible truth is indicated by the fact that at least one-fifth of the Bible was, at the time it was written, an anticipation of the future. Of this extended material much has now been fulfilled, and much remains to be fulfilled. In each step of human progress it has pleased God to declare beforehand precisely what He was about to do.[5]

Miracles also were used as visitations and accompanying signs as testimonials to the fact that God has spoken in revelation. In fact, the expression "signs and wonders" became familiar to remind observers, and then later the readers of Scripture, that God had sealed His revelation by miracles. Before leaving Egypt, Moses was allowed by the Lord to perform signs in the sight of the people (Ex. 4:30). The Lord promised to multiply His signs (7:3). He later said these signs were part of His glory (Num. 14:22), referring to them as His works (Deut. 11:3). Moses reminded a later generation of Jews that with an outstretched arm "and with great terror and with signs and wonders" the Lord brought His people out of Egypt (Deut. 26:8).

Before all Israel, Jesus went about doing great miracles and signs (John 3:2; 11:47). They accompanied His spoken revelations and proved His messiahship (3:2). In fact, because of the Lord's predictive words, Nathanael who would be a future apostle said, "Rabbi, You are the Son of God; You are the King of Israel" (1:49). In other instances, the Lord chided the nation because of their hardened spiritual condition. Without such manifestations, the people would not believe (4:48). In like manner, following the ascension of Christ, special visitations accompanied the apostles, including Paul, to prove to the people that they were the true representatives of the Lord. About some of his own works, Paul wrote to the Corinthians, "The signs of a true apostle were performed among you with all perseverance, by signs and wonders and miracles (2 Cor. 12:12; see also Rom. 15:19).

Because such signs accompanied Paul's ministry, he could write revelation truth with "the authority which the Lord gave me" to the church of Corinth (2 Cor. 13:10). It may be safely said that prophets and apostles, whose ministries were verified by signs and wonders wrote the greatest portions of revelation found in the Scriptures.

Revelation Is Both Rational and Reasonable

To say that revelation is rational in the apologetic sense is to say, "All truth is given by revelation, either general or special, and it must be received by reason."[6]

> Reason is the God-given means for discovering the truth that God discloses, whether in His world or His Word. While God wants to reach the heart with truth, he does not bypass the mind along the way. In this modified sense, there is great value in Christian rationalism.[7]

In a similar way, the written revelation is reasonable in that its message can be discerned by sound judgment, logic, and intelligent inferences. Though the human heart is darkened (Rom. 1:21) and the mind is depraved (v. 28), people can believe the message of Christ and salvation found in the Bible because of the inner interpretive work of the Holy Spirit by which the Word of God becomes understandable (1 Cor. 2:10–13). Stating it another way, though people cannot comprehend spiritual truth by themselves and though their minds are blinded to the reasonableness of the Bible, it becomes acceptable and believable through the Spirit's work. However, human belief is a conscious act not a passive one.

Isaiah wrote, "'Come now, and let us reason together,' says the LORD, 'though your sins are as scarlet, they will be as white as snow'" (1:18). Isaiah asked Israel to think through their spiritual plight. He pleaded that they be rational regarding sin in the nation. "The Lord in His grace is willing to bestow favor and pardon if His people will but reason concerning the matter of their sin."[8] The verb *yākaḥ* ("to reason") means "to prove, decide, or adjudge."[9] Though sinful and unable to decide for the good, people are still responsible to think through their spiritual situations. They will remain rebellious until the Spirit moves them to reason toward God. Paul also wrote:

> If you confess with your mouth Jesus as Lord, and believe in your heart that God raised Him from the dead, you shall be saved; for with the heart a person believes, resulting in righteousness, and with the mouth he confesses, resulting in salvation. For the Scripture says, "Whoever believes in Him will not be disappointed." (Rom. 10:9–11)

In the modern neoorthodox view, Jesus is the only Word of God. Christ may give witness to the written Word, and the Scriptures may become the Word to the reader. However, in themselves, they are not the Word of God. If this is true, the Bible may be unreasonable until made reasonable. Evangelicals denounce this teaching because the Scriptures themselves reject such a view.

> The Bible nowhere protests against the identification of Scripture with revelation, but rather supports and approves this identification. The neo-orthodox tendency to look upon Scripture as simply witness to revelation, in fact, contravenes the historic Christian view that the Bible itself is a form of revelation specially provided for man in sin as an authentic disclosure of the nature and will of God.[10]

Reason and reasonableness play a part in spiritual matters. This is not the case in other religions of the world. They present themselves as virtually fictional. Their stories and mythologies insult the searching mind. By all standards, they are unreasonable in their theologies.

Biblical revelation forms the communication link of truth to the mind. The capacity to receive such truth is presupposed. Animals cannot understand nor receive such higher abstract spiritual truth. The Spirit of God acts upon human spirits so they may be taught the deep things of God, beginning with salvation. No one knows the thoughts of God but the Spirit of God (1 Cor. 2:11). We receive the Spirit that we might know the things freely given to us by God (v. 12). Nevertheless, the Holy Spirit enlightens us with revelation that is reasonable. Charles Hodge adds to this and writes:

> We can affirm nothing of that of which we know nothing. The first and indispensable office of reason, therefore, in matters of faith, is the cognition, or intelligent apprehension of the truths proposed for our reception. . . . [Man] is not called upon by his Creator to believe without knowledge, to receive as true propositions that convey no meaning to the mind.[11]

We still must keep in mind how inferior reason can be without revelation. In this regard, Chafer writes:

> Man's true estate under reason and when isolated from revelation is partially demonstrated by the lowest forms of heathenism. . . . Never have these systems [of pagan religion] been able to perfect a code of moral duty nor could they discover any authority for their faulty precepts. Similarly, the light of nature and the aid of reason have been too feeble to dispel uncertainties concerning the life beyond the grave.[12]

Revelation and Inspiration

The doctrine of inspiration was dealt with in detail in chapter 6. It is enough here to state that there is a difference in what the two words infer. Technically speaking, revelation is the imparting of spiritual truth that people by themselves could not have discovered. God gives that revelation through inspiration of the prophets or apostles. Basically, the two doctrines differ by their objectives. As already stated, the objective of revelation is the communication of knowledge not discoverable by the human mind. However, the objective of inspiration is to secure infallibility in the entire body of truth that God wishes people to receive. This, as mentioned, includes predictive prophecy. However, it also includes the poetry, the narrative, and historic sections of Scripture.

The Spirit superintended the writers to assure their message was completely from God. In doing this, the Spirit of God worked mysteriously in that the styles, feelings, insights, and experiences of the authors were left intact. The message flowed through their conscious minds. Their words became the very words God wished to be recorded in written form.

The effect of revelation was to render its recipient wiser. The effect of inspiration was to preserve him from error in teaching. The same person often enjoyed these two gifts at the same time. That is, the Spirit often imparted knowledge, and controlled it in its communication orally or in writing to others. This was no doubt the case with the Psalmists, and often with the Prophets and Apostles. Often, however, the revelations were made at one time, and were subsequently, under the guidance of the Spirit, committed to writing. . . . If the sacred writers had sufficient sources of knowledge in themselves, or in those about them, there is no need to assume any direct revelation.[13]

Progressive Revelation

Special revelation is *progressive,* which means God gave more and more details about Himself and His plans over a long period of time. From the writings of Moses until the completion of the Book of Revelation, the Lord unfolded all that He wished human beings to know. He revealed facts about His own attributes and His nature that we describe as the Trinity. He unfolded progressively the plan of earth history that included His dealings with the children of Abraham. The person of the Messiah, His attributes, His death, burial, and resurrection were given in various segments in the Old Testament. His coming kingship and rule were likewise revealed through almost all of the prophets. Lockyer well notes:

> To those who come to the Scriptures with an open mind and reliance upon the Holy Spirit for illumination, there comes the ineffaceable conviction that they present not a "heterogeneous jumble," as critics affirm, of ancient history, myths, legends and religious speculations and superstitions, but a gradual unfolding of the plan and purpose of God, a progress of revelation and doctrine.[14]

This does not mean that doctrinal truth changes or evolves. However, it means that more truth is added on what is already known. For example, looking at the nature of God, some argue that the Jews simply "matured" in their view about Him over the time that He went from a primitive deity to the Jehovah of the Scriptures. This is simply not true nor does it properly represent the concept of progressive revelation.

There is a sense of maturity in revelation, but this does not mean that earlier messages or information was faulty. It only means that the truths presented became complete, especially in the final composition of the inspired books of the New Testament. Ramm summarizes:

> By progressive revelation is not meant that the Biblical revelation is a process of evolution in the cultural or religious sphere. This idea of the evolution of religion in the Scriptures was a means of denying the real revelatory content of Scripture and of undermining the uniqueness of Biblical revelation.

> This perspective of Progressive Revelation is very important to the interpreter. He will expect the full revelation of God in the New Testament.[15]

As an example of progressive revelation, note Mark 4:28. Chafer remarks, " 'First the blade, then the head [of the corn], then the mature grain in the head.' Each book of the Bible avails itself of the accumulated truth that has gone before, and the last book is like a vast union station into which all the great highways of revelation and prediction converge and terminate."[16]

Theological Concept of Revelation

To Adam and Eve before the Fall, God revealed Himself through direct, intimate contact. He apparently spoke with our first parents in ongoing fellowship and communion. However, after the Fall, the race even more needed a word from God. Chafer notes:

> To the latter must be given the added truth regarding sin and redemption. God has spoken. To this end the Bible has been written, and the revelation to man of that great body of truth which man could not acquire for himself and which the Bible discloses is its sublime and supreme purpose.[17]

He adds:

> In its theological usage, the term *revelation* is restricted to the divine act of communicating to man what otherwise man would not know. This extraordinary form of revelation, since it originates with God, is, of necessity, largely dependent on supernatural agencies and means. Nothing could be more advantageous to man, nor is there aught more certain than the fact that God has spoken to man.[18]

Other religions have people seeking after God or the gods. In most religions there is very little that shows God directly relating to His world. Credible revelation is doubtful and sketchy at best. The Hindu Vedas, with overwhelming mysticism, speak of hosts of divine beings. In the primitive religions of the American Indians, a crowd of lesser spirits surrounds the Great Spirit, representing animism and the phenomena of nature.

In time, ancient religions became polytheistic on an extensive scale with "every phase of nature, sky, sea, and earth, every phase of human life, its habits, accidents, and impulses, being provided with a special guardian and controlling deity."[19]

However, biblical revelation of the one true God is far above what other religions have to offer. Knowledge of the infinite God does not arise spontaneously in the human mind. The knowledge of God in the revelation of Scripture so differs from any other religious writings that a comparison is logically impossible.

> Without revelation man would never have been able to acquire any knowledge of God. In addition, even after God has revealed Himself objectively, it is not human reason that discovers God, but it is God who discloses Himself to the eye of faith. . . . The position must be maintained, however, that theology would be utterly impossible without a self-revelation of God. Moreover, when we speak of revelation, we use the term in the strict sense of the word. It is not something in which God is passive, a mere "becoming manifest," but something in which He is actively making Himself known.[20]

Though this statement by Berkhof speaks strictly about revelation found in the Word of God, there are three other ways that God has specifically made Himself known that need to be explored. He has revealed 1) some things about His activities in nature; 2) through direct communication and the theophanies; and 3) He has shown Himself in a specific way through His Son Jesus Christ. These ways will be considered after examining revelation through the written Word.

The Written Revelation

God revealed Himself to the prophets and apostles. He did this through oracles (2 Kgs. 9:25), mental visions (Dan. 7:1), dreams (Dan. 1:17), revelations (2 Cor. 12:1), through control of their minds (Acts 11:28), and by direct vocal communication (1 Sam. 3:4). The Lord told the prophets to record His words (plural, 2 Sam. 7:17; 1 Chr. 17:15) but also His total thoughts described with a singular "the word" (Jer. 32:6). At times God used angels such as Gabriel to deliver special messages, as to the prophet Daniel (Dan. 8:15–19).

The overall message, including the specific words of the Bible, forms the full body of divine revelation. We refer to this as supernatural or specific written revelation. The Word of God stands alone in its message and in the way it was transmitted to humanity. The Scriptures were intended to reveal the nature of God, the sinfulness of people, and the way of redemption ultimately through the sacrifice of Christ. God gave the Law, the Prophetic Books, the Gospels, the Epistles of the New Testament, and, finally, the outline of the end of history found in the Book of Revelation.

All these things unfolded in history through the centuries. The unfolding was progressive, being finalized at the writing of the Apocalypse of John. This revelation from God was put into written form. From this came the issues of inspiration, canonicity, and divine authority.

> The true believer has always maintained that in the Bible we have a revelation of God, in fact, the clearest and only inerrant revelation. . . . It records, for instance, the knowledge of God and His dealings with the creature which men of old gathered . . . The Christian, therefore, turns to the Scriptures as the supreme and only infallible source for the construction of his theology.[21]

General Revelation

This type of revelation is also called natural revelation because it can come through the wonders of the natural universe. The psalmist said, "The heavens are telling of the glory of God; and their expanse is declaring the work of His hands" (Ps. 19:1). Through this witness of creation to human beings, Paul said God's invisible nature, eternal power, and deity are "understood through what has been made, so that they are without excuse" (Rom. 1:20). The psalmist added that all the natural bodies in the universe give praise to the Lord (Ps. 148). They do this because He "created" and "established" them, and His glory is revealed "above earth and heaven" (v. 13).

Some also argue that God's providential activity in world history becomes a form of revelation. The people of God can see this as they read Scripture. Job confirmed this when he said God "makes the nations great, then destroys them; He enlarges the nations, then leads them away" (Job 12:23). The psalmist added, "God is the Judge; He puts down one and exalts another" (Ps. 75:7; cf. Rom. 13:1). Paul declared God "made from one man every nation of mankind to live on all the face of the earth, having determined their appointed times and the boundaries of their habitation, that they would seek God, if perhaps they might grope for Him and find Him" (Acts 17:26–27).

The Lord's revelation of His attributes in creation is meant to stir the minds and consciousnesses of the human race to consider Him (Rom. 1:20). But since none seek after God with their own volition (3:11), such revelation docs not bring the world to repentance. Concerning conscience, the apostle Paul went further and wrote in Romans 2:15 that God's Law is actually written in the hearts of humanity, "their conscience [collective or accumulated knowledge] bearing witness and their thoughts alternately accusing or else defending them." (The term *conscience* "possibly is of popular derivation and might have been quite common in popular Hellenistic philosophy. [*Suneidēsis*], following the basic meaning of the verb [*sunoida*], means 'human knowledge of something.' It also refers to 'moral consciousness' (usually of a bad deed)."[22])

Though Jesus did not use the word *conscience*, He spoke of the coming of the Holy Spirit to "convict the world concerning sin and righteousness and judgment" (John 16:8). The word *convict* (*elegchō*, "to bring to light, expose") implies that the world is strongly made aware of these issues. And though this conviction of itself does not bring individuals to the point of repentance, it does give a platform for their responsibility and a basis for their future judgment.

The apostle Paul had strong words to say about the conscience. He wrote that in the last days, human beings will pay attention to "doctrines of demons, by means of the hypocrisy of liars seared in their own conscience as with a branding iron" (1 Tim. 4:1–2). He noted that to the unbelieving:

> Nothing is pure, but both their mind and their conscience are defiled. They profess to know God, but by their deeds they deny Him, being detestable and disobedient, and worthless for any good deed. (Titus 1:15–16)

Despite this fact, revelation given to the conscience has been called the "reflection of God in the soul."[23] This revelation:

> Reveals to us not only that he is, but also that he sharply distinguishes between right and wrong (Rom. 2:14–16), that he always does that which is right, and that he also holds the rational creature

responsible for always doing the right and abstaining from the wrong. It also implies that every transgression will be punished.[24]

However, our natural minds do not want to agree with these revelations. Humans believe they are autonomous and the sole determiners of what takes place in their lives.

Because of the illumination of the message of the Scriptures, believers may have a better appreciation of the meaning of such general revelation. However, since sin entered the realm of humanity and brought about acute spiritual blindness, this natural revelation does not penetrate the hearts of those who are without Christ. Such blindness makes it impossible to read the divine script in nature.

> General revelation does not afford man the reliable knowledge of God and spiritual things that he needs for salvation. It is therefore inadequate as a foundation for the Christian faith. . . . The Christian, because he is a Christian and has a converted mind, not a reprobate mind, understands general revelation better through the Word of God, and thus he is able to see God's finger in nature and in history.[25]

Special Revelation

The Bible tells us about the God of the universe in unusual and specific ways. For example, the Lord God manifested Himself in dramatic moments through what are called theophanies or "divine appearances." He also spoke between the angelic cherubim carvings on the ark of the covenant in the tabernacle (Ps. 80:1; 99:1) and appeared in the fire, clouds, and smoke (Gen. 15:17; Ex. 3:2; 19:9, 16ff.).

> He appeared as the angel of the Lord, not as a created angel. In some instances the angel of the Lord is distinguished from God (See Exod. 23:20–23; Isa. 63:8–9) but he also is identified with God in such verses as Genesis 16:13; 31:11, 13; 32:28.[26]

Even though God does not have a physical, human body, He often came to significant individuals in bodily form in order to relate to them. For example, He came to Enoch and Noah (Gen. 5:24; 6:9); and He spoke to Noah (6:13; 7:1), to Abraham (12:1), to Joshua (Josh. 1:1), to Gideon (Judg. 6:25), to Samuel (1 Sam. 3:4), and to David (1 Sam. 23:9–12). In the New Testament, He spoke to Peter, James, and John (Mark 9:7), to Philip (Acts 8:29), to Paul (9:4–6), and to Ananias (v. 10).

The Lord appeared in storms (Job 38:1); was heard as a voice (Gen. 2:16; 3:8–19); communicated through the lots of the Urim and Thummim (Num. 27:21; Deut. 33:8); worked in dreams (Num. 12:6; 1 Sam. 28:6; Joel 2:28); and through visions (Isa. 6; Ezek. 1—3).

God also communicates His thoughts through the Holy Spirit. Though this was especially mentioned in the New Testament (Mark 13:11; Luke 12:12; John 14:17; 15:26; 16:13), the Spirit was also involved in direct communication in the Old Testament. The tabernacle builders were filled with the Spirit and endowed with wisdom to build according to the Lord's instructions (Ex. 31:3). He gave instruction (Neh. 9:20) and admonishment (9:30) and often came upon certain people to specifically direct their actions (Judg. 11:29).

As already pointed out, the Lord also spoke through signs and miracles; but sometimes such dramatic events confirmed one with whom the Lord was working, such as with His Son and the apostles. Nicodemus recognized this fact when he said to Jesus, "You have come from God as a teacher; for no one can do these signs that You do unless God is with Him" (John 3:2). And Paul told the Corinthians, "The signs of a true apostle were performed among you . . . by signs and wonders and miracles" (2 Cor. 12:12).

Revelation Through Christ

The Lord Jesus Himself plays a vital role in revelation. In looking at Him as He is revealed in Scripture, we gain insight into the person of God the Father. Because of the special relationship of Father and Son, Jesus is the One most capable of explaining Him to the human race. He explained (*exēgeomai*, aorist tense), "interprets, leads out, describes" God to us because "no one has seen God at any time" (John 1:18). Through Christ we gain a glimpse of the heavenly Father who so dearly loves us.

The word *exēgeomai* is often translated "to tell a narrative" or "to relate" (Luke 24:35). Jesus was the exegesis of God. He was the narration of God and, as the human Word of God, was the ultimate disclosure of God Himself. Jesus the beloved then had "made God known." As the Word, He was God's self-expression.[27]

As the Word, Jesus not only revealed the Father, but He also played a part in the giving of written revelation. He can be called the ultimate, living Word *from* God. With wording similar to Genesis 1:1, the apostle John wrote, "In the beginning was the Word, and the Word was with God, and the Word was God. He was in the beginning with God" (John

1:1). In his first epistle, John repeated this thought but elaborated further when he wrote, "What was from the beginning, what we have heard, what we have seen with our eyes, what we have looked at and touched with our hands, concerning the Word of Life" (1 John 1:1). The apostle again wrote that Christ was with the Father but now was manifested to us (v. 2). And in John's vision of Christ's return, he added, "His name is called The Word of God" (Rev. 19:13).

Some have speculated that John had in mind that the Greeks were seeking for the ultimate expression of truth, which they called "the word (*logos*)." Others have reasoned that John was addressing a Gnostic tradition. It is certain that John did not have the Gnostics or the Greeks in mind when he wrote concerning "the Word." The Old Testament is full of references to the "word of the Lord." John more likely had in view that Jesus was the ultimate fulfillment and completion of the message of revelation. Carson notes that John

> rises to the level of historical particularity. Precisely because the Evangelist's readers are familiar with the Old Testament, he concludes by briefly articulating the relationship between Jesus Christ and the revelation that has already been given, especially in the covenant mediated through Moses (1:16–18).[28]

Though not accepted by the Jews, the Samaritan woman had tremendous Old Testament insights about the Lord. Before she fully recognized Him as the Messiah, she said to Jesus, "When that One comes, He will declare all things to us" (John 4:25). While not explained here, she must have had in mind great yet-to-be-revealed spiritual truths and revelations. Others agreed as they listened to Jesus, for "many more believed because of His word" (v. 41).

The writer of Hebrews also understood the role of Jesus in revelation. He wrote, "In these last days [God] has spoken to us in His Son" (1:2). But Christ was the very deity Himself. The writer added, "He is the radiance of His [God's] glory and the exact representation of His nature, and upholds all things by the word of His power" (v. 3).

Though the last book of the Bible is called "the Revelation of Jesus Christ" (Rev. 1:1), it is also a revelation *from* Christ Himself. The passage goes on and says that God gave this message about His Son to Jesus Himself in order that He might in turn pass it down to John the apostle (v. 1). Likewise, the messages to the seven churches (chaps. 2—3) came directly from Jesus. For example, John wrote, "The One who holds the seven stars in His right hand . . . says this:" (2:1). "The first and the last . . . says this:" (2:8). "The One who has the sharp two-edged sword . . . says this:" (2:12), etc. Since Revelation is such a dramatic presentation of Christ and the last days, it seems appropriate that He would have a direct part in the final prophetic message of Scripture.

The Scope of Revelation

The entire Bible, from Genesis to Revelation, is the inspired Word of God. But in the strictest sense, the entire Bible is not revelation. It contains exciting chapters about history, poetry, narration, and prophecy that simply might have been observed without a revealing from God. However, the Lord superintended what was written down so that we might have all He wished for us to know. For our purposes here, however, it is perfectly legitimate to call all of Scripture the revelation of God.

By theological definition, divine revelation was the communication of God to humankind of the truths about Himself, His plans, and His will, and concerning people and their need for redemption. None of these truths could have been known through nature or natural revelation. Biblical revelation was imparted by the Holy Spirit to give an understanding about God, about the origin and focus of human life, and about the only way to approach God, which is through His Son Jesus Christ. Divine revelation then was

> "the discovery afforded by God to man of Himself, or His will, over and above what He made known by the light of nature, or of reason." God is, He created the universe, He created man, He created man in His image, for His companionship, His glory, His pleasure, man is His offspring (Gen. 1:1, 26–27; 3:8; Isa. 43:7; Rev. 4:11; Acts 17:29), and the Bible professes to be a revelation from God to His intelligent creatures.[29]

These and many other subjects are imparted in both a systematic and chronological manner in the Old and New Testaments. Beginning with origins (Gen. 1), all the way into eternity (Rev. 22), the truth is woven and tied and linked together throughout the sacred pages. The Lord has revealed Himself and His plans through the ancient prophets and His Son (Heb. 1:1–2) with the mouths of the holy prophets of old (Luke 1:70), who were moved by the Holy Spirit (2 Pet. 1:21).

With a poetic flare, Miller declares that revelation is: 1) possible because of a powerful God, 2) necessary because of the helplessness of mankind, 3) probable because God loves His creatures and wishes to save them, 4) credible because God's honor is at stake with His name behind His revelation, 5) reasonable because He imparts only what is true, and 6) certain because revelation from God is "fully substantiated by its miracles, its fulfilled prophecy," and because of its worldwide propagation.[30]

Old Testament

The Hebrew word *gālāh* is the most common word used to describe revelation. It is used this way about twenty-one times in the Old Testament. At its root the word means "nakedness" with the idea to uncover that that is hidden. In the Qal verb form, it may be translated "to reveal." In the Piel verb form, it

> always denotes "to uncover" something which otherwise is normally concealed. Thus it means "to open" the eyes—to see an angel (Num. 22:31) or wonderful things in the law (Ps. 119:18); "to make known, revealed, manifest": of Jeremiah in his complaint to the LORD (Jer. 11:20; 20:12), of the LORD in his revelation of peace and truth to Israel (Jer. 33:6) and his righteousness to them (Ps. 98:2).[31]

Before Saul came to Samuel, the prophet *received* the message he was to give to this first king of Israel (1 Sam. 9:15). When the Lord through the prophet Nathan told David he would be given a royal house (lineage), David said, "For You, O LORD of hosts, the God of Israel, have made *a revelation* to Your servant," (2 Sam. 7:27). To the prophet Amos, it was said, "He [God] *reveals* His secret counsel to His servants the prophets" (Amos 3:7). Job's friend Elihu said the Lord "opens [*gālāh*] the ears of men, and seals their instruction" (Job 33:16). Finally, one of the most poignant verses about revelation is Daniel 10:1: "A message *was revealed* to Daniel, . . . and the message was true and one of great conflict, but he understood the message and had an understanding of the vision."

Other important Old Testament words also convey the idea of divine revelation: *rā'āh, yāda', and lāmad.* The word *rā'āh* means "to see, show" as in Daniel 8:15, "When I, Daniel, had *seen* the vision, I sought to understand it." The Hebrew words translated "seer" and "vision" are derived from *rā'āh.* The word *yāda'* means "to know" as in Psalm 25:4, "*Make* me *know* Your ways, O LORD." The word *lāmad* means "to teach," as in Psalm 25:4, "*Teach* me Your paths."

Two other important Hebrew words convey the thought of giving forth revelation. One is *dābār* ("word" as in "the *word* of the Lord"), and the other is *torah* ("law, instruction"). The two are often brought together in one passage: "Hear the *word* of the LORD, you rulers of Sodom; give ear to the *instruction* of our God" (Isa. 1:10). Warfield writes:

> Both terms are used for any Divine communication of whatever extent; and both came to be employed to express the entire body of Divine revelation, conceived as a unitary whole. In this comprehensive usage, the emphasis of the one came to fall more on the graciousness, and of the other more on the authoritativeness of this body of Divine revelation; and both passed into the New Testament with these implications.[32]

Hundreds of other expressions in the Old Testament point to the giving of revelation directly to the prophets. For example: "The word of the LORD which came to Hosea" (Hos. 1:1); "Then the LORD said to me" (3:1); "Hear this, O priests!" (5:1); "The word of the LORD that came to Joel" (Joel 1:1); "declares the LORD" (2:12); "Thus says the LORD" (Amos 1:6); "Hear this word" (4:1); "Thus He showed me" (7:7); "Thus says the Lord GOD" (Obad. 1:1); "The word of the LORD came to Jonah" (Jon. 1:1); "The word of the LORD which came to Micah" (Mic. 1:1).

New Testament

The New Testament also has more than one word or expression to describe revelation. One of the most common is the verb *apokalupto* ("to reveal") with the noun *apokalupsis* ("revelation"). These words carry the thought "to disclose that which is hidden" or "from the hidden."

The apostle Paul wrote that the mystery concerning Christ and His church was hidden, "which in other generations was not made known to the sons of men, as it *has now been revealed* to His holy apostles and prophets in [by] the Spirit" (Eph. 3:5). Paul's point was that the church, made up of Jew and Gentile, was not found in the Old Testament. It is something brand new in God's divine program.

Concerning revelation, the apostle noted regarding spiritual truths that "God *revealed* them through the Spirit" (1 Cor. 2:10), and specifically Paul wrote that God "*reveal{ed}* His Son in me so that I might preach Him among the Gentiles" (Gal. 1:16). He added that he could but would not boast of receiving special visions and *revelations* from the Lord (2 Cor. 12:1) and that he was given an abundance of such *revelations* as an apostle (v. 7). Besides *apokalupsis*, other Greek words are used:

1. *Deiknumi*. "To show." In the Book of Revelation, this word is often used to describe prophecies that are revealed to John to be

recorded for our benefit. John is *shown* "what must take place after these things" (Rev. 4:1). He is *shown*: future judgment (17:1), the bride of the Lamb (21:9), the new Jerusalem (v. 10), the future river of water coming from the new Jerusalem (22:1), and "the things which must soon take place" (v. 6).

2. *Laleō.* "To speak." This expression was graphically used to describe the imparting of revelation in the Book of Hebrews. The author wrote, "God, after He *spoke* long ago to the fathers in the prophets in many portions and in many ways, in these last days has *spoken* to us in His Son" (1:1–2). He added, "We must pay much closer attention to what we have heard" (2:1) because the word was "*spoken* through angels" (v. 2). He said that salvation "first *spoken* through the Lord" "was confirmed to us by those who heard" (v. 3).

Revealing a Mystery

The Greek word *mustērion* ("mystery") is used twenty-eight times in the New Testament and refers to that which was before hidden but is now revealed. By the use of this word, the idea of revelation is specifically emphasized. Certain distinct doctrines would not have made sense if they had been revealed at some early period of time. The human mind simply could not have understood these truths unless they were presented in a fresh context. Chafer writes:

> The New Testament use of the term relates it to some work or purpose of God hitherto unrevealed. It may be related to something which needs to be understood but must have a key (Rev. 1:20). . . . The New Testament mysteries are not indeed secrets to be withheld, but to be published (1 Cor. 4:1).[33]

Many mysteries were revealed in the New Testament:

1. *The deeper things about the kingdom were kept hidden until Christ gave them to His disciples* (Matt. 13; Mark 4:11; Luke 8:10). These were intangible spiritual concepts that would have been difficult for Old Testament saints to comprehend. The facts of the kingdom were spelled out in detail in the Old Testament, but the full spiritual nature of the kingdom was withheld. Even as Christ spoke about kingdom mysteries, He did so in parable form. The average person in Israel was blinded to the issues of the kingdom and could not understand (Matt. 13:13). But it was granted to

the disciples that they should know the mysteries (things previously hidden) about the kingdom (v. 11).

2. *That Israel would be hardened toward the gospel was not previously fully known.* Paul wrote, "A partial hardening has happened to Israel until the fullness of the Gentiles has come in" (Rom. 11:25). He did not want the believers in Rome "to be uninformed of this mystery" because they thought their acceptance of the gospel made them better than the Jews. The apostle explained that a judicial blindness had come on Israel until the Lord is through with the Gentiles.

3. *Paul called the gospel itself a great mystery not previously revealed.* The full doctrine of the gospel was revealed specifically to Paul, that is, "the preaching of Jesus Christ, according to the revelation of the mystery which has been kept secret for long ages past" (Rom. 16:25). The gospel is "the mystery of His will" (Eph. 1:9). Paul asked the Ephesian church to pray for him that that he would have boldness in the utterance of the truth. He reminded them that he was an ambassador in chains (6:20) but desired to continue "to make known with boldness the mystery of the gospel" (v. 19).

Referring again to the full doctrine of the gospel, the apostle Paul called faith a mystery (1 Tim. 3:9); that is, it was not specifically revealed in the Old Testament that salvation could be secured by simply trusting in the Messiah.

4. *In relation to the gospel being a mystery, the nature of the church was also called the same.* Paul wrote, "By revelation there was made known to me the mystery" (Eph. 3:3), that is "the mystery of Christ" (v. 4), "to be specific, that the Gentiles are fellow heirs and fellow members of the body, and fellow partakers of the promise in Christ Jesus through the gospel" (v. 6). Paul referred to the fact that the church is made up of Jews and Gentiles. This was a foreign concept to the Jews and not revealed in the Old Testament. They could not conceive being joined together in the same spiritual body with those they considered pagans.

In 1 Corinthians 2, Paul continued this thought and said, "God's wisdom [is] a mystery, the hidden wisdom, which God predestined before the ages to our glory" (v. 7). This gospel was not revealed in other ages nor understood by the present rulers. If they had known who Jesus really was, he added, they would not have crucified Him, the Lord of glory (v. 8).

5. *The dramatic change that will take place at the Rapture is called a mystery by the apostle* (1 Cor. 15:51–52). He wrote, "Behold, I tell you a mystery; we will not all sleep, but we will all be changed, in a moment, in the twinkling of an eye, at the last trumpet; for the trumpet will sound, and the dead will be raised imperishable, and we will be changed." This is tantamount to saying that the doctrine of the Rapture itself is a mystery. This passage fits perfectly with what Paul wrote in 1 Thessalonians 4:16–17. When the trumpet sounds, the dead will be raised first, and "we who are alive and remain will be caught up together with them in the clouds to meet the Lord in the air." That the church, the body of Christ, would be so dramatically delivered was never before mentioned, though the mere fact that there would be a Rapture was previously revealed when the Lord told His disciples that He would prepare a place for them in His Father's house. He added, "I will come again and receive you to Myself, that where I am, there you may be also" (John 14:3). Since the time of the Rapture is not known and since that generation of disciples and believers were not so dramatically taken home, we still wait for that promise of sudden, miraculous delivery from this world.

6. *Paul wrote that "the mystery of lawlessness is already at work" in the world* (2 Thess. 2:7). He had previously written that someday the "man of lawlessness, the son of destruction," would come "who opposes and exalts himself above every so-called god or object of worship, so that he takes his seat in the temple of God, displaying himself as being God" (v. 4). Paul was, of course, speaking of the Antichrist who is fully revealed in his activities in Revelation 13. The apostle added that this one will come in the power of Satan, but his doom is certain when Christ returns (2 Thess. 2:8).

7. *Paul wrote to Timothy, "By common confession, great is the mystery of godliness"* (1 Tim. 3:16). He added that Jesus "was revealed in the flesh, was vindicated in the Spirit, seen by angels, proclaimed among the nations, believed on in the world, taken up in glory." The mystery seems to be about the marvel of the incarnation of Christ, the spread of the truth, and the ascension of the Lord

back to glory. Paul put all of this together into a summary statement. Hence, the godliness mentioned here appears to be a reference to the nature of Jesus and His work on earth. This passage was possibly part of an ancient hymn or a doctrinal statement recited by the early church. Ellicott says:

> For the glorious truth which the Church of God pillar-like upholds, is none other than that stupendous mystery, in other ages not made known, but then revealed—the mystery of Christ, in all His loving manifestations and glorious triumph. Yes, confessedly great—so great that the massive grandeur of the pillar is only in proportion to the truth it supports.[34]

8. *Babylon the Great, the Mother of Harlots, was called a mystery by the apostle John* (Rev. 17:5). He added, "The mystery of the woman and of the beast that carries her" (v. 7). Babylon here represents the world's false religious system that will be supported by the beast, the Antichrist, and the ten-nation confederation ruling during the Tribulation. The mystery could be the fact of the importance given to the Mother of Harlots that was totally unexpected and certainly not fully explained in the Old Testament. Until this revelation, John and his peers may never have anticipated such a union of all false teachings under one system.

In each case, these mysteries are about revelations given in the New Testament but not foretold in the Old Testament. Though many other truths could be classified as new revelations, these were so spectacular, they were given this designation of "mystery."

The Breadth of Revelation

The breadth of the subject material of Scripture points to its divine origin. Thousands of subjects, doctrines, personalities, and divinely superintended events are described in the Bible. However, some doctrines and revelations enlarge and confirm the fact that this book is from God.

For example, the Bible contains sixty-six books written by probably thirty-nine authors who prophesied over fifteen hundred years. This gives us a continuous history but without error or contradiction of doctrine. Yet there is also progression. Each book becomes a chapter that plays its role in the chronology of the whole revelation. "No other religion but Christianity shows 'a steady historical progress of the vision of one infinite

Character unfolding itself to man through a period of many centuries.'"[35] Though written for all peoples of the world, the Bible was delivered basically to one nation—Israel. Because the revelation of God's Word was so real, the prophets and priests held the books in the highest and most holy esteem. They preserved and guarded these books with the utmost care. However, once the revelation was complete, the world benefited by the results. This preservation of the Bible, through the caretaker attention of the Jews and later the church, is a providential miracle in itself.

Furthermore, the basic facts about the nature of the Bible point out that it is the Word of God. It has an overwhelming manifestation as having been authored by God Himself. It speaks truth about both the outward, visible world and the hidden, spiritual world. The message of the Bible is impossible to counterfeit by the evil intention of fraud. It is not a book of wild, fictional tales. Instead, it demonstrates that it has come to us in history past. And, undeniably, the Bible speaks to the hearts and souls of those who read it.

Within the Bible, profound and spectacular demonstrations show that this is a revelation from God:

1. *The story of creation.* Though the modern skeptic refuses to give any credence to the Genesis story of creation, the account still stands as reasonable and plausible. It rises above all the speculations about beginnings found in any other ancient writings. As given by Moses, the account is pure and straightforward. And though the creation of the universe and humans was an awesome and infinitely complicated affair, the written Word with sublime but simple dignity points to the larger steps the Lord employed in the creation of all things (Gen. 1:1—2:25). Proverbs concludes, "The LORD by wisdom founded the earth, by understanding He established the heavens" (3:19).

2. *The attributes of God.* The human mind could not conceive of God who exists in all His glory. Though faint echoes about the true God were in the misty recollections of pagan theology, none of their descriptions of deity come close to the awesomeness of the God of the Scriptures. From Genesis to Revelation, the Lord is omnipotent, omnipresent, and infinitely holy beyond comprehension. His glorious attributes eclipse the sinful character of humans. He is just and merciful and cannot tolerate the slightest expression of sin in His presence. The psalmist cried, Let the

people "praise Your great and awesome name; holy is He" (99:3), and "Exalt the LORD our God and worship at His holy hill, for holy is the LORD our God" (v. 9).

3. *The Trinity.* A conclave of a thousand theologians could have never conceived the doctrine of the Trinity. Yet from cover to cover, the Word of God attests the tri-unity of the Lord. No one verse tells it all. One must view the entire tapestry of passages to begin to understand this doctrine. Each prophet and apostle contributes by inspiration some small aspect of this truth until the teaching on the nature of God is complete. The doctrine of the Trinity helps demonstrate the nature of Scripture as divine revelation.

4. *The nature of humanity.* What book written by man so unashamedly reveals the sinfulness and terrible cruelty of the human species? There is none. As well, the failings of the prophets and writers of the Scriptures are exposed without hesitation. At least one author of the Bible, if he were not under the direction of the Spirit of God, would surely have loved to proclaim his own greatness or at least downplay his own sinfulness. Nevertheless, this is not found in the writings of the Bible. The weaknesses and imperfections of the most pious personalities in the Scriptures, including the prophets and disciples, are exposed and revealed. Total depravity is an inescapable truth of the Word of God. The most honored of personalities admitted their sins. David called himself a worm (Ps. 22:6); Isaiah confessed his unclean lips (Isa. 6:5); and Paul admitted his unworthiness as an apostle (1 Cor. 15:9).

5. *The plan of history.* Only the Bible unfolds in minute detail the destiny of humanity. It shows accurately the spread of tribal peoples across the face of much of the earth (Gen. 10, the table of nations). With uncanny certainty, the prophet Daniel predicted the rise and fall of the four great powers of the Western hemisphere and the Middle East. He wrote of Babylon, Medo-Persia, Greece, and Rome (Dan. 7). He predicted the division of the Grecian kingdom into four parts (8:22) and the final formation of Rome into ten nations. The scattering and regathering of Israel are given special emphasis in the Word of God. These and other details about the rise and fall of nations point to the fact that the Bible is divine revelation. The Lord said that He is the

only God who can proclaim and declare "the things that are coming and the events that are going to take place" (Isa. 44:7).

6. *Final destiny*. Not only does the Word of God write the last chapters of world history, but it also warns humanity in detailed revelation of the coming judgment. This judgment will end history as we know it. Yet it speaks of God's mercy in the salvation provided in Christ. However, it warns of a terrible end for those who reject Him (Rev. 21:8). These sobering doctrines cannot be ignored. If the Bible comes to us by divine inspiration, it forces human beings to make a decision to accept or reject these revelations about their personal, eternal destinies. The Word of God is either revealed truth or it is not.

7. *The spiritual world*. Almost all other religions present a shallow or fictional view of the spiritual world that we cannot understand with our human senses. Yet the Bible not only reveals God's own nature and future earthly events but also about how humanity can have personal relationships with Him. In the Upper Room discourse, Christ revealed that no one can come to God the Father but through Him (John 14:6). A believer in Christ can know the Father equally as well (v. 7). In other words, Christianity is not simply an intellectual body of revealed facts but a living relationship with the one true God. The written Word leads the child of God to an actual spiritual relationship with the Lord. Christ's disciples can know the Father personally and have a personal, abiding relationship with Jesus (15:4) but also enjoy the Spirit of God as Helper in the spiritual life (14:17, 26).

God Has Revealed Himself

No matter how many demonstrations can be listed that verify the Bible as revealed truth, the natural mind remains in rebellion, searching for any excuse to keep from submitting to the Bible and to the God of the Bible. The lost have no hope and are without God in the world (Eph. 2:12). They indulge their hearts and minds and are "by nature children of wrath" (v. 3). Illumination of truth begins when persons are made "alive together with Christ" (v. 5). By this work of opening our eyes to revelation, God "has shone in our hearts to give the Light of the knowledge of the glory of God in the face of Christ" (2 Cor. 4:6). By this we are able to see eternal things (v. 18). Lightner well summarizes:

It is clear that in this life we will never know God fully. Truly He is incomprehensible. As people, we possess all the limitations common to humanity. As God, the Lord possesses perfections and completeness to an infinite degree. Nevertheless, God can be known sufficiently for salvation and for living the Christian life. God has made Himself known through nature and also in the written Word. Because He has revealed Himself, He holds people responsible for the knowledge He has given them about Himself. And because God has spoken, people are without excuse for not knowing Him (see Rom. 1:18–20).[36]

FOR DISCUSSION

1. What is important about the doctrine of divine revelation?

2. What is the neoorthodox view of the Word of God?

3. What is implied by the words *rational* and *reasonable*?

4. Define and describe *progressive revelation*.

5. What is meant by *special revelation* and *general revelation*?

For Further Study

Bibliology Texts

Warfield, Benjamin Breckinridge. *The Inspiration and Authority of the Bible*. Philadelphia: Presbyterian and Reformed, 1960.

Commentaries

Carson, D. A. *The Gospel According to John*. Grand Rapids: Eerdmans, 1991.

Ellicott, Charles John, ed. Ellicott's *Commentary on the Whole Bible*, 8 vols. Grand Rapids: Zondervan, 1959.

Lightner, Robert P. *The God of the Bible and Other Gods*. Grand Rapids: Kregel, 1998.

Slotki, I. W. *Isaiah*. London: Soncino Press, 1972.

Unger, Merrill F. *Unger's Commentary on the Old Testament*. Reprint. Chattanooga, Tenn.: AMG, 2002.

Dictionaries

Geisler, Norman L. *Baker Encyclopedia of Christian Apologetics*. Grand Rapids: Baker, 1999.

Hermeneutics

Ramm, Bernard. *Protestant Biblical Interpretation.* Grand Rapids: Baker, 1986.

History

Murray, Alexander S. *Who's Who in Mythology.* New York: Wings Books, 1988.

Language Studies

Balz, Horst, and Gerhard Schneider, eds. *Exegetical Dictionary of the New Testament.* 3 vols. Grand Rapids: Eerdmans, 1994.

Theology

Berkhof, Louis. Systematic Theology. Grand Rapids: Eerdmans, 1994.

Calvin, John. *Institutes of the Christian Religion,* trans. Henry Beveridge. Reprint. Grand Rapids: Eerdmans, 1993.

Chafer, Lewis S. *Systematic Theology.* 8 vols. Grand Rapids: Kregel, 1993.

Elwell, Walter A., ed. *Evangelical Dictionary of Theology.* Grand Rapids: Baker, 1997.

Harris, R. Laird, ed. *Theological Wordbook of the Old Testament.* 2 vols. Chicago: Moody, 1981.

Hodge, Charles. *Systematic Theology.* 3 vols. Grand Rapids: Eerdmans, 1981.

Lockyer, Herbert. *All the Doctrines of the Bible.* Grand Rapids: Zondervan, 1964.

Strong, Augustus Hopkins. *Systematic Theology.* Old Tappan, N.J.: Revell, 1979.

Thiessen, Henry C. *Lectures in Systematic Theology.* Grand Rapids: Eerdmans, 1990.

Chapter Five

The Doctrine of Inspiration

*A*mong the many works of the Holy Spirit, two are closely related as to how we were given the sacred Scriptures. Though interrelated and interdependent, they are nonetheless distinct in bringing about the canon of the Bible. Historically, these two works are termed *revelation* and *inspiration*. Other works of the Spirit related to the application of the Word are *conviction* and *illumination*. But since these activities refer more directly to the Spirit's work of regeneration (or possibly illumination), a detailed look at these terms will be left to another discussion.

A distinction should be made between divine revelation and inspiration. The ancient prophets received a revelation from God. God spoke to them and disclosed His message and His purposes, which they could not have discovered on their own. The message that He gave was certain and trustworthy. Moses, for example, received revelation and then by the work of inspiration made it known to others, and yet the two are distinguishable. Edward J. Young makes this clarification:

> It is true that the two are very closely related, and it is true that in the broad sense inspiration is a form or mode of revelation. At the same time, it is well to keep in mind the fundamental distinction that, whereas revelation is essentially the communication of knowledge of information, inspiration is designed to secure infallibility in teaching.[1]

Inspiration is not the same as illumination. Christians experience illumination because they are indwelt by the Spirit of God who brings understanding of sin and guides them into walking in truth. This work

55

of the Spirit is subject to degrees, depending on the believers' spiritual state and maturity. Nevertheless, inspiration is not subject to degrees, seeing that in every instance the breath of God expressed itself fully and accurately through the human instrument.

Revelation concerns the Holy Spirit's work of disclosing divine truth to people. *Illumination* concerns the Spirit's work of enabling people to understand that truth. *Inspiration* concerns the Spirit's work of enabling human authors to accurately receive and record that truth.

Inspiration Defined

A rather simple definition is taken from Gaussen's classic work: Inspiration is "that inexplicable power which the Divine Spirit put forth of old on the authors of holy Scripture, in order to provide guidance even in the employment of the words they used, and to preserve them alike from all error and from all omission."[2] Another brief definition is as follows: "Inspiration is a supernatural influence of the Holy Spirit upon divinely chosen men in consequence of which their writings become trustworthy and authoritative."[3]

Frank E. Gaebelein penned another definition that has served this author well since college days:

> The doctrine of plenary inspiration holds that the original docu-
> ments of the Bible were written by men, who, though permitted the
> exercise of their own personalities and literary talents, yet wrote
> under the control and guidance of the Spirit of God, the result being
> in every word of the original documents a perfect and errorless
> recording of the exact message which God desired to give to man.[4]

A good definition of divine inspiration must include the following elements:

1. The supernatural, personal, and direct activity of the Holy Spirit of God.

2. The personal and genuine participation of human writers.

3. Supernatural guidance as to the individual words of the Bible (verbal).

4. A disallowing of any errors or omissions (inerrancy).

5. Extending to the totality of the Scriptures (plenary).

6. Relating only to the original autographs.

7. Communicating the exact message God intended to give to people (infallibility and authority).

The purpose of this chapter is to explore and substantiate these major elements by noting both what is meant and what is not meant when we speak of the Holy Spirit's work of inspiration.

Inspiration Explained

Though numerous passages on this subject are in both the Old Testament and New Testament, two passages are generally recognized as the most important, since they emphasize the two elements of the divine and the human in inspiration.

Second Timothy 3:16

Let's look at this verse in its context:

> You, however, continue in the things you have learned and become convinced of, knowing from whom you have learned them, and that from childhood you have known the sacred writings which are able to give you the wisdom that leads to salvation through faith which is in Christ Jesus. All Scripture is inspired by God and profitable for teaching, for reproof, for correction, for training in righteousness; so that the man of God may be adequate, equipped for every good work. I solemnly charge you in the presence of God and of Christ Jesus, who is to judge the living and the dead, and by His appearing and His kingdom: preach the word; be ready in season and out of season; reprove, rebuke, exhort, with great patience and instruction. For the time will come when they will not endure sound doctrine; but wanting to have their ears tickled, they will accumulate for themselves teachers in accordance to their own desires; and will turn away their ears from the truth and will turn aside to myths. (2 Tim. 3:14—4:4)

It is clear from the context, and particularly the immediately preceding verse, that what is referred to as "Scripture" in 2 Timothy 3:16 are the holy writings of the Old Testament. Our English word *inspired* comes from the Latin *inspiratio*, which means to "breathe in" or "into." The word inspired can thus be misleading as a description of what actually occurred in the giving of the Scriptures.

The Greek word translated *inspired* is *theopneustos* from the word for "God" (*theos*) and the word for "breath" or "breathing" (*pneō*). Hence, the word *theopneustos* literally means "God-breathed." The emphasis then is not to breathe *in* or *into* but rather to breathe out, i.e., to exhale. Commenting on the word *theopneustos,* Warfield writes:

> The Greek term has, however, nothing to say of inspirating or of inspiration: it speaks only of a "spiring" or "spiration." What it says of Scripture is, not that it is "breathed into by God" or is the product of the Divine "inbreathing" into its human authors, but that it is breathed out by God, "God breathed," the product of the creative breath of God.[5]

It needs to be acknowledged that in context 2 Timothy 3:16 refers primarily to the Old Testament writings. The New Testament uses the Greek word *graphē* ("writing") fifty times, all of which refer primarily to the Old Testament, though the entirety of the canonical Scripture cannot be ruled out. It could be affirmed that the construction used in verse 16 has a broader meaning that would allow for the inclusion of the New Testament writings. The construction *pasa graphē* ("all Scripture") can have a characteristic idea so that the phrase can mean "all that have characteristics of canonical Scripture." Also, *graphē* is used in reference to New Testament writings in 1 Timothy 5:18 and 2 Peter 3:16.

Paul was not simply giving us theological information about the nature of the Scriptures, but rather his intent in the context was that we should see the purpose of the Scriptures for our good, just as it had been for Timothy (cf. 2 Tim. 3:14–15). It is "profitable for teaching, for reproof, for correction, for training in righteousness; so that the man of God may be adequate, equipped for every good work" (2 Tim. 3:16–17).

Now it might be useful to point out that inspiration guarantees the accuracy, not necessarily the truthfulness, of all that is written. Verbal inspiration does not mean that every sentence of the Bible in isolation from its context is God's Word. Not everything contained in the Bible is affirmed by the Bible itself. Some words cannot be taken as God's words. They are included in order to be contradicted, not endorsed. For example, the Scripture sometimes contains only the best of human reasoning (e.g., some statements in Ecclesiastes); at other times, it contains false conclusions (e.g., the words of Job's friends); and at other times outright lies (e.g., the words of Satan to Eve). Nevertheless, even these things were recorded for our instruction. In such cases, the statements must be tested by the clear affirmations of Scripture in other places.

"The inspired Word of God is what is being affirmed, whether as instruction, command or promise."[6] "Whenever the Bible states a fact as a fact, . . . it must be true whether this is in a revelation of God's own being, His moral standards, or His prophetic program, or whether it involves history, geography, or facts that are related to science."[7] "Verbal inspiration means that what the Holy Spirit has spoken and still speaks through the human authors, understood according to the plain, natural meaning of the words used, is true and without error."[8]

Second Peter 1:21

Once again, we should see this verse in its larger context:

> For we did not follow cleverly devised tales when we made known to you the power and coming of our Lord Jesus Christ, but we were eyewitnesses of His majesty. For when He received honor and glory from God the Father, such an utterance as this was made to Him by the Majestic Glory, "This is My beloved Son with whom I am well-pleased"—and we ourselves heard this utterance made from heaven when we were with Him on the holy mountain. And so we have the prophetic word made more sure, to which you do well to pay attention as to a lamp shining in a dark place, until the day dawns and the morning star arises in your hearts. But know this first of all, that no prophecy of Scripture is a matter of one's own interpretation, for no prophecy was ever made by an act of human will, but men moved by the Holy Spirit spoke from God. But false prophets also arose among the people, just as there will also be false teachers among you, who will secretly introduce destructive heresies, even denying the Master who bought them, bringing swift destruction upon themselves. And many will follow their sensuality, and because of them the way of the truth will be maligned. (2 Pet. 1:16—2:2)

Whether the process was oral or written, the declaration is that these men were "moved by the Holy Spirit." The word translated *moved* (*pherō*) was the word for carrying a burden, so to speak. The human writers were carried along as a burden to a prescribed destination. The word was also used of a ship being propelled by the wind in its sails as it moved toward an intended goal. Therefore, the writers of Scripture were carried to the end that the Spirit of God intended, like passengers on a boat who are inevitably carried to their destination.

> As *theopneustos* indicated that the Scriptures originated with, and are therefore the Word of God, *phero* ("borne along") indicates the fact that the Spirit so wrought in the holy men of God as to secure

through them an inerrant record of the mind of God . . . While *phero* indicates the divine control of the human authors, it allows in its breadth of expression for an indefinite variety of ways in which the end shall be attained.[9]

Other passages support the concept of a dual authorship, even referring to the act of writing (Luke 1:70; Acts 1:16; 3:18; 1 Cor. 14:37; Gal. 1:11–12; Heb. 1:1–2; 1 Pet. 1:10, 12; Rev. 21:5; cf. Ex. 17:14; 24:4; Deut. 27:8; Isa. 30:8; Jer. 30:2; John 5:46). J. I. Packer addresses one of the common criticisms of this position:

> The inspiring process, which brought each writer's thoughts into such exact coincidence with those of God, necessarily involved a unique oversight and control of those who were its subjects. Some moderns doubt whether this control could leave room for any free mental activity on the writers' part, and pose a dilemma: either God's control of the writers was complete, in which case they wrote as robots or automata (which clearly they did not), or their minds worked freely as they wrote the Scriptures, in which case God could not fully have controlled them, or kept them from error. Exponents of this dilemma usually hold that the evidence for errors (false statements purporting to be true) in the Bible is in fact as conclusive as the evidence for spontaneous self-expression by its human writers. But our first comment must be that this is not so. Man has assumed that Scripture errs, but it cannot in principle be proved, any more than it can be proved that Jesus was not morally perfect. Both questions are actually settled farther back: if Jesus was God incarnate, He could not but be morally perfect, and if Scripture is the Word of the God of truth, it cannot but be true and trustworthy at all points. Moreover, the dilemma rests on the assumption that full psychological freedom of thought and actions, and full subjection to divine control, are incompatible; and this is not true either. If the inspiration of the prophets was what all Scriptures say it was, it is absurd to deny that the whole Bible could be similarly inspired.[10]

While the work of inspiration is beyond human comprehension or explanation, it makes clear that the human authors were not left to their own devices and were not simply exercising ordinary power. God was working through them, breathing out His word with them as the channels.[11]

The inspiration of the Scripture is a miracle—a miracle by which God conveys to us His perfect revelation designed to meet our deepest needs. It is much like the miracle of the incarnation, and it is possible to draw something of an analogy between the two. The writer to the Hebrews made much of this comparison. "God, after He spoke long ago to the fathers in the prophets in many portions and in many ways, in these last days has spoken to us in His Son, whom He appointed heir of all things, through whom also He made the world" (Heb. 1:1–2).

As in the incarnation (the Living Word), the human and the divine were joined, the result being the impeccable (sinless) person of Jesus Christ. So in the Scriptures (the Written Word), the human and the divine were joined, the result being an inerrant record of the exact message God desired to communicate to us. Though the comparison is not exact, there is clearly here a parallel in God the Spirit's working to guarantee the perfection of the result. Stott draws many of the critical items together:

> This then is the apostolic claim: that the same Holy Spirit of God, who searches the depths of God and revealed His researches to the apostles, went on to communicate them through the apostles in words with which He Himself supplied them. He spoke his words through their words so that they were equally the words of God and the words of man. This is the double authorship of Scripture . . . It is also the meaning of "inspiration." The inspiration of Scripture was not a mechanical process that bypassed God's personhood or the writers'. It was intensely personal; for it involved a Person, the Holy Spirit, speaking through persons, prophets and apostles, in such a way that His words were theirs and their words were His simultaneously.[12]

The cautionary words of Lewis Sperry Chafer are also appropriate at this point:

> As to *how* the divine revelation was given to the human author, none other than God or the elect man could know. It was wholly within those personal and sacred relationships into which none other might intrude. Here the devout soul will hesitate, and the prudent will at least respect the silence of God. . . . The Scriptures give abundant teaching as to the *fact* of inspiration but do not offer explanation of this phenomenon. The *how* of every miracle is wanting, and inspiration is a miracle. Concerning this and all miracles man is called upon to *believe* and not to *elucidate*.[13]

What Inspiration Is Not

The divine miracle of inspiration has led to attempts to explain its inscrutability. A review of these will help us understand the biblical doctrine by examining what inspiration does *not* mean.

It Is Not Simply Human Genius

Human genius is a natural ability or talent, however extensive it may be in some cases. One of the extreme views teaches that the Bible is merely like any other human book of merit. Though some divine influence may have given the writers an unusual ability of expression, it is no more than a human production and like other such books, particularly those expressing ancient concepts, is subject to error.

Inspiration in the sense we are using it here is supernatural in character. It was an endowment given to the writers of the Old and New Testaments, enabling them to write these books. The common utterance of these writers, "Thus says the Lord" (and similar utterances), indicates a source far beyond human invention that differs not only in degree but also in kind.

It Is Not Simply a Heightened (Christian) Spiritual Genius

This is a revision of the first one noted, contending that the Bible is not unlike other human books of merit in that in some special way God endued the authors with unusual insights and, like all good gifts that come from God, may be used to His glory. The biblical writers were "inspired" only in the same sense in which Christians of all ages have been inspired. Like the first theory noted, this one also ignores the claims of the biblical writers. Further, it offers no security against error, would apparently allow for additional "scripture," and confuses inspiration with illumination. At this point, we again emphasize that *the object is not the inspiration of the human authors but the books*—not the *writers* but the *writings*. It centers not on human instruments but on the record.

It Is Not Simply an Assertion of Partial Inspiration or Degrees of Inspiration

Another theory asserts that only parts of the Bible are inspired or that various parts are subject to degrees of inspiration. These classifications are determined by the nature or content of the material. The highest degree would be of truth previously unknown or undiscoverable by human means. A second level would be a guard against any "serious error" in the recording of facts already known or discoverable. A third level would be simply a matter of "divine authority" given to portions composed without any divine "intervention" or "guidance." In addition to the objections noted above, we might ask who decides on what degree each portion should be assigned and on what basis. It would appear that this theory also confuses degrees of value with degrees of inspiration.

It Does Not Simply Mean the Bible Contains the Word of God or Becomes the Word of God

The question is sometimes asked: Is the Bible the Word of God, or does it only contain the Word of God? If the question implies that God spoke every word in the Bible and hence every word is true, the answer is no. If, on the other hand, the meaning is that God, by the Holy Spirit, caused every word in the Bible, true or false, to be accurately recorded, then the answer is yes. The record includes the lies of Satan, the words of false prophets, the best of human philosophizing, and yet they are God's words in that he caused them to be recorded for our profit. In this sense, the Bible does not merely contain the Word of God; it is the Word of God.

A form of this theory advanced in this century is that of neoorthodoxy, particularly in the teachings of Karl Barth. While not disallowing supernatural elements in the composition of the Scriptures, Barth claimed the Bible contained errors and so could not be accepted as literal truth in its entirety. However, since the Bible is the record of the revelatory acts of God, He can speak through the Scriptures and use them as a means for communicating His truth to us individually. The Bible is thus a channel for divine revelation, and by this theory, its content *becomes* true only as it speaks to and is comprehended by the individual reader or hearer. Like the preceding theories, it appoints the individual as the final authority as to what is true.

It Is Not Simply the Inspiration of Ideas (Concept Inspiration)

This theory asserts that God gave only thoughts or concepts to the writers and then permitted them to express (record) these thoughts in their own words as they could remember and record them. This view allows for and acknowledges errors in the Scriptures, though no serious error. It is contended that we can have confidence with regard to salvation issues, though there are errors with regard to historical, geographic, and scientific matters.

However, the Bible itself directly contradicts the idea that only concepts were communicated to the human writers. Repeatedly, emphasis is given to the very words, even the parts of words of Scripture. Moreover, is it really possible to convey errorless thoughts without the employment of errorless facts? Does this not depend on the cruciality of the message? For example, plotting a course from here to a distant planet might be more critical than getting directions from the Chicago Loop to one of the suburbs. Stott correctly observes, "Words are the units of which sentences are made up. Words are the building blocks of speech. It is therefore impossible to frame a precise message without constructing precise sentences composed of precise words."[14] Stott then goes on to illustrate:

> Think of the trouble we all take to compose a cable or telegram. Let us say we've got only twelve words. All the same, we are determined to send a message which will not only be understood, but which will not be misunderstood. So we draft it, redraft it and draft it again. We scratch out a word here and we add a word there until we have polished our message to our satisfaction. Words matter. Every speaker who wants to communicate a message that will be understood and not misunderstood knows the importance of words. Every preacher who takes pains to prepare his sermons chooses his words with care. Every writer, whether of letters or articles or books, knows that words matter.[15]

One of the repeated refrains of the Scripture is that the very words are by God's direction. God directed Moses as to the words (Ex. 4:12, 15; cf. 3:12–18), and we are told that Moses did write the words as the Lord commanded (Ex. 17:14; 24:4; Deut. 27:8; cf. John 5:46). It was said of Jeremiah that the Lord put His "words" into his mouth. John was commanded to "write, for these words are faithful and true" (Rev. 21:5). Christ spoke of the eternal importance of even the smallest letter or the small stroke of a pen in making one letter distinct from another (Matt. 5:17–18). In Galatians 3:16, Paul's whole argument rested on the distinction between the singular and plural of one word.

The importance of the inspiration of words as opposed to merely concept-of-thought inspiration is well stated by Miller:

> It is sheer nonsense to talk about inspired thoughts apart from inspired words. Dean Burgon, one of England's greatest scholars, said, "You cannot dissect inspiration into substance and form. As for thoughts being inspired apart from words that give them expression, you might as well talk of a tune without notes or a sum without figures. No such dream can abide the daylight for a moment. It is as illogical as it is worthless, and cannot be too sternly put down."[16]

It Is Not Verbal Dictation (Mechanical Inspiration)

Muslims believe that Allah dictated the Koran to Mohammed, word by word in Arabic. A similar theory asserts that the Spirit of God dictated every word of the record to the biblical writers much as a boss might dictate letters to an assistant. Though this theory is certainly safe in preserving the errorless and authoritative character of the Bible, it fails to offer an adequate explanation for the differences in the styles of writing that appear in the Scriptures and those aspects that reflect the individual personalities of the human writers. One theologian asserts that God, knowing the writers' individualities, employed their unique characteristics in His dictation. Without denying that God knows men more accurately than any person possibly could, this explanation suggests something of deception on the part of the Spirit. It gives the appearance of genuine human involvement when indeed it was essentially excluded. With the possibility of a few minor exceptions, the biblical writers appear to have been in full possession of their faculties and individual distinctiveness while the Spirit was communicating His words by means of their words. Verbal dictation fails to do justice as well to what was noted earlier from 2 Peter 1:21. As a single illustration, would not Paul's heartfelt plea for Israel lose its meaning if it was dictated by God (Rom. 9:1–3)? This theory places strange limitations on a sovereign and wise God.

> Representations are sometimes made as if, when God wished to produce sacred books which would incorporate His will—a series of letters like those of Paul, for example—He was reduced to the necessity of going down to the earth and painfully scrutinizing the men He found there, seeking anxiously for the one who, on the whole, promised best for His purpose; and then violently forcing the material He wished expressed through him, against his natural bent, and with as little loss from his recalcitrant characteristics as possible. Of course, nothing of the sort took place. If God wished to give His people a series of letters like Paul's He prepared a Paul to write them, and the Paul He brought to the task was a Paul who spontaneously would write just such letters.[17]

Packer makes an observation that reminds us of God's ways of working. "Inspiration took many psychological forms; here, as elsewhere, God showed Himself a God of variety. The basic form of the process was *dualistic* inspiration, in which the recipient of revelation remained conscious throughout of the distinction between himself, the hearer and reporter, and God, the Speaker to and through him."[18]

It Is Not an Assertion That Every Word of the Bible Is Literally True

Biblical writers used many different literary forms or genres. Each of these must be interpreted according to its unique rules—history as history, parable as parable, apocalyptic as apocalyptic, poetry as poetry, and so on. What is inspired is the *natural* sense of the words according to the intentions of the author, whether literal or figurative.

It Is Not an Assertion That Our Present Translations Are Inspired

The record to which inspiration applies is the original record—the autographs of Moses, David, Solomon, Daniel, Luke, John, Paul, and the others. Likely no copy, and certainly no translation, is absolutely without error, considering the fallacies and propensities of humankind. Some would then say that this makes pointless our whole insistence on inspired (and thus inerrant) Scripture, for to insist on the inerrancy of a parchment that no living person has ever seen is merely an academic question and of no value. However, such a contention is an affront to the very character of God. James M. Gray recounted the following story.

> Some years ago a "liberal" theologian . . . remarked that it was a matter of small consequence whether a pair of trousers were originally perfect if they were now rent. To which the valiant and witty David James Burrell replied, that it might be a matter of small consequence to the wearer of the trousers, but the tailor who made them would prefer to have it understood that they did not leave his shop that way. And then he added that if the Most High must train among knights of the shears, He might at least be regarded as the best of the guild, and One who drops no stitches and sends out no imperfect work.[19]

Special Witnesses to the Inspiration of the New Testament

By this time, it should be clear that our only reliable source for information on the inspiration of Scripture is Scripture itself. Who better than God would know and be able to reveal the nature of His revelation to men and women? Yet in the minds of most, this immediately raises the charge of circular reasoning: The Bible is inspired by God. How do you know? Because it says it is.

Without going into an extensive response to this charge, a few simple observations can be made.

1. Self-testimony cannot be ruled out unless it is disproved. Just as in a court of law a person is permitted the right to give self-testimony, so also should the Scripture be allowed to speak for itself. Such testimony is open to proper challenge on the content, but the self-testimony must be permitted.

2. Some truths, particularly about people, will never be known apart from self-testimony. Should not God be permitted to tell us about Himself, particularly about His character, i.e., that He cannot lie? We are often led to believe that the primary determining factor as to what we may accept is its acceptableness to the modern person, whose untrustworthy character is beyond question.

3. The real issue is whether the Bible is to be regarded and accepted as a trustworthy teacher on any subject of substance. Just as the testimony of a person who lies about himself is of little value, how can we trust Scripture if it cannot be regarded as trustworthy when it testifies to itself?

4. One's basic presuppositions and commitments are crucial. Edward J. Young puts it succinctly:

    > We are in reality face to face with the question of theism. Unless we first think rightly of God, we shall be in error upon everything else. Unless we first think rightly of God, we shall indeed be in error when we come to consider His Word. We Christians need not be ashamed to proclaim boldly that our final persuasion of the Divinity of the Bible is from God himself. God, in His gentle grace, has identified His Word for us; He has told us that the Bible is from Himself. Those who know Him not may depreciate this doctrine of the internal testimony of the Spirit; those who are His know that God has truly brought them out of darkness into light.[20]

To conclude, then, this brief response to the challenge of circular reasoning, note Young's further words:

> It is then from God Himself that we learn the true character of the Scriptures. In the very nature of the case it must be so. Only God can identify what He himself has spoken. If man, unaided, could identify God's Word, man would have powers that are God's alone.

And if man really has these powers, God, whatever else He might be, would not be the One of whom the Bible speaks.[21]

The Testimony of Jesus Christ

Note the words of Jesus:

> Do not think that I came to abolish the Law or the Prophets; I did not come to abolish but to fulfill. For truly I say to you, until heaven and earth pass away, not the smallest letter or stroke shall pass away from the Law until all is accomplished. Whoever then annuls one of the least of these commandments, and teaches others to do the same, shall be called least in the kingdom of heaven; but whoever keeps and teaches them, he shall be called great in the kingdom of heaven. (Matt. 5:17–19)

Christ's View of the Nature of the Scripture. In these words, our Lord clearly expressed the full authority and eternal character of the words God gave as recorded in the Old Testament Scriptures. These words partake of the very character of God in that they are true, authoritative, and eternal, and He is committed to their fulfillment as expressive of the divine will. For Jesus to appeal to the Scriptures was to end all argument as He did in response to Satan's temptations in the wilderness. Jesus repeatedly asserted, "It is written" (Matt. 4:4, 7, 10; cf. Luke 4:4, 8, 12). That He placed all Old Testament writings in the category of Scripture is further affirmed in Luke 24:44–45; cf. 24:27.

Following a discussion of Jesus' words in John 10:35, which include the phrase, "The Scripture cannot be broken," Gaussen asks, "Is it possible to admit that the Being who makes such use of the Scriptures *does not believe in their plenary verbal inspiration?* In addition, if He could have imagined that the words of the Bible were left to the free choice and pious fancies of the sacred writers, would He ever have dreamed of founding such arguments on such a word? The Lord Jesus, our Savior and our Judge, believed then in the most complete inspiration of the Scriptures; and for Him the first rule of all hermeneutics, and the commencement of all exegesis, was this simple maxim applied to the most minute expressions of the written word, *'and the Scripture cannot be broken'.*"[22]

Christ's View of the Holy Spirit's Future Work. Jesus Christ preauthenticated the writing of the New Testament by the apostles. They would speak and write "with the authentication and authority of Christ, and the inspiration of the New Testament Scriptures partakes of the peculiar quality of being a work of the Holy Spirit as the person of the Godhead sent into the world at Pentecost."[23] This may be seen in the following ways:

1. Jesus chose certain men to receive additional revelations and to serve as His witnesses to these things (Matt. 28:19–20; John 15:27; 16:13; Acts 1:8; cf. Acts 9:15–17).

2. When they spoke for Him in the Spirit, Jesus gave their words exactly the same authority as His own (Matt. 10:14–15; Luke 10:16; John 13:20; 17:20; cf. 1 Cor. 14:37; Rev. 22:19).

3. Jesus declared that He had much more to say to His disciples that they were not able to bear at that time (John 16:12).

4. Jesus promised that when the Spirit came, "He will guide you into all the truth," and "He will disclose to you what is to come" (John 16:13). René Pache summarizes these points well:

> It is evident that none but the Holy Spirit could meet the needs of the four evangelists in their staggering task: that of recounting the essentials in the life of Christ, of reproducing exactly His words, of choosing the most significant events for the blessing of centuries to come, of passing over numerous details (John 20:30; 21:25) and of recounting facts which were unwitnessed (such as the temptation in the desert). Moreover the four accounts were all to harmonize in complementing one another. . . . As for the rest of the New Testament, the apostles plainly would never of themselves have been able to preach the wisdom of God, mysterious and hidden as it is (1 Cor. 2:7), to unveil the mystery of Christ unknown even to the angels (Eph. 3:3–11), to exalt the excellence of the new covenant (Heb. 5:11; 8:6) or to reveal future and eternal things (Rev. 4:1—22:21).[24]

The Testimony of the Apostles

In addition to what has been noted above, the writers of the New Testament were conscious of the authority of their writings, that they were adding to the body of the Scriptures by the direction of the Holy Spirit, and that its content had equal authority. For example, Paul claimed, "The things which I write to you are the Lord's commandment" (1 Cor. 14:37). In correcting the Corinthians he wrote: "Which things we also speak, not in words taught by human wisdom, but in those taught by the Spirit, combining spiritual thoughts with spiritual words" (1 Cor. 2:13). The gospel he preached carried the authority of heaven as received by "revelation from Jesus Christ" (Gal. 1:11–12; cf. vv. 7–8, 15–16). He informed the Thessalonians that "what commandments we gave you [were] by the authority of the Lord Jesus" (1 Thess. 4:2) and "by the word of the Lord" (1 Thess. 4:15). He declared the source of his authority to command their obedience: "Now we command you, brethren, in the name of our Lord" (2 Thess. 3:6; cf. vv. 12, 14).

The New Testament writers further declared the inspiration of one another's writings. In 1 Timothy 5:18, Paul cited a quotation from Deuteronomy (25:4) and another from Luke (10:7) and in a single sentence called them both "Scripture." Peter, while acknowledging his difficulty in understanding all that Paul had written, placed those writings in the category of "Scripture": "And regard the patience of our Lord as salvation; just as also our beloved brother Paul, according to the wisdom given him, wrote to you, as also in all his letters, speaking in them of these things, in which are some things hard to understand, which the untaught and unstable distort, as they do also the rest of the Scriptures, to their own destruction" (2 Pet. 3:15–16).[25]

Inspiration Demonstrated

Years ago, Edward J. Young offered these words of warning, which are as challenging today, if not more so, as they were then.

> The church is indeed at the crossroads. Shall she listen to God or to man? Will she receive what the Spirit says concerning inspiration, or, turning back upon Him, will she cleave unto man? This is the choice to be made. Sad is it, however, that many do not realize the necessity for making a choice. Having their vision obscured by the dense fog that modern theology is casting over the way, many do not realize that there is a crossroads. They are not aware that they must decide which road they will follow. Unless something is done, they will travel on, taking the wrong turning, until the road leads them at last into the valley of lost hope and eternal death.[26]

Who then shall have the final word on His own Word if not God Himself? To turn aside from that witness is ultimately to reject the only dependable and true guide for this life and the next. We would share the conviction of Pache who wrote:

Let no one say then that we cannot demonstrate the inspiration of the New Testament by its own declarations. This is the reproach that had already been addressed to Jesus: "Thou bearest witness of thyself; thy witness is not true. Jesus answered and said unto them: Even if I bear witness of myself, my witness is true; for I know whence I came, and whither I go" (John 8:13–14). None but God can reveal His unsearchable person and perfections. In addition, Jesus alone can speak of what He is, with the claim: "The witness which I receive is not from man" (5:34). When we accepted Him by faith, He gave us life and convinced us of His deity. In like manner, the Scripture touches the heart and spirit of the sincere reader. The Lord who inspired it and who gives it life makes His voice heard from heaven by means of it—that voice which the good Shepherd's true sheep instinctively know. They believe and are convinced, not through any rationalistic argument, but because they have met the living God who has saved them.[27]

Once we have set forth what the Scripture says, we can go no further. We may still have questions, but they are questions that for the present we cannot answer. Our duty is to believe and bow in humble acceptance before the truth that God has chosen to reveal. Scripture has spoken, and it has spoken about itself, permitting us to learn much about its inspiration. Though it has not told us all, it has told us more than enough to trust and obey. God by His Spirit has spoken. Let us pay close attention to His voice and so walk in the path of truth. Drawing upon the wisdom of the poet, we need to trust in the Lord with all our hearts and not lean on our own understandings. In all our ways, let us acknowledge Him and know assuredly that He will direct our paths (Prov. 3:5–6).

> How firm a foundation, ye saints of the Lord,
> Is laid for your faith in His excellent Word!
> What more can He say than to you He hath said,
> To you who for refuge to Jesus have fled?
>
> Anonymous

The Means of Inspiration

Direct Voice. The Lord spoke directly with Adam (Gen. 3:9), Eve (v. 16), and to the serpent that beguiled Adam and Eve to sin (v. 14). What was said is recorded for us as Scripture. From Cain on (4:6), He spoke directly to almost every major figure found in the Book of Genesis. In the burning bush, the angel of God visited Moses (Ex. 3:2) and then called his name from the midst of the fire (v. 4). The five books of the Pentateuch are filled with the Lord speaking directly to Moses, Aaron, Miriam, and others. By voice, God addressed Joshua when He called him to be Moses' successor (Josh. 1:1).

Many verses illustrate how the Lord directed the leaders of old to do His bidding. Much of what He said to them was recorded and kept for us as Holy Scripture. The major and minor prophets were vocally addressed over and over by the voice of God. One of the most dramatic instances was when God called Ezekiel to the office of prophet. Ezekiel saw the vision of the wheel within the wheel (Ezek. 1:13–19) and then heard a voice "like the voice of the Almighty" (v. 24) which said, "Son of man, stand on your feet that I may speak with you!" (2:1). In Jeremiah we read, "The word of the LORD came to Jeremiah" (33:1), and, "Thus says the LORD of hosts" (v. 12). Such statements are scattered throughout the prophetic writings.

Though not always as dramatic as the experience of Ezekiel, all the prophets heard the voice of the Lord giving them important instructions and prophecies. It is this overabundance of revelations that makes our Old Testament energized with direct messages from the living God of the universe.

The angel of the Lord spoke several times in the Book of Matthew to those who would be the actors on stage at the birth of Jesus. At the baptism of Jesus, God the Father spoke audibly and said, "This is My beloved Son, in whom I am well-pleased" (Matt. 3:17). This and many other statements were written down and became part of the inspired record.

In the writings of the apostle Paul, he generally opened his letters with, "Grace to you and peace from God our Father and the Lord Jesus Christ." The Lord was speaking through the very thoughts and words of Paul, who then put them down on parchment and sent the messages to specific church audiences. The writer of the Book of Hebrews used a different formula, but he still showed the Lord's direct address to the author's Jewish readers. He wrote, "Now the God of peace, . . . equip you in every good thing to do His will, working in us that which is pleasing in His sight" (Heb. 13:20–21). The apostle James also showed the stamp of approval and apostolic mandate from the Lord, when he wrote in his epistle, "James, a bond-servant of God and of the Lord Jesus Christ, to the twelve tribes who are dispersed abroad, greetings"

(James 1:1). Peter began his letters with a similar authoritative greeting (1 Pet. 1:1; 2 Pet. 1:1).

The Book of Revelation has the most direct address of any of the New Testament books. John wrote that "the Revelation" *concerning* Jesus Christ was authorized by God to show, through the instrumentality of an angel, to John himself "the things which must soon take place" (Rev. 1:1). Revelation then closes with a direct statement from Jesus: "He who testifies to these things says, 'Yes, I am coming quickly'" (22:20).

Visions. Most of the Old Testament words for *vision* are derived from the Hebrew verbs *ḥāzāh* and *rā'āh* (both mean "to see"). The first time one of these words is used in this way is when "the word of the LORD came to Abram in a vision" (Gen. 15:1), though the text does not tell what he actually saw. In this vision, however, the Lord also spoke to Abram and gave him more information about the fact that he would not remain childless.

In the Old Testament, the word *vision(s)* is used over eighty times. The word is used only eighteen times in the New Testament, and most of those references are in the Book of Acts. Many of the vision revelations in the New Testament were given to the apostle Paul. For example, when he was threatened by the Jews in Corinth, "The Lord said to Paul in the night by a vision, 'Do not be afraid any longer'" (Acts 18:9). The last vision mentioned in Scripture is found in Revelation 9:17.

Dreams. Unlike visions, *dreams* constitute revelation while the recipient is asleep. The first time such a method of communicating the divine message was used was when "God came to Abimelech in a dream of the night" (Gen. 20:3). What the Lord said was written down and became part of the Genesis record put together by the prophet Moses.

Dreams may also come to unbelievers from lying and evil sources. Jude wrote that sinful people who "indulged in gross immorality" (v. 7) may also in the same manner "by dreaming, defile the flesh, and reject authority, and revile angelic majesties" (v. 8).

Angels. Throughout Scripture angels were used as the revelatory emissaries from the Lord. Angels are referred to almost three hundred times, with a majority of these references having to do with the communication of revelation.

Many verses mention "the angel of the Lord"; in most instances, that would be the preincarnate Christ. The most compelling proof is found by comparing Exodus 3:2 and 14 and John 8:58. In Exodus 3:2 as God appeared and spoke to Abraham, He was designated "the angel of the

LORD." In verse 14, the angel of the Lord told Abraham, "I AM WHO I AM." Christ told the Jews, "I say to you, before Abraham was born, I am" (John 8:58). Jesus was directly referring to the Exodus encounter between God and Moses. The disbelieving Jews got the point and "picked up stones to throw at Him" (v. 59) because they realized that He was claiming to be God, i.e., the angel of the Lord.

Animation. The Book of Daniel tells the dramatic story of Belshazzar and the writing on the wall during his banquet feasting. Because the king had exalted himself "against the Lord of heaven" (5:23), "the hand was sent from Him [the Lord], and this inscription was written out" (v. 24). Daniel interpreted the writing: The kingdom of Belshazzar was numbered, found deficient, and would be given to the Medes and Persians (vv. 26–28).

Transportation of the Prophet. Many prophets received messages by visions. By means of such a vision, the prophet Ezekiel was lifted up by the Holy Spirit and transported "to the exiles in Chaldea" (Ezek. 11:24). But the apostle John was actually taken into heaven to receive the message of "a throne . . . standing in heaven, and One sitting on the throne" (Rev. 4:2).

John described this incredible event: "Behold, a door standing open in heaven, and the first voice which I had heard, like the sound of a trumpet speaking with me, said, 'Come up here, and I will show you what must take place after these things'" (v. 1). John added, "Immediately I was in the Spirit; and behold, a throne" (v. 2).

The Trinity in Inspiration

In the inspiration of Scripture, the work of giving revelation is a task of all three persons in the Godhead.

God the Father. Using the word *Scripture* for all the books of the Old Testament, Paul told us that it was God-breathed [*theopneustos*] or *inspired* (2 Tim. 3:16). God the Father was the ultimate author of the Old Testament revelation. For example, the prophecy of the virgin birth of Christ (Isa. 7:14) was a message "spoken by the Lord through the prophet [Isaiah]" (Matt. 1:22). The Lord is also said to have spoken through Hosea (11:1), saying, "Out of Egypt I called My Son" (Matt. 2:15).

In the Old Testament, what the Lord said to Moses was written down and kept as the authentic message and law as from the very mouth of God Himself. As Moses faced death, he told the Israelites, "Take this book of the law and place it beside the ark of the covenant of the LORD your God, that it may remain there as a witness against you" (Deut. 31:26).

In expressing His judgment, the Lord said, "I will bring upon that land all My words which I have pronounced against it, all that is written in this book which Jeremiah has prophesied against all the nations" (Jer. 25:13). God told Jeremiah, "You shall prophecy against [Israel] all these words" (v. 30). Notice the importance of all the words (plural). God wanted every word to be spoken, because they represented His message to His own people. Again through Jeremiah, the Lord said: "'They have not listened to My words,' declares the LORD, 'which I sent to them again and again by My servants the prophets; but you did not listen,' declares the LORD" (Jer. 29:19).

Psalm 119, the longest psalm in the Bible, extols the virtues of the Word of the living God. In 176 verses, the psalmist said that the Old Testament contains God's truth for living. God's Word is described by terms like law, testimonies, precepts, ways, commandments, judgments, word, statutes, and ordinances. In verse after verse, the psalmist declared how important God's word was to him: "I trust in Your word" (v. 42), "I will keep Your law" (v. 44), "Your commandments . . . I love" (v. 48), "I will meditate on Your statutes" (v. 48).

In the New Testament, the writer of Hebrews summed up many of these same thoughts and wrote, "For the word of God is living and active and sharper than any two-edged sword, and piercing as far as the division of soul and spirit" (4:12). The early church, for the most part, realized that the apostles were also speaking the message of God the Father. Paul wrote to the Thessalonians, "You received the word of God which you heard from us, you accepted it not as the word of men, but for what it really is, the word of God, which also performs its work in you who believe" (1 Thess. 2:13).

Even Revelation, the last book of Scripture, states that in its message God was declaring "to His bond-servants, the things which must soon take place" (Rev. 1:1). The Bible comes directly to us from God the Father.

God the Holy Spirit. The Word of God also tells us that the Scriptures came about by the dramatic work of the Spirit of God. Certain verses ascribe the work of God in inspiration specifically to the Holy Spirit. For example, the writer of Hebrews paraphrased the text of Psalm 95:8, and said, "Therefore, just as the Holy Spirit says" (Heb. 3:7). Quoting Jeremiah 31:33–34, the author of Hebrews wrote, "The Holy Spirit also testifies to us: for after saying; . . . He [the Spirit] then says" (Heb. 10:15–17).

At the close of the Book of Revelation, the Holy Spirit and the bride say to an unbeliever who may be reading the book, "Come" in order to receive salvation and the water of life (Rev. 22:17). Earlier in Revelation, the Spirit also gave direct addresses to the seven churches (chaps. 2—3), "He who has an ear, let him hear what the Spirit says to the churches" (2:7, 11, 17, 29; 3:6, 13, 22). Peter told us the "prophets who prophesied of the grace that would come to you, . . . seeking to know what person or time the Spirit of Christ within them was indicating as He predicted the sufferings of Christ and the glories to follow" (1 Pet. 1:10–11). He later stated, "Men moved by the Holy Spirit spoke from God" (2 Pet. 1:21).

In the Old Testament, the prophets spoke of being inspired and directed by the Holy Spirit to communicate the Lord's message to the people of Israel. Micah wrote, "I am filled with power—with the Spirit of the LORD . . . to make known to Jacob his rebellious act" (Micah 3:8).

God the Son. The Book of Revelation has the most compelling evidence of the work of inspiration of Scripture by the Lord Jesus. John the apostle told us that God presented the Revelation *about* Jesus Christ to Him, the Son, in order that He would then *show* that revelation to John to record (Rev. 1:1). Further, the salutation at the beginning of the book came "from Jesus Christ, the faithful witness" (v. 5).

In Revelation 2—3, letters of exhortation were given to the seven churches by the Holy Spirit *and* by the Lord Jesus. Each "letter" began with Jesus' own message to the individual congregation. In the conclusion of each letter, Christ said, "He who has an ear, let him hear what the Spirit says to the churches." And along with the Holy Spirit, Christ gave the final appeal to unbelieving readers of the Book of Revelation, "And the Spirit and the bride say, 'Come.' And let the one who hears say, 'Come.'" (22:17).

FOR DISCUSSION

1. In a paragraph, define what is included in the doctrine of inspiration.

2. What is the problem of holding to *mechanical inspiration?*

3. Concerning the internal testimony of the Scripture to its own inspiration, how do we answer the charge of *circular reasoning?*

4. Summarize the various ways that scriptural inspiration came about.

5. Discuss the involvement of each person of the Trinity in the inspiration of the Bible.

For Further Study

Bible Introduction

Gaebelein, Frank E. *Exploring the Bible.* Wheaton, Ill: Van Kampen, 1950.

Bibliology Texts

Gaussen, Louis. *The Inspiration of the Holy Scriptures.* Chicago: Moody, n.d.

Lightner, Robert P. *The Saviour and the Scriptures.* Philadelphia: Presbyterian and Reformed, 1970.

Miller, H. S. *General Biblical Introduction.* Houghton, N.Y.: Word-Bearer, 1944.

Pache, René. *The Inspiration and Authority of Scripture.* Chicago: Moody, 1969.

Packer, J. I. *God Has Spoken: Revelation and the Bible.* Grand Rapids: Baker, 1994.

Stibbs, Alan M. "The Witness of Scripture to Its Inspiration." In *Revelation and the Bible,* edited by Carl F. H. Henry. Grand Rapids: Baker, 1958.

Stott, John. *God's Book for God's People.* Downers Grove, Ill: InterVarsity, 1982.

Warfield, Benjamin Breckenridge. *The Inspiration and Authority of the Bible.* Philadelphia: Presbyterian and Reformed, 1948.

Young, Edward J. *Thy Word Is Truth.* Grand Rapids, Eerdmans, 1957.

Dictionaries

Elwell, Walter A., ed. *Baker Encyclopedia of the Bible.* Grand Rapids: Baker, 1988.

Harrison, Everett F. *Baker's Dictionary of Theology.* Grand Rapids: Baker, 1960.

Theology

Chafer, Lewis Sperry. *Major Bible Themes.* Grand Rapids: Zondervan, 1975.

Chafer, Lewis Sperry. *Systematic Theology.* 8 vols. Dallas: Dallas Seminary Press, 1947; Grand Rapids: Kregel, 1993.

Feinberg, Charles, ed. *The Fundamentals for Today.* Kregel, 1958.

Walvoord, John F. *The Holy Spirit.* Findlay, Ohio: Dunham, 1958.

Chapter Six

The Formation of the Canon of Scripture

*A*s we now have it, the Bible contains sixty-six books written by approximately thirty-nine authors over a period of fifteen hundred years. As the canon came together, most of the writings of Scripture were received without debate or question. In isolated cases, some books were questioned as to their authenticity. However, such scrutiny and challenge in time brought forth a unanimous consensus as to what constituted the books of both the Old and New Testaments.

Unity of Scripture

Written by shepherds, fishermen, kings, sages, farmers, priests, and military generals, the Bible constitutes a unity unequalled in the annals of literature. Even the most skeptical must hunt to find supposed contradictions. There is clearly a unity of purpose, character, and aim throughout the Word of God.

The spiritual and moral utterances stand in perfect harmony. Readers sense they must continue into the New Testament from the Old in order to discover the completion of the drama that began in history hundreds and thousands of years previously. Thus, the New Testament completes the revelation of the past and unites the entire Bible into a perfect whole. In this unity, Scripture stands unique. No modern or ancient religious parchments contain such a consistent system of belief. The main reason that seems so obvious is that the divine Author is the Lord Himself. "All Scripture is inspired by God" (2 Tim. 3:16).

The inexperienced reader of the Bible may perhaps be struck at first by its diversity and multiplicity. But as soon as he has laid hold on

79

some of the connecting elements and has become aware of the stur-
dy structure of revelation, he will marvel at its profound unity . . .
Thus the Scriptures bear in their unity the marks of the One who
inspired them from first to last.[1]

Credibility of the Authors

One important factor in the internal evidences for the reliability of the
books of the Old and New Testaments is the credibility of the authors
who wrote them. Consider the following:

1. They were men of discernment. Though coming from varied
   backgrounds, the prophets and apostles were capable mentally
   and spiritually of giving forth God's Word. The professions or
   origins of almost all of them are recorded for us to scrutinize. For
   example, though Moses, the writer of the first five books of
   Scripture, was an Israelite, he was raised as a prince in the house-
   hold of Pharaoh (Ex. 2:10); the prophet Samuel was raised in an
   average but polygamous home, yet was called of God at an early
   age (1 Sam. 1:1–18; 2:18; 3:1–19). Ezra was a prophet, priest,
   and scribe; Nehemiah held a responsible position as servant to
   the king of Babylon. Job, probably the author of his own book,
   was a wealthy and respected member of his community. David
   and his son Solomon were both important kings and leaders.
   David served as a prophet and compiled most of the psalms
   while his son Solomon authored or edited the majority of the
   proverbs in the book that bears his name. Though morally
   imperfect, these and other men were dramatically used of God
   as the human authors of the Old Testament.

2. They were men of honesty. The prophets and apostles could not
   be bribed. They spoke the truth even though it imperiled their
   lives with the threat of death, as in the example of Daniel who
   could not be bought by King Belshazzar. Daniel in defiance said
   to him when promised purple and gold clothing for interpreting
   a prophecy, "Keep your gifts for yourself. . . . I will read the
   inscription [on the wall] to the king and make the interpretation
   known to him" (Dan. 5:17). They were also honest about their
   own faults and feelings. From David's repentance in Psalm 51 to
   Solomon's conclusions on the vanity of his worldly pursuits in
   Ecclesiastes, the authors of Scripture were honest concerning

their own failures to live righteously. You will not find such honesty in the writings of other kings of their day.

3. They were men of holiness. This does not mean that they lived perfect, sanctified lives, but it means that as they spoke and wrote for God, their messages were protected and guided by the Holy Spirit. Peter said in his second message to the Jews in Jerusalem that heaven received Jesus "until the period of restoration of all things about which God spoke by the mouth of His holy prophets from ancient time" (Acts 3:21). In both large and small ways, all the prophecies of the Old Testament predicted the coming of the Messiah and the kingdom age, that is, the restoration of the kingdom begun by David. Peter continued the same prophetic theme, and in that context wrote in his epistle about the sanctified men of old: "You should remember the words spoken beforehand by the holy prophets . . . 'Where is the promise of His coming?'" (2 Pet. 3:2, 4).

    Paul placed the writing apostles on the same level as the holy prophets. In teaching about the mystery of Christ, the newly revealed church, he said, "Which in other generations was not made known to the sons of men, as it has now been revealed to His holy apostles and prophets in the Spirit" (Eph. 3:5).

4. The Gospel writers wrote in harmony about the life of Christ. Though at some point they had access to common material, their individual credibility, honesty, and consistency of message have stood the tests of much criticism. While enough differences between them show no forced collusion, sufficient concurrence make the falsehood of what they wrote infinitely improbable. Basically, the Gospels are independent witnesses; the limited number of apparent discrepancies between them are easily reconcilable. The fact that the authors were friends of Jesus does not lessen the value of their individual and combined testimonies.

5. The historical facts the writers recorded conform to the collateral facts and circumstances of setting with the witness of secular history. The biblical narrations do not rise out of a historic vacuum but instead have the imprint of fact stamped on every page. Though secular and antibiblical scholars attempt to say differently, the history of the Word of God stands the tests of time.

For decades the naturalistic theories of how the Old Testament came together attempted to destroy the credibility of this portion of the Bible. The documentary theory said the Scriptures were actually written late and were pieced together by scribes who attempted to create an authoritative book from scraps of myth and distorted history. But after years of such efforts, Archer can write:

> Thus it has come about that in case after case where alleged historical inaccuracy was pointed to as proof of late and spurious authorship of the biblical documents, the Hebrew record has been vindicated by the results of recent excavation, and the condemnatory judgments of the Documentarian Theorists have been proved without foundation.[2]

Geisler and Nix add:

> When a survey is made of all of the books of the New Testament, a claim is found in each individual book for its own divine origin and authority, either directly or indirectly. So, then, both in all of its parts and as a whole the New Testament claims to be the inspired Word of God.[3]

Though Unger applies the following three steps to the canonization of the Old Testament, they certainly apply as well to the New Testament:

> First, divine inspiration and consequent authority, which make them canonical. Second, human recognition of this inspiration and authority by providential interposition. Third, eventual collection into a canon. It must be remembered, however, that canonicity was neither dependent on human recognition nor eventual collection into an arranged grouping. It was something inherent, intrinsic and vital in the writings themselves by virtue of their being the inspired Word of God.[4]

Validity of the Old Testament

All evangelical scholars agree that the first five books of Moses, the Torah, were well entrenched as inspired very early in Israel's history. Though liberal form criticism has not died, the validity of all the Old Testament manuscripts continues to rise above attempts to discredit the exalted position these works hold.

> The Old Testament Scriptures were written with the definite purpose of being held sacred and divinely authoritative. Therefore,

they possessed the stamp of canonicity from the moment of their appearance . . . This view is the simplest and most satisfactory of all, adequately accounts for all the facts, and is in agreement with the doctrine of plenary verbal inspiration as set forth in the Scriptures.[5]

However, the liberal claim persists that the prophetic writings were not added to the canon until about 300 to 200 B.C. The argument insists that many prophets along with their messages were rejected and therefore excluded from the body of inspired literature. This is a fallacious argument that further states:

> Not until the power and prestige of the prophets were enhanced towards the close of the exile and during the restoration were the prophetic writings collected and subsequently canonized.[6]

However, the New Testament clearly blankets the ministry and message of the prophets. It does not grant or give room for a period in which the rabbis or other godly men had to ponder as to which prophet was accepted or rejected. The New Testament speaks of the holy prophets (Eph. 3:5; 2 Pet. 3:2), the slain prophets (Rom. 11:3), the prophets of old who prophesied of grace to come (1 Pet. 1:10), who desired to know the time of Christ's suffering (v. 11), and who served not themselves but believers (v. 12).

Unger well argues, "Why would 'many years have to slip away,' for instance, before the book of Malachi, written about 445 B.C., would be received as worthy of canonical status?"[7] Against the critics, he says:

> This erroneous pre-supposition loses sight of the essential character of Biblical inspiration. Inspired Scripture possesses intrinsic binding authority and did not have to wait for either a long or short period of time to give it this quality, nor is this quality dependent on the popularity or nonpopularity of the prophet, nor on the reception or rejection of his message.[8]

Close of the Old Testament

Though the argument may rage as to when the Hebrew canon of Scripture was closed, most conservative scholars say that it was finalized several hundred years or more before the time of Christ. For example, 1 Maccabees (168–63 B.C.) mentions Daniel and Psalms. And since the Dead Sea Scrolls (circa 130 B.C.) quote many biblical books, it appears to have been settled by that period. The tripartite division of the Old Testament was clearly accepted by the time of the Gospels. Luke 24:44 refers to "the Law of Moses and the Prophets and the Psalms."

Josephus (A.D. 37–95) in his work *Against Apion* mentions the three-fold division of the Old Testament books. He refers to only twenty-two books. This is not unusual, however, because many are grouped and classified differently. The oldest full catalogue is found in the list of Bishop Melito of Sardis (circa A.D. 170): The five books of Moses—Genesis, Exodus, Leviticus, Numbers, Deuteronomy—Joshua, Judges, Ruth, four of Kings, two of Chronicles, Psalms, Proverbs of Solomon, Ecclesiastes, Song of Solomon, Job; the Prophets—Isaiah, Jeremiah, the Twelve (minor prophets) in one book, Daniel, Ezekiel, Ezra. Nehemiah was probably included with Ezra, Lamentations with Jeremiah. Only Esther may have been omitted; however, it could have been included with another book.

The Jewish Masoretic scholars (*masorah*, "oral tradition") who were the textual scribes (between A.D. 500–950) include all thirty-nine books of the Old Testament though catalogued differently. In modern Hebrew Bibles by A.D. 1517, the books were divided into the thirty-nine volumes that are accepted today.

Validity of the New Testament

When considering the canonicity of the Scriptures, the tendency is to cite the church councils to prove the genuineness of the biblical documents. However, it must be recognized that the Scriptures speak internally for themselves. The books carry the weight of authenticity. In addition, the early believers, long before the councils were convened, accepted them as divine truth. This, of course, applies to both the Old and New Testaments.

The councils made proclamations about the Bible because confusion was arising as to the nature of some books. Some scholars argued that the gnostic books and pseudepigrapha should be included in the canon. The councils established guidelines but did not establish the fact that the biblical books were inspired. The acceptance of the early church and of those who were there, and the strength of the internal evidence are the most important determining factors. The Westminster Confession of Faith (A.D. 1647) states:

> The authority of the Holy Scripture, for which it ought to be believed and obeyed, dependeth not upon the testimony of any man or church, but wholly upon God (who is truth itself), the Author thereof; and therefore it is to be received, because it is the Word of God.[9]

Having agreed to this, curious minds will find value in reading what others who have gone before have surmised. There is also apologetic value in showing what is found in the earliest evidence as to which writings were considered part of Scripture and which writings were not. A confirmation of minds and hearts is important because we live far away from the generations that first received the books of David, Daniel, Matthew, and Paul. The true Author of the Bible is the Holy Spirit of God Himself. But to follow the trail of the human authors as to when and how they wrote is important. However, again, the final arbitration will not come through human judgment but from God.

Looking at external and historical evidences, we note that Clement of Rome (died A.D. 101), Ignatius of Antioch (martyred A.D. 115), and Polycarp (A.D. 80–166), were all friends and companions of the apostles and other important leaders. Together they left quotes and allusions from the New Testament except for 2 Peter, Jude, 2 and 3 John.

Papias (A.D. 80–164) was called by Irenaeus a "hearer of John." Though sometimes his testimony is controversial, he leaves for the church a stamp of trustworthiness in regard to the writings of the Gospels. Irenaeus (A.D. 120–200) mentions all the Gospels by name and specifically the Book of John. Irenaeus writes of John who leaned on Jesus' breast and the fact that this apostle published a Gospel while living in Ephesus in Asia. Irenaeus was also a friend of Polycarp who knew John.

Marcion (circa A.D. 140) accepted only the Gospel of Luke and ten of Paul's writings as scriptural. He was a gnostic who rejected other books for his own personal doctrinal reasons. Yet he confirms that for the church, the apostolic writings were seen as a complete and whole rule of teaching. The Muratorian canon in the West and the Peshitta version in the East (both dated around A.D. 160) list all the New Testament books except 2 Peter. Tertullian (A.D. 160–230) holds to the genuineness of twenty-one of the twenty-seven books in our present canon. He speaks of the books as constituting the "New Testament."

In terms of how the New Testament was viewed as compared with the Old Testament, Justin Martyr (died A.D. 148) noted that on Sundays the "memoirs" of the Lord, along with the Old Testament prophets, were read to all those who gathered in one place. With this statement, it seems clear that the early church viewed the New Testament manuscripts on the same level as the older Testament and appealed to both as authoritative and sources of blessing.

Close of the New Testament

In spite of much discussion, the issue of the canon of the New Testament was coming to an end by the time of Augustine. There was still some question about the Book of Hebrews and its authorship. Augustine said Paul wrote it. In his early writings through A.D. 406, he included it as Pauline; but he wavered in his middle years and felt the author was anonymous. But he never doubted its canonicity.

> The Council of Hippo (393) was probably the first church council to lay down the limits of the canon of scripture: its enactments are not extant, but its statement on the canon was repeated . . . [in] the Third Council of Carthage (397) . . . Here Hebrews is ascribed to Paul, but listed separately from the thirteen letters which bear his name . . . What was important was that nothing should be read as holy scripture which was not listed in the canon.[10]

The canonical writings, then, are these:

- *The four Gospels; Matthew, Mark, Luke, John*
- *The Acts of the Apostles*
- *The thirteen epistles of Paul*
- *Hebrews*
- *James*
- *The two epistles of Peter*
- *The three epistles of John*
- *Jude*
- *John's Apocalypse*

Finally, one must be careful not to give the wrong impression about the nature of canonicity of the New Testament. Though some books were questioned, all were accepted by many from the beginning of their composition. When issues were raised later, discussion, prayer, and research were carried on to settle the issue. "Like the Old Testament books, there is ample evidence available to confirm that the inspired books were received immediately as such, circulated, and even collected."[11] But because the books were written in different geographical areas (Palestine, Asia Minor), and then they spread quickly to other nations and peoples, questions were raised in order to verify and authenticate the inspired letters.

> Though a few of the books were debated over time, by the era of Eusebius (340–201 A.D.), all twenty-seven books were acknowl-

edged, though he admits that James, 2 Peter, 3 John, and Jude were "spoken against" by some. However, whatever doubts existed in his day gradually faded during the next fifty years, when Athanasius (c. 367), the "Father of Orthodoxy," clearly and emphatically listed all twenty-seven books as canonical.[12]

Apocrypha and Pseudepigrapha

To understand the formation of our biblical canon, it is helpful to know how various books have been classified throughout their history. The books that are part of our Bible were initially classified into two categories: the homologoumena and the antilegomena. The homologoumena ("one voice") are the books that were unanimously adopted into the canon. The antilegomena ("spoken against") are the books that were adopted into the canon and are part of the Bible today but were opposed by some in the beginning. The books in this group are Esther, Proverbs, Ecclesiastes, and Song of Solomon in the Old Testament and Hebrews, James, 2 Peter, 2 and 3 John, Jude, and Revelation in the New Testament.

As various books were determined to be nongenuine and not part of the Bible, they were classified into two categories: the Apocrypha and the pseudepigrapha. The Apocrypha ("hidden") referred to those books that had doubtful authenticity or were spurious. However, the term *apocrypha* is now often applied to what is specifically called the Old Testament Apocrypha, the eighteen books written during the so-called "400 years of silence" between the end of the Old Testament and the prophecy of the birth of John the Baptist. The pseudepigrapha ("false writings") referred to those books that were pseudonymous. Instead of putting their own names on the books, the authors claimed they were written by particular prophets or apostles in an attempt to give their work the needed authority and credibility.

Old Testament Apocrypha and Pseudepigrapha

The eighteen books of the Old Testament Apocrypha are listed below. These books were included in the Septuagint, the ancient Greek translation of the Old Testament.

- *1 & 2 Esdras*
- *1, 2, 3, & 4 Maccabees*
- *Letter of Jeremiah*
- *Baruch*
- *Prayer of Manasses*

- Wisdom of Sirach (Ecclesiasticus)
- Wisdom of Solomon
- Additions to Esther
- Additions to Daniel
  The Prayer of Azariah
  Susanna
  Bel and the Dragon
- Tobit
- Judith
- Psalm 151

After some debate and discussion by rabbinical authorities, a general consensus was reached as to which books were not to be included in the Old Testament Scriptures. Despite their inclusion in the Septuagint, both the Jewish and Protestant communities classified the Old Testament Apocryphal books as nongenuine. In fact, by the time of the New Testament, there is no evidence that anyone seriously considered them to be inspired books, and the Old Testament Apocrypha was never quoted in the New Testament. Since these works represent the Jewish people during their intertestamental period struggles, however, they are given a degree of importance as literature and religious history.

Interestingly, though a few fragments from the Apocryphal books were found in the Dead Sea Scrolls, there were no commentaries to these books, as might have been expected. Geisler and Nix list five other cogent reasons for rejecting these works (pp. 173–75):

1. In some of the books, there are teachings that seem to support "prayer for the dead" (2 Maccabees 12:45–46) and "salvation by works" (Tobit 12:9).

2. A lot of the material can be classified as extremely fanciful and fictional. This can be found in Bel and the Dragon, Additions to Esther, Prayer of Azariah, Susanna, Tobit, and Judith. In addition, in some of the writings there is an unbiblical emphasis on mysticism and exaggerated angelology.

3. Much of the teaching of the Apocrypha is at times immoral. God assisted Judith in a deed of falsehood (Judith 9:10, 13), while both Ecclesiasticus and the writing Wisdom teach a morality founded on expediency. As well as the low morality, there are many historical and chronological errors, almost too many to count.

4. The words of Josephus in his *Against Apion* (1:8) are important. He recorded that the prophets wrote from Moses to Artaxerxes (circa 445 B.C.) and then notes, "It is true our history hath been written since Artaxerxes very particularly but hath not been esteemed of the like authority with the former by our forefathers, because there hath not been an exact succession of the prophets since that time." The Talmudist adds a similar thought, "After the latter prophets Haggai, Zechariah, . . . and Malachi, the Holy Spirit departed from Israel."[13]

   In Josephus' quote, he is virtually repudiating the Apocrypha books, testifying that they have not been accepted on equal footing with "like authority" or with the "exact succession" of the received prophets and their books.

5. Without question, all of the Apocryphal books are nonbiblical and noncanonical. Overall, and in the larger view of biblical history, the people of God have never accepted them as such. The Jewish scholars of Jamnia (A.D. 90) rejected them. Many of the early church fathers rejected them also, such as Origen, Cyril of Jerusalem, and Athanasius. Though Augustine accepted them, he was opposed by the great scholar and translator of the Latin Vulgate, Jerome (A.D. 340–420).

In the great Counter-Reformation war, the Council of Trent (A.D. 1546) gave most of the books of the Apocrypha full acceptance for the Roman Catholic Church. This was an attempt to blunt the force of the reformers who were not in favor of giving these writings any spiritual credence or authority. But, too, this was a way to oppose Martin Luther who renounced the idea of prayers for the dead and works salvation, both of which are given high regard in the Apocryphal books. Sometime around 1827, the Apocrypha was omitted from almost all English Bibles printed. With the 1885 edition of the Revised Version and the 1901 printing of the American Standard Revision, they were completely omitted from all but Roman Catholic editions of the Bible.

Other spurious writings from Old Testament times are classified as pseudepigrapha and include the following:

- *The Books of Adam and Eve*
- *1 Enoch*
- *2 Enoch*
- *The Assumption of Moses*

- *The Martyrdom of Isaiah*
- *The Psalms of Solomon*
- *The Apocalypse of Baruch*
- *Testaments of the Twelve Patriarchs*
- *The Book of Jubilees*
- *The Sibylline Oracles*

Though there is also no evidence that the Old Testament pseudepigrapha were considered inspired books, they were quoted in several minor references in the New Testament. Jude 1:14–15 seemed to allude to both the Book of Enoch (1:9) and the Assumption of Moses (1:9). An allusion is also found in 2 Timothy 3:8 to the Penitence of Jannes and Jambres.

However, the New Testament also referred to other religious or historical writings such as the poets Aratus (Acts 17:28), Menander (1 Cor. 15:33), and Epimenides (Titus 1:12).[14] Yet this does not mean it considered them inspired canonical literature. And nowhere in these quotes were they cited by the formula "it is written" or "the Scriptures say."

New Testament Apocrypha and Pseudepigrapha

As mentioned above, the authority of seven books of our New Testament was disputed for a time. However, following the Council of Carthage (A.D. 397):

> The trend was reversed. It seems clear that the question was not one of inspiration, but interpretation and association with particular doctrinal emphases that occasioned the dispute. Once the air was cleared of these, the authentic apostolic authority of Revelation was vindicated.

> As with Revelation, so with all of the disputed books: once the question of authenticity or genuineness was settled, there was no problem about the canonicity. If it was clear that a "prophet of God wrote a book" and it told the "truth about God, man, etc.," then it was recognized to be the "word of God."[15]

Because many spurious books of New Testament times were pseudonymous and because the term *apocrypha* is more general but was sometimes used of the Old Testament Apocrypha, the terms pseudepigrapha and Apocrypha are often used interchangeably to describe these spurious works. The books of the New Testament pseudepigrapha could number as high as 280, as listed by Photius in the ninth century. However, the most well-known, some of which are listed below, only number around thirty-seven.

- *The Gospel of Thomas*
- *The Gospel of Peter*
- *The Gospel of Joseph the Carpenter*
- *The Passing of Mary*
- *The Gospel of Nativity of Mary*
- *The Gospel of Barnabas*
- *The Gospel of Andrew*
- *The Acts of Peter*
- *The Acts of Thomas*
- *The Lost Epistle to Corinthians*

These particular books have been classified as fanciful at best but contain little genuine or lasting value to the church. Eusebius called them "totally absurd and impious." No orthodox church father, canon, or council gave them serious consideration. They are full of heretical teachings from the Gnostics, Docetists, and other cults and groups. They may have been referred to by historians and commentators but without any recognition of authority.

A few books of the New Testament Apocrypha enjoyed a wider appreciation. For a certain length of time, some churches believed they were canonical, but in time they were finally rejected. Some were even considered canonical by a few of the church fathers, but in time the church at large decided against them, and they were judged faulty. "Still, local acceptance and wide circulation of some of these books manifest their value as well as their esteem."[16] These books include:

- *Epistle of Pseudo-Barnabas*
- *Second Epistle of Clement*
- *Shepherd of Hermas*
- *Didache, Teaching of the Twelve*
- *Epistle to the Corinthians*
- *Apocalypse of Peter*
- *The Acts of Paul and Thecla*
- *Epistle to the Laodiceans*

Because they fill in some details about the patristic and apostolic periods, these books hold some religious and historical value for church history. However, they are not considered totally trustworthy even in their history. Though they sometimes make reference to the canonical Scriptures to enhance their own value, none enjoyed more than a local or temporary recognition.

Transmission of the Bible

It is beyond the scope of this book to go into the incredible story of the preservation and transmission of our books of the Bible. Because of the mountains of texts, versions, and scriptural fragments that must be digested, it would appear to be an impossible task. But by the careful work of scholars who gave a lifetime of study to the process, we have arrived at almost perfect Hebrew and Greek manuscripts of God's Word.

At first, the liberals and skeptics of the Enlightenment period tried to disprove divine superintendence of the transmission of the text by arguing that the errors found in such a body of material were too great to sort out. They brought discouragement by their humanistic approach to scholarly textual studies. Nevertheless, the "problem" of so many texts proved to be a blessing. By careful classification and intense study, the actual wording of our Bible became more assured.

The study of transmission and preservation of the New Testament begins with the fact that there are two hundred thousand texts with variant readings. However, after careful analysis, these so-called errors turned out to be but ten thousand supposedly significant problems. In other words, the 190,000 other variants can be spotted, identified, and explained.

Westcott and Hort, considered outstanding experts on the subject, point out that only about one-eighth of the variants have much weight. Moreover, many of these simply have to do with spelling and style. The results of their study confirm that we have about 98.33 percent of the New Testament as it was written.[17] Though individual Greek scholars may argue over such variants even today, the science of this study, called lower textual criticism, helps to further satisfy textual questions.

Because the Jews were so careful in their copying of the holy Hebrew Bible, transmission mistakes were kept to a minimum. The Masoretic scholars were meticulous in avoiding errors. With the Dead Sea Scrolls (circa 130 B.C.), the scholarly world was shocked at how close such old copies of the Old Testament were in line-for-line agreement with the Masoretic tradition. In the Dead Sea Scroll text of Isaiah 53 with 166 words, only seventeen letters were in question. Ten of these had to do with different spellings, and four were different because of stylistic changes, such as conjunctions. With this kind of comparison that spans almost one thousand years, it may be that there exists almost 95 percent of the Old Testament as originally composed by the authors. Some scholars, such as Grudem, argue that we have close to 99 percent of the original words of the Bible.

> For over 99 percent of the words of the Bible, we know what the original manuscript said. Even for many of the verses where there are textual variants (that is, different words in different ancient copies of the same verse), the correct decision is often quite clear (there may be an obvious copying error, for example), and there are really very few places where the textual variant is both difficult to evaluate and significant in determining the meaning. In the small percentage of cases where there is significant uncertainty about what the original text said, the general sense of the sentence is usually quite clear from the context.[18]

No other body of transmitted ancient literature can come close to being as intact as the Judeo-Christian Bible. The passing down of both the Old and New Testaments is a miracle of God's providence and care of His Word to humanity.

FOR DISCUSSION

1. In your own words, discuss the credibility of the human authors of the Scriptures.

2. What was important about the apostle John in relation to what some church fathers confirmed?

3. When and how was the canon of the New Testament closed?

4. What are some of the more compelling arguments that show the Old Testament Apocrypha books were not viewed as canonical?

5. Define and describe the pseudepigrapha writings.

For Further Study

Bible Introduction

Archer, Gleason L. *A Survey of Old Testament Introduction.* Chicago: Moody, 1994.

Geisler, Norman L. and William E. Nix. *A General Introduction to the Bible*. Chicago: Moody, 1971.

Unger, Merrill. *Introductory Guide to the Old Testament*. Grand Rapids: Zondervan, 1978.

Bibliology Texts

Bruce, F. F. *The Canon of Scripture*. Downers Grove, Ill: InterVarsity, 1988.

Pache, René. *The Inspiration and Authority of Scripture*. Chicago: Moody, 1969.

Dictionaries

Tractate "Sanhedrin," *Babylonian Talmud*, VII-VIII.

Language Studies

Westcott, Brooke Foss, and Fenton John Anthony Hort, eds. *The New Testament in the Original Greek*. New York: Macmillan, 1928.

Theology

Grudem, Wayne. *Biblical Doctrine*. Grand Rapids: Zondervan, 1999.

Schaff, Philip, ed. *The Creeds of Christendom*. 3 vols. Grand Rapids: Baker, 1990.

Chapter Seven

The Church Fathers and the Bible

*T*he church fathers, who were much closer to the events of the New Testament than we are today, studied the New Testament texts with varied limitations imposed upon them. For example, they had no commentaries, or certainly very few, to draw on to aid in their judgments. The biblical manuscripts did not have chapter or verse divisions. To study the Bible in a systematic fashion was laborious and tedious. This lack of instruction led them to twist certain teachings to fit the mood of their day. We can see both their doctrinal progression and often their deviation into erroneous beliefs. Still, their thoughts are valuable for us today.

On the issue of the Word of God, the church fathers wrote their views with clarity and unanimity about inspiration and the work of the Holy Spirit in giving us the Scriptures. Below are excerpts from their valuable writings that confirm how the early church viewed the Holy Scriptures.[1]

First Thessalonians 2:13

Paul wrote, "We also constantly thank God that when you received the word of God which you heard from us, you accepted it not as the word of men, but for what it really is, the word of God, which also performs its work in you who believe."

> There are numberless instances in the Scriptures where similar statements are made about the word of God. (Augustine, *On the Trinity* 15.11.20)

When the [Thessalonians] had received from the apostle the word by hearing it, [they] received it not as the word of men but, as it truly is, as the word of God (Augustine, *On the Predestination of the Saints 19.39*)

Second Timothy 2:15

Paul wrote, "Be diligent to present yourself approved to God as a workman who does not need to be ashamed, accurately handling the word of truth."

[We are] to do all in our power that we may be called "workmen who need not to be ashamed, handling rightly the word of truth." (Origen, *Against Celsus 5.1*)

Many distort the text of Scripture and pervert it in every way, and many additions are made to it. [Paul] has . . . said . . . "rightly dividing," that is, cutting way what is spurious, . . . With the sword of the Spirit, cut off from your preaching . . . what is superfluous and foreign to it. (Chrysostom, *Homilies on 2 Timothy 5*)

Paul's intent here is to urge Timothy to teach with a correct purpose, so that the word is not undermined. (Theodore of Mopsuestia, *Commentary on 2 Timothy*)

Second Timothy 3:16–17

Paul wrote, "All Scripture is inspired by God and profitable for teaching, for reproof, for correction, for training in righteousness; so that the man of God may be adequate, equipped for every good work."

[If a man] should sit and meditate upon the Holy Scriptures, he would not comprehend all the force of the depth of the words. And man cannot rise up to the wisdom of God. (Aphrahat, *Demonstrations 22.26*)

By Scripture we may disapprove what is false, be corrected, be brought to a right understanding, and be comforted and consoled. (Chrysostom, *Homilies on 2 Timothy 9*)

The Scripture is "given by inspiration of God," as the apostle says. The Scripture is of the Holy Spirit, and its intention is the profit of men. . . . Such a gift as this, however, is not within any man's [limited mind] to lay hold of. (Gregory of Nyssa, *Against Eunomius 3.7.1*)

The Scriptures are holy, they are truthful, they are blameless. . . . So we have no grounds at all for blaming Scripture if we happen to deviate in any way, because we haven't understood it. When we do understand it, we are right. . . . When we have gone wrong, we don't make out Scripture to be wrong, but it continues to stand up straight and right, so that we may return to it for correction. (Augustine, *Sermons 23.3*)

Second Timothy 4:2

Paul wrote, "Preach the word; be ready in season and out of season; reprove, rebuke, exhort, with great patience and instruction."

> Whether you are in danger, in prison, in chains or going to your death, at that very time do not hesitate to admonish. Do not withhold your admonition [from Scripture]. (Chrysostom, *Homilies on 2 Timothy 9*)

> He further comments: But let instruction about love of truth from above have no set hour—let all the time belong to it. "In season, out of season, reprove, entreat, rebuke," Scripture says. And the prophet, "On [God's] law he will meditate day and night." And Moses too asked the Jews to do this continually. (Chrysostom, *Homilies on John 18.4*)

First Peter 1:10–12

Peter wrote, "As to this salvation, the prophets who prophesied of the grace that would come to you made careful searches and inquiries, seeking to know what person or time the Spirit of Christ within them was indicating as He predicted the sufferings of Christ and the glories to follow. It was revealed to them that they were not serving themselves, but you, in these things which now have been announced to you through those who preached the gospel to you by the Holy Spirit sent from heaven—things into which angels long to look."

> Here it is stated that the prophets spoke with wisdom and that the Spirit of God was in them because they belonged and were subject to Christ. (Clement of Alexandria, *Adumbrations*)

> The Spirit of Christ predicted his sufferings to Isaiah: "He was led like a sheep to the slaughter," and he predicted the resurrection to Hosea: "On the third day we shall be raised up before him, and we

shall go on to know the Lord, and we shall find him like the ready morning." (Oecumenius, *Commentary on 1 Peter*)

. . . the things which the prophets foretold about the future glory, for they were revealed to them. And the saints have preached the good tidings "by the [S]pirit of God sent from heaven." (Ambrose of Milan, *Letters to Laymen* 66)

Second Peter 1:20–21

Peter wrote, "But know this first of all, that no prophecy of Scripture is a matter of one's own interpretation, for no prophecy was ever made by an act of human will, but men moved by the Holy Spirit spoke from God."

The prophets heard God speaking to them in the secret recesses of their own hearts. They simply conveyed that message by their preaching and writing to God's people. They were not like pagan oracles, which distorted the divine message in their own interest, for they did not write their own words but the words of God. (Bede, *On 2 Peter*)

This [passage] means that the prophets received their prophecies from God and transmitted what he wanted to say, not what they wanted. They were fully aware that the message had been given to them, and they made no attempt to put their own interpretation on it. If they could not bring themselves to accept what the Spirit had said to them, then they kept their mouths shut. (Oecumenius, *Commentary on 2 Peter*)

[The prophets] were not speaking to themselves but serving the Holy Spirit. What is the interpretation of their words if not the works that Christ revealed when he came? (Andreas, *Catena*)

The Holy Spirit filled the hearts of the prophets when he wanted to. It was not in their power to teach whatever they wished; rather they taught by the illumination of the Holy Spirit and said only what he told them to. We say this just in case there might be someone who feels the urge to interpret Scripture for himself. Some interpret Peter's words to mean that the Spirit inspired the prophets in much the same way as the flutist blows into his flute, so that the latter were no more than mechanical instruments in God's hands, saying what the Spirit told them to say without necessarily understanding or believing it themselves. This is ridiculous. (Bede, *On 2 Peter*)

The prophets knew that they were inspired by the Holy Spirit, even if they did not always understand the full significance of what they were told. (Oecumenius, *Commentary on 2 Peter*)

Peter, the chief apostle, bears witness when he says that no prophecy ever came by man, but holy men of God spoke, moved by the Holy Spirit. (Symeon the New Theologian, *Discourses 34.5*)

Second Peter 3:15–16

Peter wrote, "And regard the patience of our Lord as salvation; just as also our beloved brother Paul, according to the wisdom given him, wrote to you, as also in all his letters, speaking in them of these things, in which are some things hard to understand, which the untaught and unstable distort, as they do also the rest of the Scriptures, to their own destruction."

It seems that some people find Paul hard to understand, no doubt because he speaks about the wisdom that comes from above, for in him Christ himself is speaking. (Cyril of Alexandria, *Catena*)

There is no book in either the Old or the New Testament which they have not perverted according to their own fantasies, by adding to it, subtracting from it or altering something which it says to make it mean something else. . . . But those who try to corrupt the Holy Scriptures and pervert the [true] faith do nothing other than condemn themselves. (Bede, *On 2 Peter*)

The Doctrine of the Early Church

The early church understood the nature of the Scriptures as inspired by the Holy Spirit and trustworthy for all matters of salvation and of Christian living. In his *Institutes of the Christian Religion*, John Calvin expressed what was understood by all divines of the centuries long before he wrote his Reformation theology. He quotes what was clearly the accepted doctrine:

Our faith in doctrine is not established until we have a perfect conviction that God is its author. Hence, the highest proof of Scripture is uniformly taken from the character of Him whose word it is. The prophets and apostles boast not their own acuteness, nor any qualities which win credit to speakers, nor do they dwell on reasons; but they appeal to the sacred name of God, in order that the whole world may be compelled to submission.

If we look at [the Scriptures] with clear eyes and unbiased judgment, it will forthwith present itself with a divine majesty that will subdue our presumptuous opposition, and force us to do it homage.[2]

Calvin then adds,

For as God alone can properly bear witness to His own words, so these words will not obtain full credit in the hearts of men, until they are sealed by the inward testimony of the Spirit. The same Spirit, therefore, who spoke by the mouth of the prophets, delivered the message with which they were divinely instructed. This connection is most aptly expressed by Isaiah in these words, "My Spirit that is upon thee, and my words which I have put in thy mouth, shall not depart out of thy mouth, nor out of the mouth of thy seed, nor out the mouth of thy seed's seed, saith the Lord, from henceforth and for ever" (Isa. lix.21).[3]

FOR DISCUSSION

1. Considering what some early church fathers had to say about the inspiration of the Bible, in what way does this give us confidence about how we understand the Scriptures today?

2. Summarize in a sentence or two the moving thoughts of John Calvin about the nature of our Bible.

For Further Study

Commentaries

Oden, Thomas C. ed. *Ancient Christian Commentary on Scripture*. 28 vols. Downers Grove, Ill.: InterVarsity, 1998–??.

Theology

Calvin, John. *Institutes of the Christian Religion*, trans. Henry Beveridge. Reprint. Grand Rapids: Eerdmans, 1993.

Chapter Eight

The Growing Attack on the Bible

A powerful assault has come against the Word of God since the times of the Enlightenment. Tenacious foes claim the Bible is simply the word of man and not the inspired message from God. Seminaries, local assemblies, and denominations soften their stance that the Holy Spirit gave us the Scriptures, and that they are reliable and inerrant in their original composition.

> What makes the present situation difficult and fraught with such dire consequences for the well-being of the Church, is that the sign-posts have been tampered with, so that they intentionally lead one astray. The guidebook and map, it is true, remain the same, and to those who will read and understand, their message is clear, for they were given by the Lord of the Church who is Truth itself and cannot lie. In fact, so accurate are they that he who follows and obeys their directions need not go astray.[1]

The central issue before the church then is whether believers in Christ can consider the Bible as a trustworthy teacher of doctrine. In other words, are we to pay attention to what it says about itself? When the Scriptures tell us plainly what kind of a book it is, are we to accept its testimony as worthy of belief? The Bible is the Word of God and true in all its aspects, or it is not.

Peter wrote that the Bible is not

> a private interpretation, and by this phrase he means that the Scripture did not come into being as the result of individuals investigating into matters and then writing down their findings. The

Scriptures are not the product of human investigation and reason. That there may be no misunderstanding on this point, the Apostle goes on to say that the "prophecy came not in old time by the will of man." . . . That is, it was not of human origin.[2]

The Scriptures tell us:

But know this first of all, that no prophecy of Scripture is a matter of one's own interpretation, for no prophecy was ever made by an act of human will, but men moved by the Holy Spirit spoke from God. (2 Pet. 1:20–21)

The language of 2 Peter 1:20–21 is clear. The Spirit of God moved those he called to speak for him. The Spirit lifted them and carried them forward, and from this they spoke what He desired. They spoke through His power and not simply from natural, human thinking.

By what the Bible tells us, inspiration is the superintendence by the Spirit of the Lord over the authors of the Scriptures. As a result, the Scriptures possess divine authority and trustworthiness. And because of this they are free from error.

Where did the modern doubt about the nature of the Bible come from? Can we identify a historic marker as the starting point?

Rationalism

Not long after the Reformation, contrary forces began working on the European mind and soul. It is true, the Reformers, such as Martin Luther and John Calvin, returned many on that continent back to a respect for the Word of God. But shortly, the philosophy of rationalism began to take over the thinking of the spiritual leaders of Europe. In religious matters, the mind, reason, and humanism replaced the authority of the Scriptures.

Descartes (1596–1650)

Many believe the era of rationalism began with René Descartes. Though born in France, he spent most of his life in Holland. A mathematician, Descartes argued that the finite soul must have a higher origin. Only a higher, perfect being such as God could create a soul. Some believe Descartes was actually an atheist but was cautious to retain his devotion to Roman Catholicism.

With Descartes, human reason replaced divine revelation in trying to understand God. Though not the first to do this, his philosophic thinking impressed many others to do the same.

Pascal (1623–1662)

Blaise Pascal was also a French citizen who was respected throughout Europe as a mathematician, scientist, and Christian apologist. Pascal was converted in 1646 to Jansenism, a movement for reformation within Roman Catholicism. For years he worked on his masterpiece, *Provincial Letters,* to reaffirm Augustine's doctrine of grace. This great work was not published until after his death. Also published posthumously was his classic work, *Thoughts,* which pitted vital Christianity against the rationalism and skepticism of his day.

Though Pascal believed in the overwhelming evidence of fulfilled prophecy, miracles, the Christian witness throughout history, and the self-authentication of Scripture, he opened the door to move away from the Bible by his belief that the evidence in the heart is the strongest proof about God. Certainly, spiritual truths proclaimed in the Bible must be received with the heart and soul of the individual, but Pascal unwittingly moved the issue of personal verification of God to subjectivity rather than objectivity. His famous saying was, "The heart has its reasons which the reason does not know."

From Rationalism to Idealism

Kant (1724–1804)

German philosopher Immanuel Kant, who attempted to reconcile empiricism and rationalism, was a native of Konigsberg, East Prussia, where he lived all his life. He was possibly one of the most influential thinkers of his day. He reacted against mystical and pietistic Christianity, thinking it was too superstitious and spiritual. He was also dissatisfied with the scholasticism that dominated Lutheranism. He argued that such rational proofs of God violated the limits of reason and had little to do with faith.

Kant felt that morality was not the true basis for Christianity. True morality was simply an unbending sense of duty to moral law. Without a doubt, Kant moved the church in Europe and Germany even closer to theological liberalism. And again, the Bible was not the centerpiece of his arguments, but instead he dealt heavily with mechanistic thinking and philosophy.

Hegel (1770–1831)

German philosopher George Wilhelm Friedrich Hegel, a German idealist and follower of Kant, had originally planned to enter the ministry but rebelled against the orthodoxy of his teachers. He entered instead into the teaching of philosophy at the Universities of Jena, Heidelberg, and Berlin. Hegel thought his philosophical arguments were supporting Christianity; however, he was robbing it of its historical and spiritual elements. Hegel thus contributed to the rise of biblical and theological liberalism and the so-called "secular religion" of his day.

To Hegel, God was simply pure reason, and Jesus was only a human teacher who acted out a rational opposition to the irrational legalism of the Pharisees. Hegel was considered a pantheist, one who denies the distinctness of God from His world. Again, reason and philosophy overshadowed the clear exposition of the Scriptures for that generation.

Schleiermacher (1768–1834)

Friedrich Schleiermacher, a German idealist and follower of Kant, was born into a pastoral family that was part of Moravian pietism. Early on, Schleiermacher was thrown into the company of the great romantic novelists and poets of Berlin, who were the leading *avant garde* intellectuals of his day. In 1804 he began teaching biblical criticism at the University of Halle.

Schleiermacher's theology steered a middle course between traditional Protestant Reformed theology based on the Bible as the Word of God and the new philosophies of the age of Enlightenment, the basis of the liberal mind-set. Since he had no answers for the vicious attacks against the inspiration and validity of Scripture, he was led to restate a whole range of Christian doctrine. God was that being upon whom people must, by feeling, utterly depend. To Schleiermacher, Jesus was not fully God and fully man in the same sense as the great theological creeds had stated. Christ was simply a mediator in the experience of people with God.

Schleiermacher pioneered the way for the later liberal views that Jesus was simply a divinely inspired man. And, of course, as theology was being destroyed, so the Scriptures were no longer considered the inspired Word of God.

Critical Biblical Scholarship

Wellhausen (1844–1918)

Julius Wellhausen became one of the most destructive Old Testament scholars for his age and even for the following generations. After being appointed professor of theology at Greifswald University in 1880, he soon resigned because he did not believe in the inspiration of Scripture. He later became professor of Oriental languages at Halle (1882), Marburg (1885), and Gottingen (1892).

Wellhausen argued that the Pentateuch was actually written by different authors who wrote over a long period of time, ending as late as the postexilic times. He saw much of the Old Testament as a patchwork of disconnected sources sewn into the fabric of human ideas, rather than divinely authored revelation.

Schweitzer (1875–1965)

Albert Schweitzer was the son of a Protestant minister in Germany. He was educated in the classical languages of Greek and Latin. He was saturated as a young man in the liberal thinking of the University of Strassburg where he studied theology and later medicine. Throughout his life, he had a driving passion for theology, medicine, and music. Much of his later life was spent as a medical missionary in Africa.

In 1906 Schweitzer wrote his most critical work about Christ entitled *The Quest for the Historical Jesus*. He argued that the Gospel records were simply the mutterings of much later apostles, who penned inaccurate information about the life of Christ. He also argued that Jesus took on the messianic expectations of the Jewish people. He believed Christ thought wrongly that the end of the world was near, with this mistaken hope dashed at the end of His life.

As Wellhausen destroyed the people's confidence in the integrity of the Old Testament, Schweitzer did likewise for the New Testament, particularly the Gospel accounts of the life of Jesus.

Deism

Deism was the bedfellow of rationalism and the Enlightenment. One of the most important of the English deists was Matthew Tindal (1655–1733) who wrote what would be called the deist Bible, *Christianity as Old as the Creation: Or, the Gospel, a Republication of the Religion of Nature*. Tindal held that no one could truly rely on the historicity of the Gospel accounts because they were beyond rational thinking and the realm of nature. Tindal rejected almost every cardinal doctrine of Christianity: the fall of Adam, original sin, the atonement, the Trinity, and the resurrection. He also rejected the teaching of the inspiration of Scripture.

For Tindal, reason was sufficient for people to know all things necessary. God was actually above and beyond His universe and was no longer involved in the world He had created. To many deists, Jesus was a fraud, an unsuccessful messianic fake who misled His disciples and those who followed later. The body of Christ was stolen, and by claiming that He had been resurrected, the apostles started a new religious belief in order to avoid working for a living.

Such a theory was proposed by Hermann Samuel Reimarus (1694–1768) in a German work entitled in English *Fragments by an Unknown Person*. His purpose was to destroy the foundation of Christianity. Albert Schweitzer admitted that the views of Reimarus inaugurated his search for the historical Jesus.

Both rationalism and deism had a profound influence on such later theories as *redaction criticism,* the study of how an author has integrated various sources to form a literary work. According to this theory, the Gospels were blown-up fabrications of some truth, rumor, and outright false theories about what Jesus said and did. His supposed miracles were the fables of His disciples and other followers.

Though classical deism is no longer with us today, it still echoes the doubts about the Bible proposed by modern liberalism. Without a doubt, those who are brainwashed in the liberal university systems of Europe and America place little if any credence in the Scriptures. Finally:

> Deists rejected any Christian claims to supernatural revelation, for God does not reveal Himself in any other way than through His creation. They rejected the possibility of miracles, for miracles would violate natural law. Belief in miracles, therefore, represents superstition and an ignorance of natural law. God has given people through reason and science the rational ability to discover in nature all that they need to know to live a full and happy life.[3]

Form Criticism

Julius Wellhausen gave birth to *form criticism,* the view that the Old Testament was simply pieced together, especially the Pentateuch, which he referred to as the "so-called" writings of Moses. According to Wellhausen, individual ancient stories were passed down orally, modified from time to time, and then written down in documents that were also later modified again and edited. The early Genesis stories were but mythological accounts.

Wellhausen applied this approach also to the New Testament and the Gospels. He argued that: 1) the original material for the gospel itself was but oral tradition circulated in small writings; 2) the material then came together and underwent revision; and 3) the material furnished information about the beliefs and circumstances of the early Church concerning Christ and possibly also some inane facts about the ministry and times of Jesus.[4]

Documentary Hypothesis

This theory suggests that various authors created the Pentateuch from oral traditions. Culling through the material, modern scholars attempted to find the element of truth in the traditional stories presented. Julius Wellhausen expanded on the work of K. H. Graf, and the two became so linked to this critical approach to study of the Old Testament that it is often called the Graf-Wellhausen hypothesis. Wellhausen's theory

> assumed that writing was relatively unknown in Palestine during the Mosaic period, and that no part of the Pentateuch could, therefore, have been found, for example, as a written form until the tenth or ninth centuries B.C. The references to the Hittites, for example, were treated with incredulity and condemned as mere fiction on the part of the late authors of the Torah; the same was true of the Horites and even the historicity of Sargon II (722–705 B.C.), since no extra-biblical references to him had yet been discovered.[5]

Working within the limitations of the nineteenth century understanding of history and archaeology, Wellhausen saw only dimly the truth about the nature of Old Testament times and events.

But times would change on the side of evangelical scholarship. There would be a resurgence of trust in the reliability of our Bible, both in the Old and New Testaments. Their truthfulness and accuracy would be vindicated by time and patience. For example, we now know more about the Hittites and Horites mentioned in the Old Testament than some American Indian tribes of a century or so ago.

> Thus it has come about that in case after case after case where alleged historical inaccuracy was pointed to as proof of late and spurious authorship of the biblical documents, the Hebrew record has been vindicated by the results of recent excavation, and the condemnatory judgments of the Documentarian Theorists have been proved without foundation.[6]

Elder adds:

> It is not too much to say that it was the rise of the science of archaeology that broke the deadlock between historians and the orthodox

Christian. Little by little, one city after another, one civilization after another, one culture after another, whose memories were enshrined only in the Bible, were restored to their proper places in ancient history by the studies of archaeologists. . . . Contemporary records of Biblical events have been unearthed and the uniqueness of Biblical revelation has been emphasized by contrast and comparison to newly discovered religions of ancient peoples.[7]

Faith History

All the theories above are based on human reason, rationalism, and the belief that God really has not spoken to humankind through the biblical records. Such thinking gives rise to the rejection of the authority of Scripture as it applies to life and eternal issues. People then do not have to put trust in Jesus Christ for personal salvation and redemption. If the truthfulness of the Bible can be diminished and the power of human intellect can be exalted, then people have no need for God.

Because of such intellectual destruction, the Bible then is simply considered as *faith history*, i.e., it only gives those who are superstitious a source for mystical and religious faith, ignoring the overwhelming evidence to the contrary. In fact, with blatant condescension, the critic labels the Bible as simply *holy history*, not to be confused with actual history. Being only *faith history,* it can be discounted at will and has no relevance except for the superstitious. The impact of these beliefs is well noted by Kenneth Hagen:

> What comes then from the Deists, naturalists, and rationalists is that the enlightened are freed from the dogmatics of Orthodoxy and any supernatural theory of inspiration. Doctrines like the divinity of Christ, original sin, atonement, sacraments, and miracles are put aside. The New Testament never meant them to be taken seriously. Views of the supernatural were regarded as superstition. Scripture was interpreted historically and critically. The "unworthy," "impossible," and "unreasonable" parts of Scripture were explained away.[8]

Even some evangelical scholars have unwittingly fallen victim to the *faith history* approach. They argue that the Bible stands apart from human history because it cannot be understood by the ordinary human mind and requires a response of faith to comprehend it. The fact is, the events of Scripture did indeed take place in time and space, and they are part of the actual drama of human history.[9] However, the illumination by the Holy Spirit is still necessary for *spiritual* enlightenment.

The Attack Against the Bible Continues

At the beginning of the twenty-first century, two main forces are coming against the Word of God. While they appear to be contrasting and even opposite critical positions, they are bedfellows in their efforts to discredit Scripture.

On the one hand, 1) postmodernism says rationalism is dead. In other words, all the original criticisms against the Bible are not important. It is the subjective "feeling" one gets from his view of God that counts. *The specific accuracy and historicity about the Scriptures are no longer important, because one cannot know absolute truth anyway.*

Then 2) the new agenda is known as form criticism. This modern version of liberalism is as deadly to the veracity of the Word of God as old-line liberalism. Modern form criticism especially attacks the historical facts about the life and person of Jesus.

Postmodernism

When critical rationalism failed, it gave way to irrationalism. Both of these views are hostile to biblical revelation, yet in opposite ways. While liberals do not believe the Scriptures are true, postmoderns simply throw out the categories of truth altogether. This philosophy is opening the church up to New Age religions, religious syncretism, and even possibly moral chaos.

Like old liberalism, postmodernism holds that there is no objective truth. Christianity is not a set of beliefs or doctrines about what is real or not. Instead, religion is a preference, a choice. People want to believe what they like, believe what they want to believe. Unlike any other period in history, many are unwilling to believe in what they do not enjoy. If there are no absolutes, the mind and the thinking processes give way to the will. People want to hear positive words from Scripture about the love of God rather than the realities of sin, death, and hell. While it is good news to hear about the grace of God, the Scriptures warn about many other realities that God wants us to know about.

> For postmodernists, morality, like religion, is a matter of desire. What I want and what I choose is not only true (for me) but right (for me). That different people want and choose different things means that truth and morality are relative, but "I have a right" to my desires. Conversely, "no one has the right" to criticize my desires and my choices.

Although postmodernists tend to reject traditional morality, they can still be very moralistic. They will defend their "rights" to do what they feel that they have a right not to be criticized for what they are doing. They want not only license but approval.[10]

Such attitudes for many Christians today constitute a virtue and are not seen as a modern way of denying the authority of the Scriptures. In this way of thinking, the idea of culture diversity means that each group or religious belief system is considered as good as any other. Islam is as valid as Christianity; the writings of Islam are as meaningful as the Bible.

Postmodernists who reject objective biblical truth have no problem with tolerating Hinduism or Buddhism, which say that the external world is just an imaginary illusion of the mind. And from Eastern religious minds, other popular kinds of religions and belief systems have come about. And many of their tenets have filtered into Christianity.[11]

New Age religions, for all of their pagan trappings, have in common the idea that the self is divine, that *you* are God, the creator of your own universe. As old as the Serpent's lie to Eve (Genesis 3:5), this idea now finds its way into self-help books, motivational tracts, and pop psychology ("You create your own reality").[12]

New Form Criticism

Besides Julius Wellhausen and his contribution to form criticism for the Old Testament, German theologian Rudolf Bultmann (1893-1976) popularized the same approach to the New Testament. The target was the Gospels. Form criticism comes from the German word *Formgeschichte* meaning "form history." Because the Gospels point to Jesus as the Son of God, the form critics say that the history of Christ was *mythologized* to create this idea from the scant information we have about Him. Thus, Bultmann went about to *demythologize* Jesus. He wanted to simply find the "truth" about the man who was called the Christ.

Today form criticism has had a reawakening with the organizing of professional meetings under the heading the Jesus Seminar. Under the leadership of liberal scholar Robert Funk, the conclave began meetings twice a year in 1985. Its initial findings concluded that only about 18 percent of the four Gospels indicate accurately what Jesus said. The gathered scholars were to vote with color-coded beads whether the words of the Lord were actually his own, allusions misquoted by followers, or myths repeated by zealous members of the early Church.

This "new" form criticism takes on a profound subjective tone where opinions determine what the life of Christ is all about. While it is easy to spot such unscholarly and unrealistic, subjective tampering with the Word of God, this approach to the study of the Bible is not fading into obscurity, but it is increasing and gaining ground. What is sad is that some evangelical Christians, who should know better, have fallen into a few of the principles that guide this thinking.

Form criticism actually has its roots in evolutionary progressions, arguing that ideas move from the more simple to the complex, i.e., the basic life of Christ was mythologically embellished and expanded. And since the liberal mind refuses to believe that God invaded history with His revelations and with His Son, to find the "historic Jesus" is the driving quest.

If the biblical doctrines of inspiration and inerrancy are further impugned as the twenty-first century gets under way, another round of liberalism will destroy the integrity of Scripture as it has done successfully in the past. Evangelical seminaries will go by the wayside, and the pastoral products will erode the faith of their congregations.

Thomas and Farnell write:

> The goal of sound hermeneutics is to avoid subjectively as much as possible and not to read into a text a foreign meaning. . . . This is an unhealthy assumption for evangelicals to make as they exegete the biblical text. . . . One can learn what Jesus taught and understand the Gospels without [form criticism], for the Gospels are not reinterpretations of the life of Christ to fit later historical circumstances in the Christian community. They present one life situation, that of Jesus Himself. To go beyond that and hypothesize an additional one impugns the text and courts hermeneutical (interpretive) disaster.[13]

Every generation of Christians has had its long list of foes that attempt to discredit the Word of God, labeling it simply the thoughts of men and not the inspired message from the Lord. The beginning of the twenty-first century is no different. Postmodernism and liberal form criticism will try to destroy the reliability of the Bible. But the Scriptures are like a rock that does not move. Through the centuries, the Bible has weathered the storms and has never become outdated in its message to hungry humanity. Since the times of the apostles, it has proven itself, enlightened hungry souls, given the gospel of personal salvation, and done its marvelous work within the hearts of believers.

Paul commended the Thessalonian church because, when the heard the Word, they "accepted it not as the word of men, but for what it really is, the word of God, which also performs its work in you who believe" (1 Thess. 2:13).

FOR DISCUSSION

1. List three men mentioned in this chapter, and explain how their theories helped destroy confidence in the Word of God.

2. Define deism.

3. What is rationalism?

4. Define and describe *the documentary hypothesis.*

5. What is meant by *faith history?*

For Further Study

Bible Introduction

Archer, Gleason L. *A Survey of Old Testament Introduction.* Chicago: Moody, 1994.

Bibliology Texts

Young, Edward J. *Thy Word Is Truth.* Grand Rapids: Eerdmans, 1960.

History

Elder, John. *Prophets, Idols and Diggers.* New York: Bobbs Merrill, 1960.

Textual Criticism

Thomas, Robert L., F. David Farnell. *The Jesus Crisis.* Grand Rapids: Kregel, 1998.

Chapter Nine

Apologetics and the Authority of the Bible

W hat is apologetics, and how is it related to the Bible and theology? How should we in the twenty-first century reply to arguments against biblical faith that neighbors and fellow workers quote from the secular media?

How should we respond to apostles of political correctness when they accuse Christianity of inherent religious bigotry? How do Christians engage unbelief in their children, spouses, or parents? What should be our answers to Christ-denying claims by the many religions and cults? Today more than ever, apologetics plays a vital role in Christian witness.

Christians of all generations have faced intense political and social challenges to major truths of the faith. Unbelief attacked the central Christian doctrine of the miracle of the resurrection (Matt. 28:12–15; Acts 17:32; 26:8). Then as now, pagan nature worship made the Creator-creature distinction almost inconceivable (Acts 14:8–18; 17:22–31). Early on, political leaders, religious teachers, and teachers of world philosophies branded early Christianity an enemy of the state and of the social and religious order of things (John 11:48–53; Acts 4:13–22; 6:11–15; 17:5–9; 19:21–41; 21:27–31).

Unbelieving family members questioned the faith of the earliest Christians (1 Pet 3:15). Present-day unbelievers, in spite of their misplaced self-confidence, are no more intelligent than their pagan predecessors centuries ago. But God has granted to the children of God sufficient revelation to assist us in speaking to the spiritual conflicts and criticisms of our day (2 Tim. 3:16–17).

In other words, apologetics is about challenging our present world with the ever-relative authority of the Word of God.

The Meaning of Apologetics

Today the English word *apology* in its everyday usage expresses regret for some wrong action as in, "I apologize." However, its earlier and specialized meaning is quite the opposite. Its specialized meaning comes from the Greek word *apologia*, from which it was transliterated. A prominent example of ancient usage is the title of Plato's dialogue, *The Apology*, which presents the courtroom defense of Socrates against his accusers.

Similar usage occurs in the New Testament (Acts 22:1; 25:16; Phil. 1:7, 16; 2 Tim. 4:16). Far from meaning regret for a wrong action, these uses of *apologia* refer to a carefully reasoned defense against questioning or wrongful accusation by recognized authorities. The word can also refer to a more informal defense outside the courtroom against personal questioning or accusation (1 Cor. 9:3; 2 Cor. 7:11; 1 Pet. 3:15). The intent of an *apologia* is to win over the people being addressed, to change their minds about what is true.

Every Christian should be ready to give a defense (*apologia*) for his or her faith (1 Pet. 3:15). Christian leaders, especially, are to be characterized by their apologetic ability to refute those who attack Christianity (Titus 1:9). In fact, we ought to be encouraged because the Bible says that no unbelievers can ever successfully justify their unbelief (Rom. 1:20). It is the unbelievers who have no answers—not the Christians. Following the prophets and apostles, therefore, we should not be afraid to reason about our faith.

To forsake all reasoning from the Bible with inquirers or accusers is to engage in fideism—the idea that faith cannot be discussed in a rational manner or argued about fruitfully. Offering only autobiographical accounts of inner feelings and personal experience without justification for the gospel is fideism, not apologetics. Tragically, fideism in practice is often a cover for weak faith.

If we avoid reasoning with outside accusers, we probably are avoiding reasoning with our own internal doubts. We may be hiding spiritually, fearful that our biblical faith might not be true after all. A genuine and maturing relationship with God inevitably involves reasoning through His Word amid the challenges of daily life.

Recall the intense reasoning of the psalmist with God over His ways and how he concludes with a deepened, restful, and worshipful faith in the Lord (e.g., Ps. 2; 10; 13; 44; etc.). God created us, after all, to set our lives on real truth that ultimately is derived only from Him.

At the bottom line, apologetics, based on the authority of Scripture, is nothing more than a focused version of our responses to everyday temptations of the world, the flesh, and the devil. No believer, therefore, should think apologetics to be a strange skill impossible to master.

Unfortunately, apologetics can attract people who are naturally argumentative and proud of their intellects. Unless based on the truths of the Word of God and done in submission to the leading of the Holy Spirit, apologetics can easily degenerate to a carnal one-upmanship, a social game that witnesses not to the life of Christ and the teaching of biblical doctrine but to plain arrogance. Peter warns us to practice our apologetics "with gentleness and reverence" (1 Pet. 3:15). The same humility toward the Lord that He requires in personal trials of faith must be present in apologetic activities, too.

The Relationship Between Apologetics and Theology

Church history shows the influence of apologetics on theology. Using the Bible as the basis of apologetics actually advanced the theological understanding of the Bible itself. When Paul headed for his Roman trial, many believe that Luke researched and compiled his two-volume theological history (Luke and Acts) to aid in Paul's defense (*apologia*). Later, additional theological advances occurred to confront heretical views of the doctrines of Christology and soteriology. But the war is unending, and every generation of believers in Christ have to be ready to respond to the torrent of doubt that constantly overflows the church of Jesus Christ. In order to answer questions and criticisms that come against our faith, we have to deepen our appreciation of God's Word.

Unfortunately, the church has sometimes unwittingly adopted bad theology while trying to engage in apologetics. Out of a desire to minimize conflict, Christian apologists often have tried to show that biblical faith fits peacefully into established non-Christian concepts. Well-known church fathers such as Augustine and Aquinas, for example, along with their great positive contributions to Christian thought, also distorted parts of biblical theology with concepts of Greek philosophy.

In recent times, the apologetic urge to fit the Bible into evolutionary schemes of natural history has seriously compromised literal interpretation and inerrancy of Scripture. We have to be careful, therefore, how we answer those who challenge us.

Holding Firm to Scripture

Criticism of the Christian faith nearly always involves some sort of question. A question often contains a subtle viewpoint that can mislead us when we try to answer it. The Bible warns us that to answer a question before one really understands it is "folly and shame" (Prov. 18:13). We all can remember trying to answer a test question in school that we did not understand and missing it by a mile. This is why, when we do biblical apologetics, we must first understand the question. We may even have to clarify and reword it before we can give a clear biblical answer.

Paul warned the church about being deceived by pagan notions of the fundamental categories of reality (Col. 2:8). Concerning beliefs about creation, the basic categories or *stoicheion* ("elementary principles") in ancient times could be earth, fire, water, air, or other created things that paganism falsely interpreted as cosmic sources and sustainers. Against this pagan viewpoint, Paul directs us to build on the truths revealed in Christ. Paul said the Lord Jesus Christ created the entire cosmos, sustains every so-called natural process, and fully reveals God's Person (Col. 1:15–17). The apostle's revelation about Jesus, not based on human speculation, is the key to interpreting history, what is and is not possible, and what is right or wrong. In Him "are hidden all the treasures of wisdom and knowledge" (Col. 2:3).

At Lystra Paul rejected the adoration of the people because of the pagan notions of deity embedded in their interpretation of what had happened. It would have been folly for him to preach Christ without first clarifying who God is. He replaced their perverted notions of deity with the biblical Creator-creature distinction. Only then would Paul respond to their thankfulness by directing it toward the God of creation (Acts 14:8–18). Similarly, in Athens Paul went to great lengths to clarify the nature of God before introducing the gospel itself (Acts 17:22–31).

The Early Church

When the early church responded to heresies about our Lord, it had to reject the basic ideas of deity that these teachings were grounded on, not just the individual heresies themselves. Various versions of Monarchianism, for example, started with the false idea of solitary monotheism, so they were unable to conceive of plurality in the Godhead. They insisted that Jesus could not be deity and yet distinct in person from the Father at the same time. This mistaken notion about the Lord Jesus survives to this day in certain Christian cults, Unitarianism, postbiblical Judaism,

Islam, and liberal theologies. After exposing the underlying false notions about the deity of Christ over some decades, the church formulated in a clear way with accurate biblical evidence the doctrines of the Trinity and the Incarnation.

Requiring an Apologetic Strategy

To use apologetics carefully without harming theological doctrine requires a strategy. Strategy is not primarily concerned with specific tactical issues such as debates over the resurrection, inspiration of the Bible, the Genesis creation story, or one's lifestyle. Strategy is concerned with how to appeal to the non-Christian in such a way that biblical doctrine and authority is not compromised in the process, regardless of the issue at hand. It focuses on how to understand biblically the true nature of unbelief.

Christians commonly use several different strategies in apologetic encounters. For purposes of discussion, we can classify present-day apologetic strategies by distinguishing the common ground that their advocates think exists between Christianity and unbelief. To have genuine communication with critics and accusers concerning their questions, there must be common ground that offers a point of contact. What is the common ground? How should we use it to build our case?

Three Apologetic Strategies

Three major ideas exist about the common ground that exists between Christians and non-Christians. Upon each of these ideas, Christians have fashioned distinct apologetic strategies. In actual practice, however, these strategies are often mixed together.

The first two strategies we will review are based on the common ground of experience and reason. These strategies are called classical apologetics. Classical apologetics asserts that you can start with factors that are independent from Christian beliefs and work your way toward convincing proof of the claims of Christianity and the Bible. The third strategy, based on the nonneutral common ground of God's revelation, is a part of presuppositional apologetics. Presuppositional apologetics asserts that you have to argue from presuppositions for the existence of the God of the Bible and the truth of Christianity.

The Neutral Common Ground of Experience

One idea of common ground holds that all humans share historical experience and events. They all experience good and evil. Not only do they have facts in common, but this empirically centered approach also holds that all people can reason correctly about these data with religious neutrality. Truthful interpretation of the facts in arithmetic, cooking, music, and science does not require belief in the Bible.

We can, it would seem, reason to the truths of Christianity from this neutral zone of shared facts. In other words, we can sit down with unbelievers, suspend our faith, and impartially seek together how to interpret the common facts of our experiences. In a culture impressed by the scientific method, this data-centered approach carries much credibility. Apologetics in this view tries to operate prior to theology and thus maintain religious neutrality.[1]

For the sake of discussion, believers agree with unbelievers that facts are objective and determine what is true. For example, isolated biblical facts, therefore, should lead to the conclusion that the gospel story is true. However, the resurrection is a fact open to historical investigation. Impartial study of the biblical documents and the claims of the early church make this doctrine certain. Ancient Near Eastern archeological facts similarly support the Old Testament. Successful apologetics will utilize the alleged neutral common ground of facts, so it behooves us to gather reference material on creation, archeology, and ancient history.[2]

Empirically centered apologetic strategy rightfully reminds us that biblical revelation is historical revelation. God actually created the universe with a history external to Himself; He did not just dream about it. His revelation to human beings made in His image was not abstract theory divorced from everyday experience.

The biblical authors would not tolerate factual errors and mistaken historical witness (Deut. 4:3, 11–12; 18:20–22; Luke 1:1–4; 2 Pet. 1:16–17). In spite of the modern misconception that ancients were indifferent to historical accuracy, biblical authors considered fabricated history to be a violation of the ninth commandment (1 Cor. 15:14–15, 32). Prophetic claims that turned out to be historically false could result in capital punishment (Deut. 18:20–22). Jesus went so far as to say if His historical witness were flawed, then no one should believe His witness concerning heavenly things (John 3:12). When we speak of Christianity, therefore, we are speaking of something as real as any other fact or experience of our lives. The biblical record is indeed historically correct.

However, we have to be careful how we think about the alleged neutral common ground of historical experience between believers and unbelievers. Universal categories contain religious and theological beliefs. These constitute the *stoicheion* of Paul's warning in Colossians 2:8: "See to it that no one takes you captive through philosophy and empty deception, according to the tradition of men, according to the elementary principles of the world, rather than according to Christ." Believers and unbelievers do not share the same *stoicheion*. Neutrality quickly disappears.

Sin affects ideas. We have to go no further than our everyday confrontation with lusts to see the principle in action. All temptations invite us to alter our theology. The fall of man profoundly illustrates the affects of sin on interpretation of facts. Paul tells us that our unregenerate minds have become vain and darkened (Rom. 1:21; Eph. 4:18). We therefore cannot naively accept the unbelievers' notions of the sensing, meaning, and interpretation of facts.

Suppose a critic of the faith holds to an empiricist view of facts. Empiricism views facts as isolated, meaningless things distributed throughout a universe of chance ("brute facts"). All we know are the sensations we experience: sight, sound, taste, smell, and touch. Any meaning given is from inside our heads. Even if we tie together this stream of sensations into a generalization, it would be contingent on the next so-called fact. Is this the kind of neutrality we—who know the Creator of the human mind and the things it senses—want to share in common with an unbeliever?

Suppose an unbeliever responded to the resurrection claim by saying, "Okay, you've convinced me that Christ's tomb became empty and an utterly strange thing happened. But you know that in this world of chance, strange things do happen. It doesn't prove that your gospel is the truth." His unbelief would absorb the resurrection fact inside itself like a giant amoeba. He would strategically envelope us. We would have won the battle over the isolated fact of the resurrection, but we would have lost the war over repentance from unbelief.

The Neutral Common Ground of Reason

The second idea of common ground is that all people share rationality. The law of contradiction—that a statement cannot be both true and false at the same time and in the same way—underlies all thinking. No one can think or communicate without it. Not only do all people have rationality in common, but this rationally centered approach also holds that they apparently use it without any specific religious commitments. It appears to be a theory-neutral tool for Christian and non-Christian alike. With it, we can sit down with unbelievers in complete neutrality and seek to create a logically consistent view of life. This strategy, however, tries to place the apologetic enterprise prior to theology.[3]

Rationally centered apologetic strategy correctly disciplines our argumentation. God is not a God of confusion (1 Cor. 14:33). Logical consistency in the Bible identified false prophets for execution in ancient Israel (Deut. 13:1–5). Logic emanates from God's very nature (2 Tim. 2:13). Jesus' replies to His critics always showed valid logic. Paul's arguments were tightly reasoned. This approach correctly notes that true knowledge must involve universal categories, not merely contingent sets of experiences. Historical facts cannot be understood without rational ideas (Rom. 1:20; Heb. 11:3).

The law of contradiction, standing by itself, is an empty calculating machine. Everyone must appeal to more than just the solitary law of contradiction. To use it in any discussion, we need to load it with the two valid statements that are being compared. We need to spell out what is meant by true and false. We must return to Paul's warning about *stoicheion* in Colossians 2:8. Our so-called neutral deductive logic turns out to be as vulnerable to theological effects as the reason-centered approach.

If we go this route, we apologists find ourselves left only with a rationally centered argument. We are no longer arguing from Scripture but simply point by point with human reasoning that only leads to a dead end.

When doing this, we focus mainly on intellectual issues, and we disregard the spiritual issues of repentance and unbelief. Only God the Creator correctly understands how limited human beings will think. The greatest intellectual thinkers finally have to come to an end of their reasoning abilities. They sin in their own ways as all of humanity.

By exalting logical consistency above the Word of God, this approach leaves non-Christians with the idea of the sufficiency of the law of contradiction that can be used prior to any theological commitment. If they are won over, they will live under the delusion that Christianity is merely the truest position so far shown by their skillful use of logic. If they are not won over, they will assume that further study will expose unanswerable contradictions in the Christian faith. In either case, rationalism has enveloped the authority of Scripture.

The Nonneutral Common Ground of God's Revelation

In one form or another, the first two apologetic strategies have characterized most of church history since the second century. Broadly speaking, they are the classic or traditional apologetic approaches.[4] During the last century or two, however, they have become less effective.

Since the so-called Copernican revolution of the German philosopher, Immanuel Kant (1724–1804), non-Christian systematic thought has been more openly grounded in people. Copernicus had revolutionized humankind's concept of the universe by substituting a heliocentric point of reference for the old geocentric one. Kant revolutionized philosophy by substituting a new starting point (the human mind) for the old starting point (the external world). According to Kant, all apparent order and logic are produced by the mind. People can know nothing of the world or God or anything else beyond their own minds.

Some have classified the approach of Kant and other rationalists as *neurotheological,* by which they intend that we simply learn by the mind alone. "The content of all knowledge comes through the senses, [and] the *form* or *structure* is provided by the . . . forms of sensation and categories of the mind."[5] They have concluded that we are simply physical and what comes forth from the mind is all that there is. Christian claims are completely encapsulated within mental experiences and cannot contain truth of the world outside. Enemies of the Christian faith have employed this subjective approach in one form or another to envelop and neutralize the gospel ever since Kant.

A third apologetic strategy has developed over the last century within Dutch Calvinist circles, culminating in the life and work of Cornelius Van Til and his disciples, most notably Greg L. Bahnsen, R. J. Rushdoony, Vern S. Poythress, and John M. Frame.[6] Van Til countered Kant's revolutionary method of argumentation with an equally revolutionary method based on Scripture. Instead of making the mind the source of order and logic, the starting point is the Bible and theology that shapes the thinking processes of the inner person. It requires theology to go before apologetics, and then shape it at every point. Only by so doing, Van Til argues, will theology be protected from compromise when Christians respond to critics' questions.

This third strategy centers on the totality of biblical revelation and contrasts it with the totality of unbelief. Belief and unbelief appear as two opposing systems. This strategy surrounds biblical miracles, such as the resurrection, with the entire biblical story from creation to consummation. It refuses to extract historical miracles out of their biblical context to be neutrally analyzed as isolated evidential pieces. This strategy is often called a presuppositional strategy.

An illustration will help show the difference between presuppositional and the normal approach to apologetics. Imagine that someone wants to remodel and redecorate his house. But he drives up to the front door with a bulldozer and starts by demolishing the entire house. Rather than remodeling and redecorating, he bulldozes the old structure in order to build a new one.

That is like Van Til's presuppositional apologetics. The entire structure of unbelief is attacked and replaced with biblical categories, biblical reasoning, biblically interpreted historical facts, and biblically based ethics. Christianity is not presented as a supplement to the notions of an unregenerate mind at enmity with God (Rom. 8:7). The God of Scripture is not added to other gods and goddesses in the pantheon of one's heart; instead, all such other authorities must bow down to Him alone (cf. 1 Sam. 5). Only after the Triune God becomes the final authority can there be genuine spiritual knowledge and eternal truth (Prov. 1:7).

Presuppositional apologetics, however, must answer some questions. If genuine knowledge only derives from biblical presuppositions, how can unbelievers know truths about life, history, science, and art? Because all humans are made in God's image and their environment is God's handiwork, they are encircled with the revelation of God's creation everywhere that is sufficiently clear to refute all claims of innocence and ignorance (Job 38—42; Ps. 19:1–4; 139:7–8; Isa. 40:21, 26; John 1:9; Acts 17:24–29; Rom. 1:18–23, 32).

Thus, in daily living all people utilize perception, logic, language, and moral judgments that make no sense whatever unless the biblical worldview is correct. Science relies on a view of logic and observations that has no meaning apart from the Bible.[7] Public discourse requires more than ideas inside the human mind. At the bottom line, unbelievers cannot live consistently with unbelief but must utilize biblical notions to get along in life.[8] Because they do so, in spite of their protestations to the contrary, unbelievers discover truths in all areas of life.

Believers and unbelievers share a large common ground with each detail radiating God's glory. However, they do not share a neutral view of it. At the heart of unbelief is a foolish suppression of God's claims at every point (Ps. 14:1–3; Prov. 18:2; Rom. 1:18). Unbelief attempts to make an existence free of responsibility to the Creator—a new world safe for sinners. Unbelief derails and perverts the primary goal of the cultural mandate into a global campaign to reinvent truth. Following the example of Satan, unbelievers try to become what they know they never can be—gods who can remake the world.

Biblical trust, on the other hand, seeks to think God's thoughts after Him in every area. Believers try to discover the truth of His design and intent in each detail. They must destroy every vain imagination and God-hating thought, starting with those in their own hearts (2 Cor. 10:5). Apologetically speaking, biblical trust must interpret all unbelief according to the Word of God rather than accept unbelievers' own self-interpretation.

While sharing common ground, both belief and unbelief are engaged in a bloody spiritual conflict. No demilitarized zones exist. If the lost come to faith in Christ, they will know that God's Word is the final authority in every area of their existence. If they do not come to Christ as their Savior, they will at least become aware of the chasm between belief and unbelief and the corresponding need to repent.

Biblical Examples of Apologetics in Action

Having in mind the three apologetic strategies developed by Christian teachers, we turn to the Scripture to observe how God and His spokesmen actually responded to critics and objections to biblical faith. Were their defenses carefully reasoned counter arguments, or did they ignore the challenges? Did they use historical facts? If so, how? What common ground or point of contact did they use? How far did they push the issue of underlying obedience or rebellion?

Response to Adam and Eve's Rejection of God's Authority (Genesis 3)

Our first parents challenged the authority of the Lord by questioning His command not to eat from the tree of the knowledge of good and evil (Gen. 3:5–6). They accepted the serpent's advice to eat the forbidden fruit over God's mandate to "not eat, for in the day you eat from it, you will surely die" (2:17). Though our parents' fall from their position of fellowship with the Lord followed, God still came to the garden to seek them. He called, "Where are you?" (3:9). He had not changed; He remained sovereign and in charge of His world. But sin drove Adam and Eve to hide from His presence. The common ground remained the same, though sin now separated them from the Lord.

A change took place, however, in the thinking of both Adam and his wife. They used a false theology that viewed God as unfair and themselves as innocent victims (vv. 10, 12–13). As the Lord probed with questions (though He knew their thoughts), they rationalized and rebelled against Him. Adam said, "The woman whom You gave to be with me, she gave me from the tree, and I ate" (v. 12). Eve replied, "The serpent deceived me, and I ate" (v. 13). Because of sin, the death threat became real. God said, "For you are dust, and to dust you shall return" (v. 19). However, the Lord portrayed a future redemption by slaying an innocent animal to clothe them from their nakedness (vv. 20–21). Grace, judgment, and truth were all present.

While God engaged Adam and Eve in a rational argument that involved spiritual, historical, and prophetic facts, He did not lower His majesty to the couple's notions of reality. He imposed His authority over the events that transpired.

Although the Fall had occurred, God periodically visited the human couple. Sin and its consequences failed to alter His control of the situation or to blot out God-consciousness in the couple. Both were so conscious of His existence that they retreated from any contact with Him. Thus, there remained common ground before and after the fall. The point of contact between God and humans continued.

Response to Job's Demand for the Right to Evaluate the Cause of His Suffering (Job 38—42)

Job and his friends are the most well-known examples of those who try to reconcile the problem of evil in the universe. They engaged in wide-ranging arguments over how sin could be rationally and ethically justified. God's response to their complaints gives another example of truth apologetics in action. As in the case of Adam, God raised theological questions to force Job's skeptical friends to rethink their arguments. He focused on issues of creation and providence, natural history, biology, geophysics, astronomy—facts about God's providence and sovereignty these men, including Job, could observe (Job 38–41).

Job finally admitted his creature status. He confessed that a man-centered viewpoint only produces words "without knowledge" (42:2–3). He repented of trying to do what centuries of unbelieving thought have always tried to do: attain a virtual omniscience to become like God, being a new lord and a new judge.

The Lord did not accept the questions about sin and His providence. In giving His final answers, God first asked Job, "Who is this that darkens counsel by words without knowledge? . . . Where were you when I laid the foundation of the earth? (38:2–4). Toward the end of His final dialogue with Job, the Lord asked, "Will the faultfinder contend with the Almighty?" (40:2), followed by Job's humble answer, "I lay my hand on my mouth. Once I have spoken, and I will not answer; even twice, and I will add nothing more" (vv. 4–5).

God first redefined the question by correcting it theologically. Then and only then, did He answer. Critics still insist Job never got an answer. What they really mean is that the answer Job received requires a bowing in humility before the awesomeness of God and His works. Those who despise the Lord and His Word resist with their hardened wills to do this. Logically valid arguments do not persuade hardened hearts.

Response to Israel's Historical Rejection of Yahweh (Deuteronomy 32)

Moses' song in Deuteronomy provides a third example of biblical apologetics in action. About to die, Moses left the nation he had helped found with a prophetic outline of their future history. This vision of Israel's future revealed that the nation would rebel against God. Moses' song depicted God's response to that defection. Israel had been founded on the Law as a treaty between itself and Yahweh God. Any violations of the treaty would be challenged by a lawsuit. Deuteronomy 32 is the first occurrence in the Bible of this God-against-Israel legal indictment. This charge was repeated in the writings of later Old Testament prophets (cf. Isa. 1:2; Mic. 6:1–2). Following Moses' example, other prophets gave divine pronouncements from the written Law against the Israelites who had lost their consciousness of who God is.

The divine legal indictment requires both historical accuracy and a Law-based interpretation of the facts for the prosecution's rationale to be valid. The Old Testament prophetic writings, therefore, never argue for the existence of God. Instead, logic argues that defection from the God of Israel leads to destruction, national catastrophe, and death. It exposes self-destructive unbelief and establishes the claim of Old Testament wisdom literature that such unbelief and disobedience is folly.[9] According to God's promise, His plan for human history through Israel will succeed (Deut. 32:43). His way is the way of spiritual wisdom.

Biblical apologetics turns apologetic defense into an assault against unbelief. Such apologetics, therefore, does not simply defend the faith; it refutes the unbelieving foundations beneath the accusations and objections of godless skepticism.

Response to Israel's Rejection of Jesus Christ Found in the Gospels

All four Gospels report the apparent failure of Jesus Christ to win national recognition of His messiahship. Many objections were leveled against His claims, especially concerning His deity. The New Testament authors repeatedly set forth the teachings and the historical facts about the life and ministry of Christ (Luke 1:1–4; John 20:30–31; Acts 1:1–3; 26:26; 1 Cor. 15:3–8; 2 Pet. 1:16–18; 1 John 1:1–3).

All these evidences, however, derive their apologetic force from the prior Old Testament framework. For example, Yahweh alone reigned over the seas (Ps. 29:3, 10; 65:7) and rebuked the waters with His voice or wind (Ex. 14:21; cf. Ps. 104:6–9). When Jesus did these same things (Matt. 8:26–27), the rationale established the divine messiahship of Christ, with logic built on the prior revelations of the ancient prophets.

Jesus insisted that the reason why unbelievers in that generation were not convinced by these historic evidences was that they had rebelled against the prior revelation: "If they do not listen to Moses and the Prophets, they will not be persuaded even if someone rises from the dead" (Luke 16:31; cf. John 5:45–47). Rejection of previous revelation establishes a pattern of thinking that automatically perverts additional revelation. The unbelievers of Jesus' day were not acting out a form of neutral ignorance as if the testimony of Jesus were unclear. Instead, those who rejected Him sought to reinterpret His life and teachings so they would not have to believe. Unbelief went into action in order to deny that He was the Messiah and the Son of God.

Jesus attributed both the positive and negative responses of the lost to the sovereignty of God in history: "I praise You, Father, Lord of heaven and earth, that You have hidden these things from the wise and intelligent and have revealed them to infants" (Matt. 11:25–26; cf. 13:10–17; John 6:44–45). Biblical apologetics succeeds, for it divides unbelief from belief.

Response to Pagan Opposition to the Gospel in Acts 17

The last example of a biblical apologetic shows how Paul responded to the pagan society he lived in. Athens easily ranked as one of the chief intellectual centers of the ancient world. The city was filled with idolatrous religions and worldviews (17:16, 22). Like pagan intellectuals throughout history, Athenians could not suppress the evidence of God-consciousness in their literature, art, and science. Paul was ready to give an answer concerning the evidence of God when called on to speak before a public forum (17:16–21, 23, 28).

The subject Paul focused on was the resurrection of Christ (17:18–19). Since he understood their pagan orientation, he knew the resurrection would not make sense. His apologetic began, not with a direct answer to their question, but with a critique of their entire world-view. Using the Old Testament revelation, he contrasted the biblical worldview with their pagan worldview point by point. He challenged their belief concerning the continuity of being, using the Creator-creature distinction of Isaiah and the psalmist (17:24–25; cf. Ps. 42:5; 50:9–12; Isa. 42:5). [10]

The apostle Paul denied paganism's deification of human intellect by referring to Solomon's confession of the incomprehensible nature of God (17:24; cf. 1 Kings 8:27). Against proud Athenian ethnical nationalism, Paul presented Moses' record of the unity of the human race (17:26; cf. Gen. 1, 9; Deut. 32:8) and his account of the paganization of civilization (17:30; cf. Deut. 4:19). Paul used Greek literature to show that underneath their paganism they really did know of the true God. The apostle then pointed out their responsibility to think according to His ways (17:28–29). He demonstrated that not only did the gospel belong to a very different worldview, but also paganism was beset with an internal contradiction between what it said and what it knew was true.

After his analysis of Athenian culture, Paul could then address the original resurrection question without theological compromise. Instead of tolerating a cyclical Greek view of history, he explained the resurrection within the presuppositions of the Old Testament view of history. The resurrection's meaning was that it constituted the final step in a historical progression toward final judgment (17:31). The response to his apologetic recalled the response to Jesus' own ministry: belief and unbelief became clearly divided (17:32).

These biblical examples of apologetics demonstrate an uncompromising adherence to biblical theology. In each case, the one doing apologetics avoids any attempt to find common ground in unbelievers' notions of the meaning of facts or an abstract use of logic. Instead, unbelieving worldviews are contrasted with the Word of God and shown to be self-contradictory and self-destructive manifestations of sin. [11] Unbelievers in each case are thus held accountable for their suppressed knowledge of God. They are left with a clear challenge to repent.

Practical Apologetics

Having reviewed the various strategies apologists use to contend for the inerrancy of the Bible and the truth of its teachings and having observed biblical examples of apologetics, let us consider some practical ways believers can argue for the truth of their faith.

Strategic Principles

First, perfectly sound arguments will not necessarily persuade. Jesus gave the clearest manifestation of truth the world would ever see but succeeded only in persuading a small number, while the majority further hardened their unbelieving hearts.

Second, to a military metaphor, we must strategically encircle unbelief by living the Christian life. Godly living cannot but help show the rational consistency of Christianity. This is worth more than a scholarly treatise. From God walking in the Garden, through the heroic lives of faith (Heb. 11; Joseph; Daniel) to thousands of Christians since the first century, unbelievers have witnessed the power of spiritually transformed lives. C. S. Lewis puts the matter this way:

> We can make people often attend to the Christian point of view for half an hour or so; but the moment they have gone away from our lecture or laid down our article, they are plunged back into a world where the opposite position is taken for granted. . . . It is not books on Christianity that will really trouble [the modern man]. But he would be troubled if, whenever he wanted a cheap popular introduction to some science, the best work on the market was always by a Christian.[12]

For an ungodly nation to hinder Christianity, it must paint the Christian message as bigoted and outmoded. It must show that Christ is not suitable for a modern, pluralistic society. The message that it is a danger threatening abortion and gay rights must be repeated.

Christians should answer by encircling unbelief with strong biblical faith and truth. Pagan caesars fear Christ because they do not want to be held accountable to an ethical and spiritual standard not of their own making.

Tactical Techniques

Biblical apologists must be good listeners and students of critical issues about the Bible. When challenged about spiritual issues, they should witness with loving hearts of compassion. When questioning doubters of the Bible, apologists should show respect to them as valued creatures made in God's image. God often used the questioning approach in the Bible.

Apologists should be able to recall Scriptural precedents for the specific areas at issue. Modern objections are not new. They are merely recent variants on age-old unbelief. Essentially, the same naturalism that infects modern scientific reconstructions of universal history had to be addressed by both Paul (Colossians) and Peter (2 Peter). Scripture offers the best and sufficient guidance in these matters (cf. 2 Tim. 3:16).

Apologists should take advantage of the library of research that Bible-believing scholars and other apologists have produced in recent years. In addition to the materials cited in the endnotes of this book, many other sources offer numerous books, audio tapes, videos, and internet courses that cover the creation/evolution debate, archeological research, defenses against higher criticism of the Bible, philosophical studies of the implications of biblical doctrines, accurate views of church history, comparative religious studies, and present-day cultural issues. Searching the internet, consulting faithful pastors or teachers, and browsing reliable Christian bookstores will quickly uncover the latest materials.[13]

Be Ready to Give an Answer

Christians find themselves giving answers to challenging questions both informally in everyday situations and occasionally in more formal situations. By observing biblical examples, we can learn how to use biblical apologetics in a logically consistent way that makes use of the abundant historical and biblical evidence available. We need to always be ready to give an answer to everyone that asks us a reason for our faith (1 Pet. 3:15). In the end, we will find our faith strengthened, our victory over everyday temptations easier, and our worship deepened.

We must remember that we can accomplish nothing without the guidance of the Holy Spirit. From the human standpoint, Christians do their best to share the Word of God with skeptics. However, final conviction is the work of the Holy Spirit who brings the lost to a saving trust in Christ. Ryrie writes about this dramatic spiritual work. He points to the

> ministry of the Spirit recorded in John 16:7–11, where Jesus says that when the Holy Spirit comes He will "convict the world concerning sin and righteousness and judgment." This is the narrowest circle of common grace because it is not experienced by everyone. However, it may be classed as an example of common grace simply because it is not something that is done only for the redeemed.[14]

FOR DISCUSSION

1. Define the word *apologetics*.

2. What is the theological meaning of the word?

3. Describe how apologetics relates to theology.

4. What is the basis of support for the practice of sound apologetics?

5. Put in your own words descriptions of the three apologetic strategies.

6. In your opinion, what are some of the strongest biblical examples of apologetics in action?

For Further Study

Apologetics

Booth, Robert R., ed. *Always Ready*. Texarcana, Ark.: Covenant Media Foundation, 1996.

McDowell, Josh. *The New Evidence That Demands a Verdict*. Nashville: Thomas Nelson, 1999.

Morris, Henry M. *The Long War Against God*. Grand Rapids: Baker, 1989.

Schaeffer, Francis. *The God Who Is There*. Downer's Grove, Ill.: InterVarsity, 1968.

Dictionaries

Milton, John. "Aeropagetica." *Great Books of the Western World*. Chicago: Encyclopedia Britannica, 1952.

History

Montgomery, John Warwick. *Where Is History Going?* Grand Rapids: Zondervan, 1969.

Van Til, Cornelius. "Once Upon an Apriori," In *Jerusalem and Athens*, edited by E. R. Geehan. Nutley, N.J.: Presbyterian and Reformed, 1971.

Related Articles

Lewis, C. S. "On Moving with the Times." *Christianity Today*, 12 March 1971.

Theology

Ryrie, Charles. *The Holy Spirit*. Chicago: Moody, 1977.

Part Two

THE INERRANCY OF THE BOOKS OF SCRIPTURE

Chapter Ten

Inerrancy of the Pentateuch

O ne of the major ongoing theological issues throughout the twentieth century had to do with the nature of the Bible: Is it or is it not what it claims to be—the very Word of God and thus an inerrant communication of His self-disclosure? Failure to arrive at a positive consensus on this issue will continue to challenge the doctrinal integrity and authority of the Bible and will contribute to the resulting paralysis of the life and witness of the church in the twenty-first century. Belief that the Bible is riddled with errors vitiates compelling reasons to proclaim the gospel message.

Most of the discussion of the inerrancy of Scripture centers on its epistemological and theological necessity.[1] The proofs are largely theological deductions based on certain New Testament texts (primarily 2 Tim. 3:16–17 and 2 Pet. 1:20–21). While this method is appropriate as far as it goes, such a limited approach ignores the global witness of the entire canon, particularly the Old Testament. The purpose of this second part of the book is to examine the evidence for the Scripture's attestations to its own inerrancy, beginning with the Torah (or Pentateuch), the foundational composition on which all the subsequent biblical witness is based.

External Testimony

Before this question is addressed, it will be helpful to briefly observe, how Moses' contemporaries and successors viewed his writings. We will review the teachings of 1) the remainder of the Old Testament, 2) post-biblical Jewish tradition, 3) the New Testament, and 4) post-New Testament Christian tradition.

The Old Testament and Mosaic Inerrancy

The universal biblical assumption is that Moses wrote the Pentateuch, a view held by virtually all Jewish and Christian scholars until the rise of eighteenth century European rationalism. This is not the place to rehearse the history of this debate (see chapter 8) or to defend the traditional, precritical point of view. Many conservative scholars have done this ably.[2] Our intention is to trace the biblical and postbiblical affirmation of the Mosaic authorship of the Pentateuch and to discover its various formulations.

As for the testimony of the Old Testament itself, one can hardly begin with a better endorsement than that given to Moses' younger colleague and theocratic successor Joshua. Immediately upon Moses' death, the Lord charged Joshua to take up the mantle of leadership with the authority of Moses as articulated in the Mosaic literary legacy, the Torah. Joshua had already been designated as the heir apparent to Moses (cf. Num. 27:18), one whose word, like that of Moses, would be authoritative (v. 21; cf. 32:28; 34:17; Deut. 3:28). He had even shared with Moses in reciting the covenantal "song of witness" to the assembly of Israel (Deut. 32:44).

The inerrancy of the Mosaic writings is implied in the statement that they represented the spoken word of God (Josh. 1:3; 8:31–35; 14:2, 6, 10; 17:4; 20:2). These writings bear divine authority because they derive ultimately from God Himself and not Moses. It is the "book of the law" which, though Mosaic, was God's mandate to Israel (Josh. 1:7–8; 8:31–32, 34). The people must love and obey God because the Law that commanded this was in the writings of Moses, that is, in the Word of God itself (Josh. 22:5; 23:6).

In David's final charge to Solomon, he urged him to "keep the charge of the LORD your God to walk in His ways, to keep His statutes, His commandments, His ordinances, and His testimonies, according to what is written in the Law of Moses" (1 Kings 2:3; cf. 1 Chr. 22:12–13). Clearly, David viewed Moses' writings as inerrant revelation. Solomon held the same view when he spoke of God's Word as having been declared through Moses (1 Kings 8:53, 56).

Later, Hezekiah was commended for keeping "commandments, which the LORD had commanded Moses" (2 Kgs. 18:6; cf. 2 Chr. 30:16), and Josiah was likewise commended (2 Kgs. 23:25). When the latter was presented with a copy of the Law found in the temple, he regarded it as the Word of God as well as the writing of Moses (2 Kgs. 23:24–25).

The chronicler stated, "Hilkiah the priest found the book of the law of the LORD given by Moses" (2 Chr. 34:14), thus equating the Law of God with the Law of Moses. Ezra (3:2; 6:18; 7:6) and Nehemiah (1:7–8; 8:1, 14; 9:14; 10:29; 13:1) shared this viewpoint, and both understood Moses' writings to be the very writings of God Himself. From beginning to end, the Old Testament speaks with one voice on the matter—the Pentateuch is the Word of God and therefore without error.

As we have noted, because the Scriptures come from the God who is truth (John 14:6; Rom. 3:4), therefore, the Scriptures themselves must be true. The doctrine of inspiration logically leads to inerrancy. And because inspiration extends equally to all parts of Scripture, the historical books are also inerrant. As Charles Hodge declares:

> It means, first, that all the books of Scriptures are equally inspired. All alike are infallible in what they teach. And secondly, that inspiration extends to all the contents of these several books. It is not confined to moral and religious truths, but extends to the statements of facts, whether scientific, historical, or geographical. It is not confined to those facts the importance of which is obvious or which involved matters of doctrine. It extends to everything which any sacred writer asserts to be true.[3]

The Scriptures claim that their contents come from God. Repeatedly, God's intervention, promises, prophecies, and words were recorded. The historical books show that God and His words were inseparably intertwined with Israel's history. With the many references to God speaking, these books implicitly claim that they are inspired and inerrant.

Critics have placed too great an emphasis on man's part in the writing of Scripture; they see apparent contradictions as human errors and mistakes in the text. Their wrong emphasis leads to wrong conclusions. The Scriptures are "breathed out" from the God who is truth and who is omniscient and omnipotent. It is no blind leap of faith to believe that the Scriptures, superintended by God Himself, are inerrant. It is true that apparent difficulties and contradictions are in the Scriptures, but these lie not in God's revelation but in human understanding of God's revelation.[4]

Jewish Tradition and Mosaic Inerrancy

So persistent and exceptional is the Old Testament attestation to Moses as the inerrant spokesman of Yahweh that there appears to be no need in postbiblical times to add to or otherwise corroborate that testimony. All the extant literature—whether apocryphal, pseudepigraphal, rabbinic, or Qumranic—assumed that the Torah is the Word of God so that further defense was deemed unnecessary.

Josephus (c. A.D. 37–100) states that God through Moses delivered the Law. In *Antiquities* III.5.3, for example, he relates, "The author of these institutions [i.e., the Sinai covenant] is barely Moses . . . but he who obliged the Nile to run bloody for your sakes." The legislation he transmitted "which appeared to be divine, made this man [Moses] to be esteemed as one superior to his own nature" (*Ant.* III.5.3). It is in his so-called treatise *Against Apion* that Josephus makes his strongest and clearest statement about the nature of Scripture. He says that the Jews have twenty-two sacred books "which are justly believed to be divine; and of them, five belong to Moses" (*Against Apion* I.8). To Josephus the words of Moses and the Word of God are indistinguishable.

The Talmud also endorses the inerrancy of the Torah in a more pointed and precise manner than most modern stalwart defenders. The great rabbi Judah (and perhaps Rabbi Nehemiah as well) suggested that Moses wrote all the Pentateuch except for the account of his own death at the end of Deuteronomy (Deut. 34:5–12). This was attributed to Joshua. The counter opinion was adamant that this was unthinkable. "Can [we imagine the] scroll of the Law being short of one letter?" it was asked. The answer was "No; what we must say is that up to this point the Holy One, blessed be He, dictated and Moses repeated and wrote, and from this point [i.e., about Moses' death] God dictated and Moses wrote with tears" (*Baba Bathra* 14a).

While one might quibble over the matter of dictation and/or Joshua's involvement, it is clear that normative Judaism held tenaciously to the position that the Torah was inerrant because it proceeded directly from God. Orthodox Judaism has never wavered on that view.[5]

The New Testament and Mosaic Inerrancy

Jesus and the apostles, in line with the Old Testament and their own Jewish tradition, held to and taught the doctrines of the inspiration and inerrancy of the Torah.[6] Holding it in the highest esteem, Jesus said he came not to abolish the Law but to fulfill it (Matt. 5:17). He followed this by the astounding declaration that neither the smallest letter nor the slightest stroke of a pen would disappear from the Law until all was accomplished (Matt. 5:18). When questioned about divorce, Jesus said, "Moses permitted . . . divorce" because of their hard hearts, thus equating the teaching of Moses with God's own Word (Matt. 19:8; cf. 22:24;

Mark 7:10; 10:3–5; 12:19, 26; Luke 20:37; John 1:17; 5:46; 7:19–23). In a remarkable juxtaposition of texts, Luke spoke of the "law of Moses" as being identical to the "Law of the Lord" (Luke 2:22–23).

Christian Tradition and Mosaic Inerrancy

It is unnecessary here to trace the doctrine of bibliology through two millennia of church history, for it has been well established that the universal Christian tradition—like the Jewish—has maintained a view of the Torah that, though lacking the specific term, can be described as "inerrancy."[7] This was true, at least until critical methodologies grounded in naturalistic and rationalistic premises no longer countenanced the possibility of such divine miraculous intervention as prepositional revelation. Only those who subscribe to the label "evangelical" or "fundamentalist" embrace inerrancy now.

The rise of skepticism has not affected the nature of the Torah, but only how those who have rejected the Bible's own testimony, along with the testimony of ancient Jewish and Christian traditions, now perceive it. To those for whom historical-critical presuppositions have little practical significance, the issue is not how its critics evaluate the Torah but how it perceives itself. Having briefly traced several avenues of external testimony to the Torah's inerrancy, it is now important to let the text speak for itself.

Internal Testimony

The internal evidence of Mosaic authorship is divided among three avenues of approach: 1) The stature, gifts, and authority of Moses as described in the narratives of the Pentateuch; 2) the self-attestation of Moses in his role as a mediator of divine revelation; and 3) literary formulae and other clues that point to the writings of Moses as being synonymous with the Word of God.

The Stature, Gifts, and Authority of Moses

From the beginning of the narrative of Moses' birth, it is clear that he was to be no ordinary man. Born in times of Egyptian infanticide directed at the Hebrews (Ex. 1:15–16), Moses, a "beautiful" child (Ex. 2:2),[8] was miraculously preserved from death, reared in Pharaoh's palace, and, according to the New Testament, heir of the privileges that royalty could enjoy in New Kingdom Egypt (Heb. 11:24–26).

Though raised as a son by Pharaoh's daughter (Ex. 2:10), Moses' heart was with his beleaguered people. Thus, he took their side, even to the extent of killing an Egyptian slave driver (2:11). In this act, his natural leadership and sense of responsibility became apparent even if his own people misunderstood it as an arrogation of unwarranted power. Their query, "Who made you a prince or a judge over us?" (v. 14) anticipated those times when Moses' God-ordained leadership would be challenged again (cf. Ex. 16:2; 17:2; Num. 11:1–3; 12:1–2; 16:1–3; 20:2–5; etc.).

Both the Egyptians (Ex. 11:3) and the Israelites recognized Moses' stature. After the Exodus, the latter came to him for justice (Ex. 18:13). As Jethro observed, Moses was God's representative, the only one authorized to communicate His decrees and laws (vv. 19–20). He could lead the people "to meet God," (Ex. 19:17) and whose intercession was essential if they were spared the impact of God's awesome glory (Ex. 20:19; cf. Deut. 5:22–27). When his own siblings challenged Moses' authority, Yahweh made it clear that ordinary prophets received revelation in visions and dreams but not so with Moses. "With him I speak mouth to mouth," God said, "even openly, and not in dark sayings, and he beholds the form of the LORD" (Num. 12:6–8). Whatever else this means,[9] it clearly speaks of the uniqueness of Moses' relationship to Yahweh as a communicator of revelation.

Deuteronomy 18:15–19 supplemented this endorsement of Moses as a great prophet from God. Here, Yahweh promised to raise up "a prophet . . . like you [Moses]" into whose mouth "I will put My words" so that "he shall speak to them [i.e., Israel] all that I command him" (v. 18). Christian interpretation is agreed that the Prophet ultimately in view is Jesus Christ (cf. Acts 3:22; 7:37).[10] The point here, however, is quite the reverse: Moses was almost Christlike in his authenticity as a bearer of the message of heaven (cf. Deut. 34:10).

The Self-Attestation of Moses

Despite his initial reluctance to serve as theocratic administrator (Ex. 3:11; 4:1, 10) and his disclaimer that he was "very humble, more than any man who was on the face of the earth" (Num. 12:3), Moses came to recognize that God had raised him up for a particular and privileged task—that of mediating revelation from God to humankind in both oral and literary form. While the latter is more relevant to our topic, the former is also necessary as the precursor to written, canonical composition.

Moses and divine communication. Having responded to the call of God, Moses became aware that God intended to continue to communicate through him to the elect nation Israel. Thus, at Sinai, Yahweh said, "I will come to you in a thick cloud, so that the people may hear when I speak with you and may also believe in you forever" (Ex. 19:9). The fact that Yahweh spoke to Moses raised his esteem in their eyes. After the initial encounter on the mountain, the record stated, "Moses spoke and God answered him with thunder" (v. 19).

This would not be a one-time event; indeed, God promised to meet Moses regularly at the tent of meeting and there speak to him (Ex. 29:42). This took place in such a dramatic form that all who saw it recognized the holiness of the experience and responded in worship (Ex. 33:9–10). As Moses related it, on those occasions "The LORD used to speak to Moses face to face, just as a man speaks to his friend" (v. 11; cf. Num. 12:8; Deut. 34:10). At the same time, there was transcendent glory in the encounter, for Moses heard the voice of God "speaking to him from above the mercy seat that was on the ark of the testimony, from between the two cherubim" (Num. 7:89).

When Moses later reflected on Yahweh's communication with him at Sinai, he said that it was done to enable him to pass on those heavenly words to the people (Deut. 5:5). Its essence was the corpus of "the commandment, the statutes, and the judgments" (that is, the covenant and all its stipulations) designed to guide the nation in being a priestly kingdom and a holy nation (Deut. 6:1).

Moses and the communication of the Law. Moses attested not only to his having received divine communication in general but also specifically to having been enlightened concerning God's purposes for His people, purposes embodied in the corpus of covenant law. Even before the Sinai revelation, Moses told his father-in-law Jethro that whenever the people had a dispute, "it comes to me, and I judge between a man and his neighbor and make known the statutes of God and His laws" (Ex. 18:16). The nature of this legislation is unclear, but it presupposes some form of direct revelation.[11]

At the moment of covenant presentation, Moses called the elders of Israel "and set before them all these words which the LORD had commanded him" (Ex. 19:7). The words in question were those of verses 4 to 6 in which Israel was offered the privilege of becoming Yahweh's servant people. After God spelled out the terms of the covenant (Ex. 20:1—23:33), Moses "came and recounted to the people all the words of the LORD and all the ordinances"—clearly words of revelation. Moses then wrote them down exactly as God had spoken them (Ex. 24:3–4).

In the plains of Moab, Moses reminded the great assembly of Israel that he had taught them "statutes and judgments just as the LORD my God commanded me, that you should do thus in the land where you are entering to possess it" (Deut. 4:5). That these were divinely inspired was clear to Moses who said, "You shall not add to the word which I am commanding you, nor take away from it" (v. 2).[12] And this is not because of Moses' innate authority, for he made it clear that these were "the commandments of the LORD your God which I command you" (v. 2).

Moses and the very words of God. Those who hold firmly to a doctrine of verbal, plenary inspiration are frequently caricaturized as espousing a dictation theory in which the prophets and apostles were only passive instruments through whom the Holy Spirit spoke without their active participation. Scripture does not teach such a view nor do thoughtful students of the Bible entertain it. However, a few texts in the Pentateuch suggest that on rare occasions God himself penned the words of divine self-disclosure. Surely, there can be no doubt of their inerrancy under such circumstances.

The texts in question have to do with the revelation of the Decalogue, the heart of the Mosaic covenant. The importance of these texts is underscored by the fact that God Himself was said to be the author and scribe. The first hint of the circumvention of human involvement is in the covenant ceremony of Exodus 24. Yahweh here said to Moses, "Come up to Me on the mountain and remains there, and I will give you the stone tablets with the law and the commandment which I have written for their instruction" (v. 12). Reference to "tablets" identifies the text with great precision. As for the meaning of the phrase, "I have written," the summation of the Sinai epiphany in Exodus 31:18 made the astounding declaration that the tablets in question were "written by the finger of God." Even taking into account the bold anthropomorphism of the passage, there remains no doubt that its intention was to assert that in some manner God Himself authored the text.[13]

Moses and literary composition. According to ancient and nearly unanimous tradition, Moses not only received orally transmitted revelation, but he wrote it down in a composition known to Jews as the Torah and to Christians as the Pentateuch. Not least among the witnesses to this tradition, the Pentateuch itself makes it clear that the words of Moses were the very words of God, that is, they were inerrant in their assertions and claims. All the books of the Pentateuch except Genesis explicitly endorsed the role of Moses in this respect; likewise, all the implicit evidence pointed to Moses as the author of Genesis.[14]

The first clear passage connecting Moses to authorship is Exodus 17:14 where God told the lawgiver to write in a book an account of the Amalekite attack on Israel at Rephidim. Their acts must be secured in writing "as a memorial" that God was going to judge the Amalekites for raising their hands against His elect. Four hundred long years passed, but at last the day of reckoning came. Samuel, prompted by Yahweh, told King Saul to annihilate the Amalekites, a command Samuel identified as "the words of the LORD" (1 Sam. 15:1). In Samuel's mind, the text Moses had written long before, which had become canonized and preserved, was nothing less than a divine message. Moses' memorandum, now part of the Book of Exodus, was at the same time God's Word.

The reader is free to disbelieve these testimonies, of course, but he or she is not free to deny that they exist and that their intention was to assert Mosaic authorship of the entire body of revelation from Mount Sinai.[15] At the very least, this portion of Scripture included the Book of the Covenant (Ex. 20—23), instructions for the manufacture of the Tabernacle and its furnishings (chaps. 25—27, 30), and regulations concerning the priesthood, sacrifices, and worship (chaps. 28—29; Lev. 1—7; 11—25). The connecting narratives and exhortations are part of the whole collection and for this reason alone must be considered as elements of the covenant text that Moses was commanded to write.

That such records were also part of Holy Scripture is clear from Numbers 33:2, for example, which referred to something as secular as the compilation of an itinerary. Having come through the Sinai wastelands—a long and arduous trek of forty-years duration—Moses is instructed by the Lord to record for posterity the various stages of the journey. Numbers 33:3–49 is the document detailing this movement, a tedious recounting of place after place from Egypt to the plains of Moab. If such information was deemed so important as to be recorded by divine command and inspiration, what can be said of the theological or spiritual content of the Pentateuch? Clearly, such sections also share the official approval of the God of truth.

Like Leviticus, Numbers closed with a statement that asserted Mosaic authorship of the book and, hence, its canonical and revelational authority: "These are the commandments and the ordinances which the LORD commanded to the sons of Israel through Moses on the plains of Moab by the Jordan opposite Jericho" (Num. 36:13).[16] The effect of this summation was to incorporate everything prior to the Moab conclave—at least, everything from Exodus 20 onward—into one massive literary composition, embracing virtually everything in the Pentateuch except Genesis and Deuteronomy. The latter abounds with its own evidentiary witness to its Mosaic authorship and inherent revelatory character.

Written revelation. The first clear reference in Deuteronomy to Moses' self-awareness that he was an inerrant spokesman for Yahweh is in 12:32 which, while not expressly speaking of written revelation, places the word of Moses on the same plane as the Word of God. "Whatever I command you, you shall be careful to do," he said. "You shall not add to nor take away from it." Such an injunction—loaded as it is with overtones of unlimited authority—would be the height of hubris were it as the edict of Moses alone.[17] Clearly, Moses spoke for God whose word is final, complete, and inviolable. The prohibition against making any change in it eloquently testified to its inerrant perfection.

While nothing could be added to or deleted from the sacred text, it had to be copied from time to time. In his instructions about Israel's future monarchy, Moses insisted that the king in days to come must "write for himself a copy of this law on a scroll in the presence of the Levitical priests" (Deut. 17:18). He urged such a ruler to carefully observe "all the words of this law and these statutes" (v. 19), intending, it seems, to include the entire corpus of Deuteronomic covenant law in his purview.[18] It is worth noting again the appeal to "words" as if to say that they, and not just a general sentiment, were important to his injunction.

The same quibbling about words and phrases appeared in the blessings and curses section of Deuteronomy where Moses threatened the nation with dire consequences if they were not "careful to observe all the words of this law which are written in this book" (Deut. 28:58). By "book" was meant the whole scope of Deuteronomy. It must be heeded in part and in whole for the revelation of God was not a vague impression susceptible to arbitrary nuances but a verbal composition identical to the purpose and even to the language of its divine author. One could violate Moses' personal wishes with impunity, but one could reject the Word of God through Moses only at his or her own peril.

Nowhere in the Pentateuch is the equation that the Word of God equals the word of Moses clearer than in Deuteronomy 30:11–14:

> For this commandment which I command you today is not too difficult for you, nor is it out of reach. It is not in heaven, that you

should say, "Who will go up to heaven for us to get it for us and make us hear it, that we may observe it?" Nor is it beyond the sea, that you should say, "Who will cross the sea for us to get it for us and make us hear it, that we may observe it?" But the word is very near you, in your mouth and in your heart, that you may observe it.

Finally, Deuteronomy, like Leviticus and Numbers, contained a summary statement concerning its own authorship as a divine and human collaboration:

> When Moses finished writing the words of this law in a book until they were complete, that Moses commanded the Levites who carried the ark of the covenant of the LORD, saying, "Take this book of the law and place it beside the ark of the covenant of the LORD your God, that it may remain there as a witness against you" (Deut. 31:24–26).

While Moses was the human instrument in writing Deuteronomy, by the work of inspiration of the Holy Spirit, the result was what God wanted to transmit to the Jewish people. What Moses wrote as a frail human being, became a part of the changeless truth of divine revelation.

Literary Formulae and Other Compositional Clues

In addition to explicit statements by and about Moses as to his receiving and recording divine revelation, abundant compositional indicators throughout the Pentateuch attested to its character as the Word of God and, as such, to its inerrancy. Throughout, the narrative was related as though it was undisputed, unqualified fact. Moses made no effort to persuade readers of this point of view, for the Pentateuch was so commonly understood to be true as to require no proof. Some principal features pointing to justification for such assumptions must now be addressed.

"Thus says the LORD." This often-used phrase and its variants occur scores of times in the Pentateuch, suggesting a consciousness by the spokesman/author that what he was communicating was, in fact, the very Word of God. One may challenge the correctness of his assertion, but it is impossible to deny that that was his conviction and the convictions of those who heard him as well. The following list of references is a sample of the use of the divine speech formula in the Pentateuch and is limited to those instances where a sustained address follows: Exodus 20:1; 25:1–2; 40:1; Leviticus 1:1; 4:1; 5:14; Numbers 1:1; 2:1; 3:5; Deuteronomy 1:3. Even a superficial perusal of these passages will show

that Moses attributed virtually everything he wrote to the revelation given him by the Lord. There is not a hint that he viewed himself as the originator of any of it.

Revelation in prehistoric times. The term *prehistoric* is used here to refer to the time before the advent of people and, therefore, prior to the possibility of human witness to events such as the creation of the heavens and the earth. In literary terms, this is embodied in Genesis 1:1—2:7. Moses was not there to observe these pristine acts nor, in fact, were Adam and Eve. The only Being present was the God who effected the creation, so only He was capable of providing information as to its origin and processes. There is, of course, no statement to the effect that God authored this text or even that He revealed it to a human scribe. In fact, no authorial clues are given except for the straightforward notation that "this is the account of the heavens and the earth when they were created" (Gen. 2:4). The question is, who wrote the account and how did he access his data?

Modern skepticism suggests that the creation story is a pastiche of sources (Gen. 1:1—2:4a by P and 2:4b–25 by J) reflecting mythopoeic ideas about origins and redacted into its present form only in the postexilic period (c. 450 B.C.).[19] Such an approach does not view the material as having any serious scientific or historical basis and, therefore, sees it as nothing more than a primitive attempt to provide a cosmic etiology. The very impossibility of human witness to the creation, in fact, gives rise to the common designation of the account as a "myth." The only alternative is to understand the creation narrative as a direct revelation of God to a human being, who then wrote of it in the account referred to in Genesis 2:4. Possibly this person was Moses himself, but more likely it was done anonymously. With other narratives also described as "accounts," they were eventually handed down to Moses who compiled them all into the composition called Genesis.[20] How and when the human ingredient was introduced is incidental to the main point here, namely, that the creation story, known only to God, was a product of the mind of God and is, therefore, without error.

Assertions of divine speech, especially in nonwitnessed contexts.[21] If the creation account in general narrates events unknown and unknowable to human beings apart from divine revelation, what is to be said of details in the narrative such as statements as to what God said or, more problematic, what He thought? Several times God "said," and creation resulted (Gen. 1:3, 6, 9, 11, 14, 20, 22, 24, 26). Other times He "called" things by some terms (Gen. 1:5, 8, 10) or issued commands as to how they were to perform (Gen. 1:28–29). Having created the separation between the seas and the dry land, "God saw that it was good" (Gen. 1:10). The same is said of vegetation (v. 12), the separation of light from darkness (v. 18), the creation of marine and aerial life (v. 21), the creation of land animals (v. 25), and, in fact, the whole work of creation (v. 31). This approbation was never stated in so many words but was always something God "saw."

At the conclusion of the flood story, the narrator says, "God remembered Noah" (Gen. 8:1). He said of the sacrifice Noah offered, "The LORD smelled the soothing aroma; and the LORD said to Himself, 'I will never again curse the ground on account of man'" (v. 21). The author knew that God was pleased and he was aware of God's secret pledge never again to bring such judgment. This ability to "read" God is possible only when God lays bare His own innermost disposition.

The anthropomorphisms of the tower of Babel anecdote do not conceal the reality of Yahweh's distress over the incident and His determination to do something about it. "The LORD came down to see the city and the tower," the author related, and then, as though listening to the heavenly council, continued by quoting God, "Come, let Us go down and there confuse their language, so that they will not understand one another's speech" (Gen. 11:5, 7). Access to this privileged conversation is explainable only as God took the initiative to inform the human reporter of such things.

A final example must suffice, one in which the Lord agonized within Himself as to a course of action. This concerns the threat to destroy wicked Sodom, the place where Lot, Abraham's nephew, had chosen to settle. Anticipating the urgency of Abraham's intercession on behalf of the place, Yahweh asked, "Shall I hide from Abraham what I am about to do?" (Gen. 18:17). Yahweh made the decision not to conceal His purposes, and He informed the patriarch of His intended action. Nowhere does the narrator hint that God revealed to Abraham or anyone else His inner conflict. It is a struggle of emotion and will known only to God until He saw fit to share it with the human penman. There could be no guesswork here or in any of the instances where God finally broke the silence and permitted entrance into His own private world. To put ideas in God's mind or to invent words as though they had come from His mouth when in fact they had not would be the height of blasphemy. Only the view that God revealed Himself in words is compatible with the nature of both God and the Bible.

Predictive prophecy. One of the most potent weapons in the armory of biblical polemics is that of fulfilled prophecy. If it can be demonstrated conclusively that a biblical prediction came to pass in the time and manner intended by its author, such a correspondence carries *ipso facto* evidence of something beyond natural happenstance; indeed, it is an argument for divine revelation, inspiration, and inerrancy. This is no less true of the converse: If a prophetic word failed in these respects, it exposed itself as a falsehood and, by extrapolation, brought down with it the integrity of the entire biblical witness.

Obviously, a predictive prophecy, if it is employed as evidence for the supernatural character of Scripture, must be one whose fulfillment has already taken place as a matter of documented record. Four of these have been selected from the Pentateuch to make the case that a certain composition can lay claim to inerrancy according to this criterion.

The first full-fledged prophecy in Scripture is the so-called *protoevangelium,* which was a primitive statement about the gospel of future salvation. It is a prediction from God in Genesis 3:15, in which He says

> I will put enmity between you and the woman, and between your seed and her seed; he shall bruise you on the head, and you shall bruise him on the heel.

A closer span between promise and fulfillment may be seen in Genesis 15:12–14. Here Yahweh informed Abraham that his descendants would be in bondage in a foreign land for four hundred years, following which they would be supernaturally delivered to return to Canaan. That is precisely what took place in history as Moses, by retrospect, was careful to point out (Ex 12:40).

In Jacob's blessing of his sons, he said of Judah:

> The scepter shall not depart from Judah, nor the ruler's staff from between his feet, until Shiloh comes, and to him shall be the obedience of the peoples. (Gen. 49:10)

The focus on Judah as the tribe from which Messiah would come finds its earliest clear expression here, but this tribal connection becomes a pervasive biblical theme culminating in Jesus. David, the founder of the messianic dynasty, was from Judah (1 Sam. 17:12). Because both Joseph and Mary were his descendants (Matt. 1:6, 16; Luke 3:23, 31), they were compelled to go to Bethlehem of Judah to be enrolled in the census (Luke 2:4). Thus, Jesus, the Son and successor of David, fulfilled the prophetic blessing concerning the royal scepter and staff from Judah (cf. Acts 2:29–36; Rev. 3:7; 5:5; 22:16).

The fourth example of a fulfilled prediction is the utterance of the Lord Himself concerning a prophet to come. Speaking to Moses, He said, "I will raise up a prophet from among their countrymen like you, and I will put My words in his mouth, and he shall speak to them all that I command him" (Deut. 18:18). Springing from this text, Jewish messianism ascribed prophetic identity and gifts to their anticipated Redeemer. The New Testament spoke to this hope (John 1:21–25; 6:14; 7:40), and the inspired apostles confirmed it by equating the promised prophet with Jesus Christ (Acts 3:17–23).

The Stamp of Supernatural Character

This study has reviewed the evidence for the inerrancy of the Pentateuch from both external and internal sources. The Old Testament beyond the Pentateuch, extra-canonical Jewish literature, the New Testament, and Christian tradition—all point to this conclusion either by explicit statement, implicit assumption, or lack of any suggestion to the contrary.

As for the Pentateuch itself, the picture could not be clearer. The role and gifts of Moses, as well as his own self-attestation as receiver and proclaimer of revelation and recorder of the sacred text, were consistently set forth. In addition, the work itself was self-authenticating. It presupposed the voice of the Lord, and in its bold prefiguring of events yet future to it—events subsequently fulfilled in meticulous detail—it bore the stamp of supernatural character. The Pentateuch claimed to be divine revelation imparted to Moses. The corollary to this claim is the inerrancy of all it taught, for there can be no inconsistency between who God is and what He says.

FOR DISCUSSION

1. What is significant about Joshua in regard to inerrancy?

2. What are the repeated claims of Scripture in regard to the doctrine of inerrancy?

3 What is the overwhelming Jewish tradition concerning inerrancy and the writings of Moses?

4. What is the testimony of the New Testament?

5. What is significant regarding the authority of Moses?

6. What did Moses testify as to his role in inspiration?

For Further Study

Bible Introduction

Allis, Oswald T. *The Five Books of Moses*. Philadelphia: Presbyterian and Reformed, 1949.

Archer, Gleason L. Jr. *A Survey of Old Testament Introduction*. Chicago: Moody, 1974, 1994.

Dillard, Raymond B. and Tremper Longman, III. *An Introduction to the Old Testament*. Grand Rapids: Zondervan, 1994.

Harrison, R. K. *An Introduction to the Old Testament*. Grand Rapids: Eerdmans, 1969.

Wolf, Herbert. *An Introduction to the Old Testament Pentateuch*. Chicago: Moody, 1991.

Bibliology Texts

Dockery, David S. *The Doctrine of the Bible*. Nashville: Convention Press, 1991.

Lightner, Robert P. *The Savior and the Scriptures*. Philadelphia: Presbyterian and Reformed, 1970.

Ryrie, Charles C. *What You Should Know About Inerrancy*. Chicago: Moody, 1981.

Stonehouse, Ned B. and Paul Woolley, eds. *The Infallible Word*. Philadelphia: Presbyterian and Reformed, 1946.

Warfield, B. B. *The Inspiration and Authority of the Bible*. Philadelphia: Presbyterian and Reformed, 1948.

Young, Edward J. *Thy Word Is Truth*. Grand Rapids: Eerdmans, 1957.

Commentaries

Ashley, Timothy R. *The Book of Numbers*. Vol. 5 of the *New International Commentary on the Old Testament*. Grand Rapids: Eerdmans, 1993.

Budd, Philip J. *Numbers*. Vol. 5 of the *Word Biblical Commentary*. Waco: Word, 1984.

Cassuto, U. *A Commentary on the Book of Exodus*. Jerusalem: Magnes, 1967.

Enns, Paul. *New International Dictionary of Old Testament Theology and Exegesis*. 5 Vols. Edited by Willem A. VanGemeren. Grand Rapids: Zondervan, 1977.

Garrett, Duane. *Rethinking Genesis*. Grand Rapids: Baker, 1991.

Hartley, John E. *Leviticus*. Vol. 4 of *Word Biblical Commentary*. Dallas: Word, 1992.

Mathews, Kenneth A. *Genesis 1–11:26*. Vol. 1 of *New American Commentary*. Nashville: Broadman and Holman, 1996.

Dictionaries

Botterweck , G. Johannes and Helmer Ringgren. *Theological Dictionary of the Old Testament*. Rev. ed. Translated by John T. Willis. Grand Rapids: Eerdmans, 1977.

Hermeneutics

Berlin, Adele. *Poetics and Interpretation of Biblical Narrative*. Sheffield: Almond, 1983.

Merrill, Eugene H. "Deuteronomy, New Testament Faith, and the Christian Life." In *Integrity of Heart, Skillfulness of Hands*, edited by Charles H. Dyer and Roy B. Zuck. Grand Rapids: Baker, 1994.

History

Crapps, Robert Wilson and David Anthony Smith. *People of the Covenant*. 4th ed. New York: Oxford University Press, 1996.

Hannah, John D., ed. *Inerrancy and the Church*. Chicago: Moody, 1984.

Theology

Hodge, Charles. *Systematic Theology*. 3 Vols. Grand Rapids: Eerdmans, 1995.

Nigosian, Solomon. *Judaism: The Way of Holiness*. Great Britain: Crucible, 1986.

Rosenthal, Gilbert S. *The Many Faces of Judaism*. New York: Behrman House, 1978.

Ryrie, Charles. *Basic Theology*. Wheaton: Ill.: Victor Books, 1988; Chicago: Moody, 1999.

Chapter Eleven

Inerrancy of the Old Testament Historical Books

The historical books begin with Joshua taking command of Israel at the death of Moses (1405 B.C.) until the Babylonian captivity and the story of Esther (ca. 605–536 B.C.). As with the writings of Moses and the Pentatauch, the historical books contain history, and often prophecy as it is revealed through various prophets. The history books tell of both the victories of the people of Israel, but also they give vivid accounts of their many failures. These chronicles tell of the people entering the land under Joshua, settling down, apostasizing, taking sides in a civil war, and finally being taken captive to Assyria (the Northern Kingdom, 722 B.C.), and then to Babylon (the Southern Kingdom, 586 B.C.). What is the value of the historical books? Howard writes, "The Bible's message is given, to a large extent, through historical writings, . . . It is through historical writings about historical events that we learn much about God and His purposes for humans. . . . Historical writings . . . provide an accurate account of the history of God's people."[1]

The Book of Joshua

The Book of Joshua continues the story of God's formation of the nation of Israel and is, therefore, inseparably linked to the Pentateuch. God had promised Abraham that He would make a great nation from Abraham (Gen. 12:1–3). By the time of Joshua, the formation of the nation had been going on for some seven centuries. People, law, and land were needed to fulfill this promise of making a nation out of Abraham. By this

151

time, God had multiplied the nation (people) and had given them their constitution at Mount Sinai (law). Now all that remained was to possess Canaan—the promised land. The Book of Joshua gave God's words, fulfilled prophecies, and references to previously given statements dozens of times. These many statements by the Lord point to the "God-breathed" nature of this book and thus to its inerrancy.

Prophecies Given Prior to Joshua's Day but Fulfilled in Joshua

- *1:1–9: Numerous times, the prediction was made that Israel would possess the land promised in the covenants (e.g. Gen. 17).*
- *2:9–11: The words of Rahab revealed the fulfillment of the prophecy that God would supernaturally instill fear into the hearts of the Canaanites prior to any military victory by Israel (cf. Deut. 2:25; 11:25).*
- *8:30–35: Joshua fulfilled a previously given command from God through Moses when he built an altar at Mount Ebal (cf. Deut. 27:1–13).*
- *16:4: The double portion of the land given to Joseph's descendents fulfilled the prophecy of Jacob (cf. Gen. 48:1–22).*
- *21:1–3: The scattering of the tribe of Levi throughout the nation of Israel fulfilled the prophecy of Jacob (cf. Gen. 49:5–7).*
- *21:43–45: The Lord fulfilled His prophecy to give Israel the land (cf. Gen. 17). Note: This passage reflects an Old Testament concept wherein the promise of God was being fulfilled and that generation was getting its share. But it was not the ultimate fulfillment of the promise since that required that the land be an everlasting, permanent possession.²*
- *24:12: God would send "hornets" (a figure of speech for a spirit of terror) to terrorize the Canaanites (cf. Ex. 23:27–28; Deut. 7:20).*
- *24:32: Joseph's bones of Joseph that had been brought up from Egypt were buried in fulfillment of Joseph's request (cf. Gen. 50:24–25; Ex. 13:19).*

Prophecies Given to Joshua and Fulfilled in Joshua's Day

- *3:8, 13: The prediction of the drying up of the Jordan River (fulfilled in 3:17).*
- *6:5: The prophecy of the falling down of Jericho's walls (fulfilled in 6:20).*
- *8:1: The prediction of the victory over the city of Ai (fulfilled 8:10–29).*
- *10:8: The Lord foretold the complete defeat of the five southern kings' coalition (fulfilled in 10:10–27).*
- *11:6: The Lord foretold victory over a coalition of kings from the northern region (fulfilled in 11:11–14).*

Fulfilled prophecy is a powerful testimony to inspiration and inerrancy. These specific prophecies have been literally fulfilled and not only testify to the supernatural nature of predictive prophecy but also to the inerrancy of the Book of Joshua.

Promises Made by the Lord to Joshua

The Lord spoke to Joshua on many occasions, and these contacts seemed to be made directly with Joshua without a prophet being involved. Though it cannot be said for certain, it seems that the means of communication was audible rather than through visions and dreams. However, we must remember that it is also true that the use of Urim and Thummim by the priest may have occurred frequently (cf. Num. 27:21). But whatever means were used, these recorded words were said to be from the Lord Himself.

- *1:1–9: God promised Joshua that He would be with him and that Joshua would be successful (cf. 3:7; 4:17–18; 5:14; 6:27).*
- *3:7: The Lord promised to validate Joshua's leadership before Israel.*
- *6:2: The Lord guaranteed victory at Jericho.*
- *11:6: The Lord spoke to Joshua, promising him military victory.*
- *19:50: Joshua received his inheritance in accordance with the Lord's promise.*

Instructions and Commands Spoken Directly to Joshua by the Lord

A number of verses record that the Lord spoke directly to Joshua, instructing him to do specific things as well as relating general truths to him. After initially encouraging Joshua to be strong and courageous (1:1–9), the Lord gave him the following detailed instructions: He was to erect memorial stones commemorating the Jordan crossing (4:1–3); to tell the priests carrying the ark to exit the Jordan River (4:15–16); to circumcise all the males in Israel (5:2); to find the person guilty of stealing items under the Jericho ban (7:13–15); and to spring the ambush at Ai and Bethel at just the right moment (8:18).

The Lord also spoke directly to Joshua, letting him know that the reproach of Egypt was gone (5:9); that the real commander of Israel was the Captain of the Lord of hosts (5:13–15); that Israel had been defeated militarily because they had sinned (7:10–12); that Joshua was to continue in the conquest of Canaan after sin had been dealt with (8:1); that more land should be taken and divided among the tribes of Israel (13:1, 7); and that obedience to the Mosaic Law was critical to living on the land (23:5–6).

Instructions and Commands Previously Spoken by the Lord and Then Repeated in Joshua's Day

On a number of occasions, reference was made to God's words previously spoken either directly by the Lord or through His spokesman Moses.

Even if the statement was not a direct quote, it still was inspired and thus inerrant.

> If a . . . writer makes a free quotation from the Old Testament, since he was writing under the inspiration of the Spirit, that free quotation becomes part of the inspired, inerrant text. The Holy Spirit . . . certainly has the right to quote Himself as He wishes and to use quotations with meanings we as uninspired interpreters might never have seen.[3]

As we would expect, these references in the Book of Joshua are almost exclusively Moses' statements. A number of them refer to commands and instructions concerning the distribution of conquered Canaan: the tribal areas for the two and a half tribes who settled east of the Jordan (1:13; 22:4 with Deut. 3:18–20; Num. 32:31); the dividing up of the land (14:2, 5 with Num. 34); the cities of refuge (20:1–2 with Num. 35:6–34; Deut. 4:41; 19:2); the Levitical cities (21:1–3 with Num. 35:2–8); and matters related to personal inheritances (14:6; 15:13 and 19:50 with Num. 14:24, 30; and 17:4 with Num. 27:1–11). There were also remembrances of Moses' words about erecting an altar at Mount Ebal (8:30–35 with Deut. 27:1–13); conquering the land in obedience to Moses' commands (11:15 with Deut. 7:1–4; 20:16–18); and warnings regarding idolatry (23:12, 16 with Deut. 7:1–6; 12:2–3). Joshua himself recounted the history of Israel from Abraham to Moses, reflecting the accounts found in Genesis, Exodus, and Numbers (24:2–10).

The Book of Joshua gives over forty references to God speaking in the current situation or to things that God said in the past. Certainly, this is strong support for the inspiration and inerrancy of this book of history.

The Book of Judges

When Joshua died, the Lord did not replace him with another leader. Rather, the Lord desired to be the leader of Israel in a theocracy. Working through the Law of Moses and the priesthood, the Lord Himself would be Israel's king. The theocracy, however, proved to be a frightening failure because Israel refused to live in obedience to God's Law. The result was that Israel walked in sinful disobedience and experienced the Lord's severe discipline. It is not surprising when we learn that during this period of three centuries, the "word from the LORD was rare in those days, visions were infrequent" (1 Sam. 3:1). Since God had given much revelation recently, this was a time for Israel to respond to that revelation.

God gave revelation to man periodically rather than in a chronological pattern. It would seem that He desired man to have opportunity for showing his manner of response to any new revelation given, before providing more. God had just preceded the judges' period with one of His most concentrated times of giving revelation (through Moses), in anticipation of the period. The period itself then was logically a time for waiting to see how man would react to what had been given, rather than a time for further revelation. Such a time, by its nature, calls for less reporting.[4]

Nevertheless, communication from the Lord is referred to over a dozen times in Judges.

Statements from the Angel of Jehovah

The most frequent theophany in the Old Testament is the Angel of Jehovah. He was the second Person of the Trinity[5] and, therefore, God spoke directly to individuals several times. He made several appearances in the Book of Judges.

The Angel of Jehovah appeared to the Israelites and warned them of judgment because of their disobedience (2:1–5). He also appeared to Gideon and told him to deliver Israel from the Midianites, assuring Gideon of victory (6:11–21). He also appeared twice to Samson's parents, announcing the birth of Samson (13:3–9), and Deborah and Barak referred to the Angel of Jehovah's words in their song (5:23).

Words from the Lord through Prophets

Words through prophets are not found often in the Book of Judges. But God did speak through the prophetess Deborah, commanding Barak to go to war against the Canaanites (4:6). God spoke through an unnamed prophet just prior to the call of Gideon. This prophet was sent to rebuke Israel for their sins and to tell them the reasons for their sufferings (6:8–10). Prophets would become more prominent in the national life of Israel in the monarchal period.

Words from the Lord in Response to Requests from His People

Several times the text said that the people "inquired of the LORD" and He responded to their requests (1:1–2; 20:18, 23, 27–28). While the method involved is not clearly specified, it most likely included the high priest and his use of the Urim and the Thummim (cf. Ex. 28:30; Num. 27:21; 1 Sam. 14:36–42; 28:6). The use of this device, however, did not rule out God's employment of dreams, visions, and audible speaking.

Words from the Lord Directly to His People

The Lord spoke to Israel, indicating His great displeasure over their idolatry (10:11–14). He also told them of their disobedience and His resulting unwillingness to give them victory over the Canaanites (2:20–23). Several times the Lord spoke directly to Gideon, telling him to destroy the altar of Baal (6:25) and to reduce the size of his army (7:2, 4, 7). In none of these cases is the method of communication stated.

Other Words from the Lord

Several times prophecies of certain victory were given and then immediately fulfilled (victory by Judah in 1:2 and fulfilled in 1:4; and victory by Barak in 4:6 and fulfilled in 4:21). Also, there was a violation of previously given commands of the Lord (2:11–19 with Deut. 7; 12; 28).

Although the occurrences were not frequent, God did speak to His people during this three hundred year period. These statements point to this book as being "God-breathed" and thus without error. It should be noted that the chronological difficulties associated with this period of the Judges have been adequately dealt with in a number of places, including Leon Wood's helpful book, *The Distressing Days of the Judges*.

The Book of Ruth

Ruth is one of the smallest books in the entire Word of God, but it is one of the most important because it forged a link in the messianic chain that led to the coming of Christ.

The time frame of the book could fit into the latter part of the Book of Judges. However, both the author and the exact date of its writing are unknown. Many suggest Ruth was probably written during the reign of David (1000 B.C.), to show how Gentile blood came into his line. Contrary to normal thinking, this argument would be a benefit because it would extend the rule of David to the peoples surrounding Israel by a blood relationship.

When a famine struck Israel, Elimelech and his wife Naomi went to Moab and remained apparently for some time (1:2). Their two sons married Moabite women. After the husband, Elimelech, and the two sons died, Naomi and her daughters-in-law, Orpah and Ruth, decided to return to Judah. Orpah became homesick on the way and returned to Moab and her gods. However, the plot thickened when, arriving in Bethlehem where David was later born, Naomi saw a match for Ruth in one of her kinsmen, a wealthy landowner named Boaz.

Ruth had earlier professed her faith in the God of Israel when she uttered those famous words, "Your people shall be my people, and your God, my God" (1:16). So it was natural for Ruth to remain in the land she had learned to love. Her affection was also strong for her godly and kindly mother-in-law, Naomi.

The great connection with royalty and ultimately the prophecy of the coming of the Messiah is brought out in the final verses of the book. Boaz and Ruth were married and conceived a son named Obed, who "is the father of Jesse, the father of David" (4:17).

Ruth's Place in the Canon

The historical accuracy of the book is firmly attested by the minutest details of harvesting and marital customs. The practice of the levirate marriage is well-known by the earliest documents of the ancient Near East. From Nuzi tablets, we see that it was common for a father to obtain a bride for his son and to specify that if the son died, the girl should marry his brother. This practice of family "protection" is similar to what happened in the Book of Ruth. Also, the practice of the removal of a shoe during the close of a special legal transaction is historically confirmed (4:8–12).

In regard to the integrity and historicity of Ruth, Archer writes:

> Ruth appears to give an accurate account of the customs during the early period. It was perfectly natural at that era (before the Moabites had become embittered by Israelite overlordship) for a Jewish family to take refuge in Moab during a time of drought and famine. Under those conditions it would be natural also for young people to fall in love and get married with the inhabitants of the land. The fact that David was descended from a Moabitess would furnish a ready explanation for his seeking refuge with the king of Moab during the time he was being pursued by Saul.[6]

The surprising fact that David would be a descendent of a Moabite woman is one proof of the historic nature of the book. An integral part of the inspiration of Scripture is that truth is not hidden. All biblical truth moves toward a divine purpose in an overall master plan, initiated and authored by the Holy Spirit.

The Providence of God

A prevailing theme of Ruth is the providence of God. Two women were cast adrift without the care of husbands, but God led them back to the family roots of Naomi and her spouse.

The name of the Lord was mentioned often in the book. Naomi decided to return to Israel when she heard that "the LORD had visited His people in giving them food" (1:6). She urged her daughters-in-law, "May the LORD deal kindly with you" (v. 8), and, "May the LORD grant that you may find rest, each in the house of her husband" (v. 9). In her aloneness, Naomi had a negative moment and cried, "The hand of the LORD has gone forth against me" (v. 13), and "Do not call me Naomi; call me Mara, for the Almighty has dealt very bitterly with me" (v. 20).

The spirituality of Boaz is also recorded when he said to Ruth, "May the LORD reward your work, and your wages be full from the LORD, the God of Israel, under whose wings you have come to seek refuge" (2:12). The common people and the elders of the area also showed a great sense of the working of the Lord. As Boaz and Ruth were about to be married, they wished for Boaz "offspring which the LORD will give you by this young woman" (4:12). When Ruth bore a son, Naomi's friends said, "Blessed is the LORD who has not left you without a redeemer today, and may his name become famous in Israel" (4:14).

Kinsman-Redeemer

One of the great values of Ruth is the amplification of the doctrine of the kinsman-redeemer that was ultimately fulfilled with the coming of Jesus. Christ became our human kinsman who came to earth, partook of humanity, and then brought about our redemption. Archer says of the Book of Ruth:

> 1. It affords a foreshadowing of the enlarged blessing to come: Gentiles are capable of being joined to the commonwealth of Israel upon condition of repentance and of faith in Jehovah. 2. God's marvelous and unexpected providence is exhibited also by the inclusion of a Gentile in the royal lineage of the Messiah (cf. Matt. 1:5). 3. The kinsman-redeemer serves as Messianic type, the *go'el* who fulfills the . . . qualifications and functions of his kinsmen. . . . Therefore, the little book of Ruth is one of the most instructive in the Old Testament concerning the mediatorial work of the Lord Jesus.[7]

Hubbard writes,

> The earliest Jewish and Christian lists of Scriptures unanimously include Ruth, though not always in the same canonical location. . . . The book's content certainly commended it as canonical. . . . [Rabbi Simeon ben Yohai] plainly affirms Ruth's canonicity with no hint of a contrary rabbinic opinion.[8]

Heuy adds,

> Ruth's place in the canon was never seriously questioned . . . Its connection with David, the frequent mention of God, and the exemplary morality of its leading characters were sufficient to secure its place in the canon. . . .
>
> The LXX, followed by the Vulgate and subsequent Western versions, placed Ruth after the Book of Judges because of the similar setting of the two books established in Ruth 1:1: "In the days when the judges ruled."[9]

The Books of Samuel

The Book of 1 Samuel records the end of the period of the Judges and the beginning of the monarchal period in Israel. Samuel himself was the last of the judges and the greatest of God's prophets since Moses. The office of prophet began with Moses (Jer. 7:25), but it is in the monarchal period that the office of prophet came into prominence since the Lord used these men to be His mouthpieces to Israel.

God's Word through Prophets

Prior to Samuel's ministry, an unnamed prophet rebuked the priest Eli with a "thus says the LORD" for not dealing properly with his sons (2:27–34). God spoke to King David through Nathan regarding the building of the temple (2 Sam. 7:4–17) and concerning his sinful behavior with Bathsheba (2 Sam. 12:1–12). The prophet Gad conveyed the Lord's word that David could select the punishment for his sin of numbering the people (2 Sam. 24:11–13). While the text does not specifically say so, God most likely communicated His will to these prophets through visions and dreams (cf. Num. 12:6 with 1 Sam. 3:15 and 2 Sam. 7:17).

God's Word through Samuel

The most significant channel of God's word to Israel in those days was Samuel himself. The Lord first spoke to Samuel when he was a child (3:4, 6, 8, 10, 15, 21). The Lord "came and stood" before Samuel, which would indicate that Samuel saw a vision (3:10). Apparently, the Lord chose to speak frequently to Samuel, and this became well known in Israel (3:21; 4:1). But it is likely that many communications from the Lord to Samuel were not recorded. The Lord spoke to Samuel several times in connection with Israel's request for a king and the selection of Saul as the first king (8:7, 22; 9:17; 10:18, 22). Samuel communicated God's word to a disobedient King Saul (13:13–14; 15:10–11) and reminded Saul of God's word about the Amalekites, which was given in the days of Moses (15:2 with Deut. 25:17–19). The Lord also instructed Samuel to anoint a son of Jesse in Bethlehem as Israel's next king, and He intervened to keep Samuel from selecting the wrong one (16:1, 7, 12).

Prophecies Made and Fulfilled in the Books of Samuel

The existence of prophecies made and fulfilled are a powerful testimony to the inerrancy of the books in which those prophecies are found. The Books of Samuel also include prophecies whose fulfillment was clear and precise.

First Samuel:

- *2:34: The unnamed prophet prophesied to Eli that his two sons, Hophni and Phinehas, would both die on the same day (fulfilled in 4:11).*
- *3:11–14: The Lord told Samuel that He was going to discipline the family of Eli (fulfilled in 4:11–22).*
- *9:15–16: The Lord told Samuel that on the following day the man who would be Israel's king would come to him (fulfilled in 9:17–18).*
- *10:2–6: Samuel prophesied to Saul that two men would meet him at Zelzah and tell him that his donkeys had been found, then that three men carrying goats, bread, and wine would meet him and give him two loaves; and finally that prophets near Bethel would sing and prophesy as they came to Saul, and Saul himself would prophesy (fulfilled in 10:9).*
- *23:4: God told David to attack the Philistines and promised victory over them (fulfilled in 23:5).*
- *28:19: Samuel prophesied that Saul and his sons would die the next day in battle with the Philistines (fulfilled in 31:2–6).*

Second Samuel:

- *5:19: The Lord promised that David would be victorious over the Philistines (fulfilled in 5:20).*
- *5:23–24: Again the Lord promised to give David a military victory over the Philistines (fulfilled in 5:25).*
- *12:1–15: The prophet Nathan, after rebuking David for his sin with Bathsheba, foretold the death of their child (fulfilled in 12:18), the trouble in David's own family (fulfilled in 13:1—18:33), and the violation of David's harem (fulfilled in 16:21–22).*

Instructions and Commands from the Lord Given to David

Toward the end of 1 Samuel, David became prominent in the story, and the Lord frequently spoke to him. In response to David's prayer about going into battle, the Lord directed him to attack the Philistines (23:2,

4). David asked the Lord about Saul's intentions when Saul was seeking to destroy him. The Lord, using Abiathar the priest and the ephod, communicated to David the information he desired (23:6–12). Again, using Abiathar, David inquired of the Lord about attacking the Amalekites who had overthrown David's city of Ziklag (30:7–20). David asked the Lord where he should live, and the Lord told him to go to Hebron (2 Sam. 2:1). The Lord responded to David's requests concerning battles with the Philistines (2 Sam. 5:19, 23). And the Lord responded to David's inquiry regarding famine in the land (2 Sam. 21:1).

Over thirty times in the Books of Samuel, there are statements that the God who cannot lie has spoken. The phenomenon of inspiration-inerrancy can be found in these historical books of Samuel.

The Books of Kings

The two books of Kings chronicle the events of the monarchal period after King David and record over sixty occurrences of the Lord speaking to and through a variety of individuals. During this era, the roles of the prophets took on new significance as they called Israel back to their constitution, gave counsel to the kings, and foretold events to come.

Appearances of the Lord with Accompanying Instructions

The Lord appeared to Solomon twice after he sat on the throne of Israel. First, the Lord appeared to him in a dream, inviting him to ask whatever he wanted from the Lord (1 Kgs. 3:5). His second appearance to Solomon was after the dedication of the temple, when the Lord accepted the king's prayer and promised blessing for obedience but discipline for disobedience (9:2–9). The Angel of the Lord appeared to Elijah the prophet twice, instructing him to intercept the messengers of wicked King Ahaziah (2 Kgs. 1:3) and to rebuke the king personally (1:15–16).

Instructions and Commands Given by the Lord

In the incidents above, no mediator seemed to be between the Lord and the individual. This does not rule out the possibility that prophets or priests were involved; it is just that none were mentioned in the text. In any case, they all were definitely messages from the Lord.

The Lord spoke to Solomon (1 Kgs. 6:11–13; 11:11); to an unnamed prophet (13:7–9); to Elijah (1 Kgs. 17:8, 21–22; 19:9; 21:17–19); to Elisha (2 Kgs. 6:32–33; 7:19–20); to Jehu (2 Kgs. 10:30); and to Isaiah (2 Kgs. 20:1, 4). These references illustrate the Lord's involvement in Israel as He spoke repeatedly to His people.

Prophecies Given and Fulfilled in Kings

Some thirty prophecies given during the days of 1 and 2 Kings were fulfilled during that same period. These many prophecies made and fulfilled bear a strong testimony to the inspiration and the inerrancy of this portion of the Scriptures.

First Kings:

- *3:5–14: The Lord promised Solomon wisdom, wealth, and fame (fulfillment seen in many places; e.g., 3:28; 4:20–34; 5:7–12; 10:4–29).*
- *11:30–32: Ahijah prophesied that Jeroboam would rule ten tribes of Israel (fulfilled in 12:15–20).*
- *13:1–2: An unnamed prophet pronounced judgment on the idolatrous altar of Jeroboam in Bethel, declaring that Josiah from the tribe of Judah would destroy it and the priests of Jeroboam and would burn human bones on that altar (fulfilled 300 years later in 2 Kings 23:15–20).*
- *13:3: The unnamed prophet prophesied that Jeroboam's altar would split apart (fulfilled in 13:5).*
- *14:5–16: Ahijah spoke of the death of Jeroboam's son (fulfilled in 14:17), the destruction of the house of Jeroboam (fulfilled in 15:29), and the captivity of the northern kingdom of Israel (fulfilled in 2 Kings 17:6).*
- *16:1, 7: The prophet Jehu prophesied the total destruction of the house of Baasha (fulfilled in 16:11–12).*
- *17:2–4: God promised Elijah that He would provide for his needs at the brook Cherith (fulfilled in 17:6).*
- *18:1: Elijah foretold the coming of rain after three years of drought (fulfilled in 18:45).*
- *20:13: An unnamed prophet told Ahab that Israel would be victorious over the army of Syria (fulfilled in 20:20–21).*
- *20:28: Another prediction was given of victory over Syria (fulfilled in 20:29–30).*
- *20:42: An unnamed prophet told Ahab that because he neglected to destroy the king of Syria, he would be judged (fulfilled in 22:37).*
- *21:17–24: Elijah predicted coming judgment on Ahab and Jezebel because they had Naboth killed and took his vineyard (fulfilled regarding Jezebel in 2 Kings 9:30–37).*
- *22:13–23: Micaiah, the prophet, told Kings Ahab and Jehoshaphat of their sure defeat in battle (fulfilled in 22:34–35).*

Second Kings:

- *1:4: Elijah told sick King Ahaziah that he would die from his illness (fulfilled in 1:17).*

- *2:1–7:* Through many unnamed prophets in ways not explained, the Lord clearly communicated that He was going to take Elijah to heaven that day (fulfilled in 2:11).
- *3:16–19:* Elisha prophesied that water would be provided for the armies of Israel and Judah and Moab would be defeated (fulfilled in 3:20, 24–26).
- *7:1:* Elisha prophesied that the siege of Samaria would end the following day (fulfilled in 7:7).
- *8:1:* Elisha prophesied a seven-year famine (fulfilled in 8:2–3).
- *8:10:* Elisha told Hazael that Ben-Hadad would die (fulfilled in 8:15).
- *8:12–13:* Elisha foretold that Hazael would become king of Syria and would commit terrible atrocities (fulfilled 8:15; 13:22).
- *9:3, 6:* Elisha foretold that Jehu would be Israel's next king and would destroy Ahab's family (fulfilled in 9:30—10:17).
- *10:30:* The Lord told Jehu that because of his obedience in destroying the house of Ahab that four generations of Jehu's descendents would sit on the throne of Israel (fulfilled in 14:29; 15:8–12).
- *13:17–19:* Elisha told King Joash of Israel that he would defeat Syria three times (fulfilled in 13:25).
- *19:6, 20, 32–34:* Isaiah foretold that Sennacherib of Assyria would not have success in his siege of Jerusalem but would return to his own country (fulfilled in 19:35–37).
- *20:1:* This is one prophecy given by Isaiah that was not fulfilled because of Hezekiah's prayer.[10]
- *20:6:* Isaiah told Hezekiah that he would live fifteen more years (fulfilled in 20:20).
- *21:10–16:* Unnamed prophets foretold of coming judgment because of Manasseh's sins (fulfilled in 24:1, 3; 25:1–30).
- *22:15–20:* Huldah the prophetess foretold that judgment would come on Judah but not in Josiah's day (fulfilled in 23:29; 25:1–21).

One cannot help but be impressed by this large number of fulfilled prophecies in the Books of Kings and recognize that God spoke clearly and without error.

Prophecies Given Previously but Fulfilled in the Books of Kings

Promises made to David concerning the temple were mentioned by Solomon at the dedication of the temple (1 Kgs. 8:20, 24–26 with 2 Sam. 7:2–16 and 1 Chr. 28:6). In his prayer at the dedication, Solomon also praised God for fulfilling His word to Israel in giving peace and prosperity (1 Kgs. 8:56 with Lev. 26; Deut. 11; 28).

Two other fulfilled prophecies reach back much further in time. God told Joshua that anyone who rebuilt Jericho would suffer the loss of his children. A man named Hiel rebuilt Jericho, and two of his sons died for it (1 Kgs. 16:34 with Josh. 6:26). King Josiah fulfilled prophecy given three hundred years earlier regarding the idolatrous altar of Jeroboam (2 Kgs. 23:15–20 with 1 Kgs. 13:1–2).

Words Given Previously by the Lord and Repeated in Kings

The Lord had spoken in the past, and these inerrant words were the basis of commands, instructions, and actions in the Books of Kings. These include statements found in the Davidic covenant (8:15, 18 with 2 Sam. 7:2–16); commands against intermarriage (11:2 with Deut. 7:1–4; 17:17); judgment on King Ahab (2 Kgs. 9:7–10; 10:1–11, 17 with 1 Kgs. 21:19–24); references to the Mosaic Law (2 Kgs. 14:6; 18:6 with Deut. 24:16); Jonah's prediction about victory (2 Kgs. 14:25); a warning about idolatry (2 Kgs. 17:12, 35 with Ex. 20:4–5; Judg. 6:10; Deut. 12:1–14); previous warnings from prophets (2 Kgs. 17:13 with Deut. 29:22–28; 1 Sam. 12:24–25); previous *written* words from God (2 Kgs. 17:37 with Ex. 24:3; 34:27); previous covenants (2 Kgs. 17:38 with Deut. 4:16–23; 6:1–9); God's commitment to put His name in Jerusalem (2 Kgs. 21:4 with 1 Kgs. 8:1, 29; 9:3).

Supernatural Authentication of God's Message and Messengers

Anyone can claim that he or she speaks for God. One way God chose to validate His words was through supernaturalism. Jesus presented this proof to validate His message and claims (John 5:36). The Books of Kings record an unusual number of supernatural events designed to authenticate the messengers of God along with their messages. These individuals spoke for God, and this reinforces the inspiration and inerrancy of these books (cf. 1 Kgs. 17:1, 3–6, 14–16, 22; 18:37–39; 2 Kgs. 1:10, 12; 2:8, 14, 22; 3:20; 4:1–7, 32–37; 5:14; 6:6, 17–20; 7:6; 20:8–11).

The Books of Chronicles

The Books of Chronicles covered the same time period as the Books of Samuel and Kings and consequently recorded many of the same events where God spoke. But little was said about the Northern Kingdom, since Chronicles emphasized the southern kingdom of Judah. These books focused on the godly kings of Judah, the priesthood, and the temple. Once again God's deep involvement with His people is seen in the nearly sixty times when He spoke to and through individuals, as well as references to His previously spoken words.

God's Word through Prophets

During the monarchy period, the role of the prophet came into new prominence, and God used numerous prophets to convey His message. The prophets gave commands, reminders, instructions, and warnings (2 Chr. 24:19; 25:15; 26:5; 33:18; 36:15–16). A number of prophets were mentioned by name as they communicated God's messages to kings, leaders, and other people: Nathan (1 Chr. 17:4); Gad (1 Chr. 21:9); Shemaiah (2 Chr. 11:2–4; 12:5, 7); Azariah the prophet (2 Chr. 15:1); Hanani (2 Chr. 16:7); Micaiah (2 Chr. 18:18); Jehu the prophet (2 Chr. 19:2); Jahaziel (2 Chr. 20:14); Eliezar (2 Chr. 20:37); Zechariah son of Jehoiada (2 Chr. 24:20); and Jeremiah (2 Chr. 36:12).

God's Word through Kings

In several places, God's word was spoken to kings without any reference to mediators. This, of course, does not mean that prophets or priests may not have been involved. God responded to David's inquiry about going to battle and gave him a plan (1 Chr. 14:10, 14–16). God also gave David the detailed plan for the temple (1 Chr. 28:11–19). God spoke directly to Solomon when He appeared to him on two different occasions (2 Chr. 1:7, 11; 7:12). God apparently gave Hezekiah orders related to the temple (2 Chr. 29:5, 25) as well as assurances regarding his illness (2 Chr. 32:24). The text also seems to indicate that God had spoken to the king of Egypt (2 Chr. 35:21–22).

Prophecies Given Previously but Fulfilled in Chronicles

Once again, fulfilled prophecy testifies to the inspiration and the inerrancy of these historical books. Samuel foretold David's ascent to the throne of Israel, which was fulfilled when David was anointed (1 Chr. 11:3 with 1 Sam. 16:13). The harsh words of Rehoboam led to the fulfillment of Ahijah's prophesy regarding the division of the kingdom (2 Chr. 10:15 with 1 Kings 11:29–37).

Prophecies Given in and Fulfilled in Chronicles

Chronicles records a number of occasions where a prophecy was made and then was shortly fulfilled. The prophet Micaiah spoke to Kings Ahab and Jehoshaphat of the coming death of Ahab and of a military defeat (2 Chr. 18:18–22 fulfilled in 18:34). Jahaziel prophesied of an unusual victory for King Jehoshaphat's forces (2 Chr. 20:14–17 fulfilled in 20:23–24). The prophet Eliezar foretold the end of Jehoshaphat's commercial venture after rebuking him for his alliance with Azariah of Israel

(2 Chr. 20:37 fulfilled in 20:37). Elijah sent a letter to King Jehoram foretelling his terrible death (2 Chr. 21:12–15 fulfilled in 21:18–19). Zechariah, son of Jehoiada, gave a prophecy that was shortly fulfilled (2 Chr. 24:20 with 24:24).

Unnamed prophets warned King Amaziah to dismiss his mercenary soldiers if he wished to have victory (2 Chr. 25:7 with 25:11–13); they rebuked him for worshipping gods of other nations and foretold his defeat and death (2 Chr. 25:15–16 fulfilled in 25:19–27). Huldah the prophetess (2 Chr. 34:22–28) declared that the nation of Judah would surely be judged (fulfilled in 36:6–21) but that godly King Josiah would not experience that judgment (fulfilled in 35:24). The prophet Jeremiah foretold the length of Judah's captivity as being seventy years (2 Chr. 36:21; cf. Jer. 29:10 with Ezra 1:1–3).

Words Previously Given by the Lord and Recorded Again in Chronicles

Instructions, commands, and warnings given by the Lord earlier were repeated in Chronicles. These words were "God-breathed" when originally given and were just as inspired and inerrant when repeated. First Chronicles records a number of such words previously given by the Lord (16:39–40; 22:8–10; 28:3, 6–7), and 2 Chronicles has even more words (6:4, 8–9, 15–17; 13:5, 11; 21:7; 25:4; 30:16; 34:14, 31; 35:6, 12).

Appearance of the Lord with Accompanying Instructions

The Lord appeared twice to Solomon, first giving him a wonderful offer and then responding to Solomon's prayer at the dedication of the temple (2 Chr. 1:7, 11–12 and 7:12–22). The Angel of the Lord also made several appearances: God spoke to the Angel of the Lord, telling him to cease his judgment on the people (1 Chr. 21:15); the Angel of the Lord ordered Gad the prophet to speak to David (21:18); and the Lord again spoke to the angel telling him to put his sword back into its sheath (21:27). The Angel of the Lord also delivered Jerusalem from the Assyrian army in the days of King Hezekiah (2 Chr. 32:21).

Authenticating Signs or the Message and the Messenger

Supernatural signs and wonders authenticated the messengers of God along with their messages. These unusual appearances and events reinforced the idea that these books were inspired and inerrant, having come from the Lord Himself. Such supernatural evidences were recorded in the Book of 2 Chronicles.

At the dedication of the temple in Jerusalem, the glory cloud of God filled the temple, forcing the priests out (5:13–14). At the time of the temple dedication, fire from heaven consumed the sacrifices on the altar (7:1–3). The glory cloud again filled the temple (7:1–2). This may have been a subsequent appearance of the cloud of glory on the same occasion of 5:13. And finally, the Angel of the Lord supernaturally destroyed the Assyrian army (32:21).

The Book of Ezra

The Book of Ezra describes in vivid detail a part of the one-hundred year period of restoration of the Jewish people back to their land. The seventy years of captivity ended in 536 B.C., and people made the first trek back to Judah under Zerubbabel a few years earlier. Various Persian kings, such as Cyrus, Darius, and Artaxerxes, played their part in the divine plan. When some fifty thousand Jews returned under the leadership of Zerubbabel, they laid the foundation of the temple in Jerusalem but did not complete it until 515 B.C.

Ezra 1—6 describes some of the initial events, with chapters 7—10 giving the story of Ezra's return to Jerusalem under the permission of King Artaxerxes. God used Ezra to bring about a spiritual revival of the people. Ezra's name means "God helps." God no doubt providentially chose Ezra to carry out an appointed role in restoring the Jewish people back in the land.

Ezra and Chronicles

In the ancient Jewish Talmud, it is possible that Ezra and Nehemiah were seen together. The Masoretic scholars also seemed to put the two books back-to-back. The ancient Septuagint and old Latin and Syriac versions as well treated the books as a unit.

The Jewish scholar Abarbanel, in his commentary on Samuel, asserted that Ezra was a continuation of Chronicles.

The Integrity of Ezra

Even critics are impressed by the book and make few objections as to the authorship of Ezra. The intrigue against the Jews by some Persian leaders fits everything we know about the history surrounding the return.

Of the integrity and spiritual prominence of Ezra, John Gill states that the book

agrees with the prophesies of Haggai and Zechariah, and serves to illustrate them; it is of use for the continuation of the sacred history, to point at the fulfillment of prophecies concerning the return of the Jews from captivity, and the rebuilding of the temple; and to give us an account of the state of the [people] in those times, the troubles and difficulties it met with, and what care was taken to keep the tribes and families distinct, that it might be known from whom the Messiah sprung.[11]

The Spirituality of the Book of Ezra

Because the book was written so close to generations who would live just before the coming of the Messiah, its historical accuracy must stand firm. And indeed the book has the stamp of divine authorship and with this the pristine accuracy of supernaturally superintended historical accounts.

The first two chapters give a detailed numerical register of family names that must reflect accuracy. Another lengthy genealogy is spelled out in chapters 8 and 10. Later generations would be able to identify relatives who were part of the contingency of returnees. Further details describe the places and movements required to establish renewed temple worship. The Law of Moses is referred to often with a careful accounting of how the sacrifices and ceremonies should go forward. The expression "it is written" (3:2–4) is repeated several times with a mention that the instructions came from "Moses, the man of God" (v. 2).

Specific names of various governors are mentioned, and those again must be actual names or the historical material would be compromised and useless. In one section (5:3–17), pagan rulers are cited: Shethar-bozenai, Tattenai, and Sheshbazzar, as well as King Cyrus and even Nebuchadnezzar. There is a constant reference to the "house of God," "the temple of God," "the God of Israel," and "the Lord God of Israel," "your God," the "God of Jerusalem," "God of heaven," and the "law of God."

Interestingly, Ezra generally described God in the third person, but then used His name in describing what He had done in the past with His people. All references to the Lord pointed to His providential activities in bringing this remnant back home to the Holy Land.

Ezra the scribe made one poignant prophetic statement as to how the Lord brought the people back to Jerusalem. He said, "But now for a brief moment grace has been shown from the LORD our God, to leave us an escaped remnant and to give us a peg in His holy place, that our God may enlighten our eyes and grant us a little reviving in our bondage" (9:8).

Ezra bears all the marks of an inspired Old Testament historical book.

The Book of Nehemiah

The name Nehemiah means "Yahweh consoles." Again, this was a fitting name for his task of helping to bring stability to the Jews who had returned to Israel. We place the period of the writing of this book at about 433–420 B.C. Nehemiah was the cupbearer to King Artaxerxes I. It was his job to drink the wine and taste the king's food to detect poisons. When Nehemiah learned that the walls of Jerusalem had not been built, the king permitted him to help rectify the problem. Though he was a servant, Nehemiah's royal position may have influenced those in Jerusalem to finish the work.

Nehemiah's leadership skills helped complete the daunting task in just fifty-two days. The people made Nehemiah governor of Jerusalem where he exhibited leadership qualities and humility. After twelve years, he returned for a brief visit to Babylon (13:6) but then returned to Judah where he led the people in a movement of solid repentance.

The Integrity of the Book

As is so often the case, critics attack this historical book in order to destroy its integrity. Some claim that Nehemiah actually comes chronologically before Ezra. They argue that contradictions of silence cannot be answered.

Evidence clearly maintains that Ezra and Nehemiah were contemporaries, but liberals say that their time periods were successive. They reason that Artaxerxes would not have sent two men to Judea about the same time equipped with the same authority. But these men were contemporaries; the evidence stands. In fact, they clearly ministered together when the Mosaic covenant was renewed and the law was read to the returning people (chap. 8). "The cumulative effect of the Biblical evidence is too strong to be shaken by mere conjecture."[12]

Remembering Moses

As with Ezra, Nehemiah set forth great prayers of humility for God's people. Nehemiah too reminded the Lord of all His promises towards Israel through Moses His servant (1:8). In fact, the Mosaic promises that the Lord would keep His people was the basis of the return and restoration to Judah. As with the Book of Ezra, Nehemiah mentioned the names of many of his contemporaries, making the events that were then taking place difficult to fictionalize. The book is saturated with historical markers to the truthfulness of all that was taking place. It contains a considerable list of names of officials and priests that give the book historic authenticity.

God dealt in a distinct and direct fashion with Nehemiah who told how God put into his mind what he was to do in Jerusalem (2:12). He said, "I told [the people] how the hand of my God had been favorable to me" (v. 18) and how "my God put it into my heart to assemble the nobles" (7:5).

As with Ezra, the book has several lengthy genealogies that verify the families who were there (7:5–73; 10:1–27), and it contains many locations that are prominent in Jerusalem. Without a doubt, the writer of this document was there and witnessed firsthand all that was taking place.

In summary: "Jewish tradition and the title of the book assign the authorship of the work to Nehemiah (1:1). . . . The book is based on historical sources. . . . There is no valid reason for rejecting the authorship of Nehemiah as tradition, usage of the first person and other internal evidences show."[13] Therefore, the book stands as part of the great body of inspired and inerrant volumes in our Old Testament canon.

The Book of Esther

The events of this book took place during the reign of the Persian King Xerxes I and cover about a ten-year period (483–473 B.C.). The Book of Esther is dedicated to the intrigue within the palace that gives us a glimpse of the inner workings of Persian royalty. But the book also places us in the midst of a remarkable drama that providentially saved the Jewish people. The Israelites would surely have been slaughtered if the evil anti-Semite Haman and others had their way.

The Jewish girl by the name of Hadassah (meaning "myrtle") or by the Persian designation Esther (meaning "star") is the heroin of the story. Because of her influence as queen, the Jewish people were spared from certain destruction.

What about the Name of God?

The great objection to this book being inspired and a part of Scripture is the fact that God is nowhere mentioned in its twelve chapters. The argument goes: If this dramatic scroll were revelation, the Lord would certainly be spoken of in its pages.

Some logical reasons have been suggested, however, why the name of God is not referred to. While the Jews were filtering back to the Holy

Land from Persia, it was still undetermined as to how and when more people could return. The Jewish population had many enemies among the Persian court rulers. Could it be that this daring story of Esther would offend Persians who would read it?

While this theory cannot be confirmed, it may be a plausible explanation for the absence of the Lord's name. The Jews believe that the author, the pious Jew Mordecai mentioned in the book,

> feared that the Book might be profanely treated by Gentiles, because of its story of the triumph of the Jews over their enemies. But whatever the reason for the omission of the Name of God, the sense of Divine providence pervades the Book. . . . [It] shows unfailing trust in God's providential care for His people.[14]

Critics who argue against the book say that the history of Persia does not record such a story nor mention the Jewish queen Esther. This is one of the standard objections of liberals who reject the book by the argument of silence. However, Esther's existence actually fits well into the chronology of the Persian period.

On the positive side,

> Much evidence does support the historicity of the facts in this book. Xerxes was a real king in Persia. His drinking parties were well known. Xerxes did have an irrational temper, occasionally exhibiting fits of rage (1:12; 7:10). He did have a palace in Susa and a large harem there. Various features of the court can also be substantiated from other sources.[15]

Canonicity of the Book

What is so impressive about the book is its long-standing popularity and acceptance among the ancient Jewish people. It is generally recognized as the best known of all the books of the Old Testament. The Feast of Purim celebrates the defeat of the enemies of the Jews in the book. Under every test of scrutiny, the book has passed muster with Jewish scholarship. Its canonicity has stood the test of time for well over two thousand years.

The integrity of the book is rarely challenged, except by those who are automatically skeptical about any book of the Bible. The author shows an intimate and detailed knowledge of Persian court life. Because of this, the book is seen as a valuable source of information, filling in many historic gaps about classical history.

The book reads and moves with a fast pace. It contains graphic descriptions, clear and concise language, few obscurities, remarkable accounts of action and movement, and drama that holds the reader spellbound from verse to verse.

Esther is listed in the Old Testament canons of both Origen and Jerome. The Jewish scholar Maimonides gives Esther a lofty position in Jewish thinking. Gill, another Jewish scholar, writes,

> As to the canonical authority of it, it has been generally received by Jews and Christians; our wise men, says Maimonides, openly and plainly affirm of the book of Esther, that it was dictated by the Holy Spirit; so Aben Ezra [says] on ch. vi. 6; and he himself affirms that "all the books of the prophets, and all the Hagiographa (or holy writings) shall cease in the days of the Messiah, except the volume of Esther; and lo, that shall be as stable as the Pentateuch, and as the constitutions of the oral law, which shall never cease.[16]

All signs point to an important scroll inspired by the Spirit of God and without error in its historical veracity. Unger considers it a literary phenomenon when given honest consideration and argues that it displays the marks of factual inerrancy. Unger adds that the author has an "undeniable knowledge" of Persia and is precise in his description of events, by which all objections simply evaporate.[17]

Validated by God's Involvement

The Bible is not a mere human book subject to mistakes and errors. The Bible is God's book. God used fallible human beings to write His book, but He kept them from error as the Holy Spirit "carried them along." They did not make mistakes in writing about justification by faith, other great spiritual truths, and historical events.

God as King of creation is in control of all that transpires on earth. The histories of nations are ultimately records of their relationships with God. But with the nation of Israel, God entered into a special covenant relationship. This relationship is described in the historical books of the Old Testament as God interacted with His covenant people. It is not surprising, therefore, that we find over two hundred references to times when God intervened in Israel's history, spoke to them, or reminded them of commands and instructions previously given.

Repeatedly, prophecies were made and prophecies were fulfilled, reinforcing the "God-breathed" character of these books. On a number of occasions, supernatural events were employed to validate that the messages being given were from the Lord. This deep involvement of God with Israel in Joshua, Judges, Samuel, Kings, and Chronicles tells us that these books fit into the category that the apostle Paul spoke of in 2 Timothy 3:16. They are "God-breathed" books. And as the apostle Peter declared, "Men moved by the Holy Spirit spoke from God" (2 Pet. 1:21). This kept them from error as they wrote.

We must conclude that the books of Joshua, Judges, and the other historical books were just as inspired and inerrant as the Gospel of John, the Book of Romans, or the Psalms.

FOR DISCUSSION

1. What are the various ways the Lord revealed Himself in the historical books?

2. Is the evidence plentiful or scant as to the inspiration of the historical books?

3. In what ways did the Lord speak to the prophets in the historical books?

4. Why is Samuel important as a prophet of God?

5. How did the Lord authenticate His message by the prophetic messengers?

For Further Study

Commentaries

Wood, Leon. *The Distressing Days of the Judges*. Grand Rapids: Zondervan, 1975.

Hermeneutics

Benware, Paul. *Understanding End Times Prophecy*. Chicago: Moody, 1995.

Theology

Geisler, Norman. *Creating God in the Image of Man?* Minneapolis: Bethany House, 1997.

Walvoord, John F. *Jesus Christ Our Lord*. Chicago: Moody, 1969.

Chapter Twelve

Inerrancy of the Old Testament Poetical Books

N ote that the Hebrew canon, called the Writings (*Kethubim*), contained the three major poetical books: Psalms, Proverbs, and Job, and the five Megilloth or Rolls: Song of Solomon, Ruth, Lamentations, Ecclesiastes, and Esther. In the Septuagint, the Writings are called the Hagiographa, but Job was considered a historical book.[1]

The Massoretes who edited the current edition of the Hebrew Bible recognized only three poetical books, Psalms, Proverbs, and Job. But in the last two hundred years, Hebrew poetry has become better understood. In form, we now can see parallelisms and rhythms. Though some use the term "meter" when describing Old Testament poetry, there is no evidence that the writers had a fixed code of prosody like the Greeks. The Hebrews,

> although they wrote under deep emotion and expressed themselves rhythmically, unconsciously producing the phenomena which were later to develop into more definite ideas of metre. In other words, there is evidence that poetry in ancient Israel had a long career and preceded [Greek] prosody.[2]

Expressing emotion, the greatness of God, and even prophetic truth, the poetry was inspired, inerrant, and preserved as Scripture by the Lord's guiding providence. We can identify with much of it through our experiences, emotions, and feelings, but the Holy Spirit must still help us to comprehend the spiritual message.

In this chapter, we want to see how ancient Israel looked at their own poetical books but we also will examine the internal evidence for inspiration and the statements dealing with inerrancy.

The Book of Job

The Book of Job stands in a lofty and unique position in the Old Testament canon. The book is outside the framework of inspired Hebrew Scripture, and yet one cannot imagine the Old Testament without this remarkable and even miraculous writing. Though some scholars say Job was written during the period of Solomon (971–931 B.C.), the majority place it just before the patriarchal age. Many markers point this way.

For example, the Book of Job makes no mention of any Old Testament characters, such as Abraham, Isaac, Jacob, or Moses. It records no outstanding events, such as Israel's escape from Egypt. Palestine, the Jewish people, or the fact that God is the Lord of the Hebrew people is never referenced.

But the following makes Job important: 1) It makes a strong prophetic statement about Job some day seeing his Redeemer and experiencing resurrection; 2) it shows there was an ancient accurate memory of the true God whom many trusted even before Abraham; and 3) it gives a pristine description of the attributes and characteristics of God prior to the writings of Moses.

Limited Knowledge about Job

Unger writes:

> The Biblical Job was a pious man who dwelt in the steppes eastward or southeastward of Palestine in the land of Uz (1:1), Teman, Shuah and Naama (2:11). There is no concrete reason for denying that Job was a real character or for maintaining that the events recorded are not historical. The reference to Job in Ezekiel 14:14, 20 and James 5:11 show that he was a historical character. There is nothing in the book itself to suggest that the account is symbolic, either in the names, places or circumstances of the narrative.[3]

Genesis 10:23 and 22:20–22 tie Uz to the Arameans. Some identify the Chaldeans with the Arameans and Uzites, but this does not make them identical. Though Uz was east of Palestine, its exact location cannot be determined. According to Lamentations 4:21, the land of Uz was located in Edom.

Though Job is commonly cited as the author of this marvelous piece of literature, we have no way to determine for sure who penned the book. (It would not be uncommon for a Middle-Eastern writer to tell his experiences in the third person.) But the story tells us of a man named Job who was no commonplace thinker. His knowledge of God could not have been created from his imagination. With all the surrounding paganism, his high view of God needs no apology. In fact, this is one of the miracles of the writing. The knowledge of the true Lord of the universe must have been transmitted down through the generations by pious and godly personalities. In New Testament terminology, Job and his friends were "born again."

The Theme of Job

"Is there retributive justice in the world?" finds [a] positive answer from [the Book of] Job. His own tragic struggle confirmed the paradox that, in appealing from the apparent injustice of God, Job found strength and support in the righteous God who would one day establish his innocence. Job denies the adequacy of material retribution. Suffering is no sure proof of sin. But there does exist retribution of a higher order: the righteous man is never completely cut off from the fellowship of God.[4]

Inspired Scripture

As long as people have pondered these things, Job has been considered a part of the Hebrew canon. In other words, in the earliest days of the people of Israel, the book was part of the spiritual tapestry of the nation. Did Moses add it to the Torah himself? Was it a part of the Exodus collection? Was it written during the time of Abraham and preserved by him or others who realized its spiritual importance and that truly it was inspired of God?

Job has had many assignments by the rabbis. Sometimes they placed the book with the poetical writings, sometimes with the historical or the prophecy scrolls. But with almost no doubts, Job has always had a home in the Jewish Old Testament canon. Smick writes:

> It is amazing that a book about a man outside the sphere of Israel's covenant bond whose experience illustrates both the highest and the lowest levels of faith became part of the Hebrew canon and was never seriously challenged. This proves that the Hebrews recognized the superior spiritual message of this book. The book did

not become authoritative by an edict of an official body like the rabbinical synod at Jamnia in 90 A.D. It was accepted as a divine word by the community of God's people at a time well before the LXX [Septuagint] was completed or else it would not have been included.[5]

The Inerrancy of Job

If the Book of Job is inspired with its undeniable prophetic utterances, it must also be inerrant. The two principles and doctrines must work together. This can be seen beginning with chapter 1.

The encounter between Satan and God (1:6—2:6) conforms to all we know from other writings about the devil and how he acts. The story begins by Satan coming before God accusing Job but also accusing God of overprotecting Job (1:10–11). In God's providence, He allowed Satan to test Job but not to take Job's life (1:12; 2:6). After Satan removed all of Job's possessions, including his family (except his wife), the devil came before God with "the sons of God" (2:1) to accuse Job again. This narration fits perfectly with what we know of the activities of Satan, his accusing of the brethren and his mode of operation. Again, the burden of disproof lies with the critic.

From chapter 3, the story with its twists and turns begins in earnest. Job's friends come to "comfort" but also to argue with him, implying that he must have done something wrong to bring on the horrible things he was suffering. The nature and attributes of God are described perfectly in conformity with how He is pictured throughout Scripture. There is no deviation.

Job spoke of God's absolute control of history and people (12:22–25). In his discourse, Job gave one of the most amazing prophecies in Scripture:

> As for me, I know that my Redeemer lives, and at the last He will take His stand on the earth. Even after my skin is destroyed, yet from my flesh I shall see God. (19:25–26)

Predicting far ahead of other Messianic prophecies, Job here gave one of the most amazing promises. Some have tried to discredit this passage, but its meaning cannot be doubted. Unger well notes:

> Job declared that he knew that his *Go'el*-Redeemer was alive, presently as a reality, existing at that time, and not someone to come into existence later, though His manifestation in human flesh

was to be an event in the future. His Redeemer was alive as the eternally existing One, the pre-incarnate Christ, the eternal Word who was with God and was God (John 1:1–3) and in the future was to become incarnate (John 1:14).[6]

Some work hard to find fault with the Book of Job. To do this, they have to go to poetic sections and claim that the writing is full of mythology. For example, such doubters of the book's authenticity cite 26:11 where the "pillars of heaven" are mentioned or where it is said that God's breath clears the heavens (v. 13). But such limited poetic expressions are swallowed up in more literal language throughout the writing. Anyone can judge that poetry was used for the sake of expression, but Job and his friends were not using such thoughts because they saw their world in this light.

In the Book of Job, the Lord and His universe are too great for interpreting such thoughts in this fashion. Anyone reading Job with an open mind must realize that poetry was used for embellishment and not for supporting the idea of a limited God and a puny universe.

Again, the weight of the argument falls on the critics. They must disprove inspiration and inerrancy in the Book of Job. They will have great difficulty, especially in light of the Redeemer passage that few can prophetically deny.

The Psalms

The 150 psalms were compiled possibly by priests or court scribes during and after David's adult life (990–965 B.C.). Seventy-three psalms are ascribed to him while many others should be also. The psalms called Songs of Ascents (going up to Jerusalem) are suspected to be by David, and at least one (Psalm 127) probably was penned by Solomon. Choir songs dedicated to the feats of David were sung by the musicians who performed at the tabernacle, such as the sons of Korah (Psalms 44—49). Moses (90), Asaph (50), and Mahalath (53), and possibly more, also composed portions of the Psalms.

In many of David's psalms, as Psalm 16, he acted as a prophet inspired by the Lord to predict Jesus' resurrection (Acts 2:24–28). As a prophet, David "knew that God had sworn to him with an oath to seat one of his descendants on his throne" (Acts 2:30; cf. Ps. 89:3–4).

Almost all the psalms describe the attributes and thoughts of God, and prophecy is included in at least half of them. Psalm 1 describes the knowledge of the Lord who "knows the way of the righteous" (v. 6).

Psalm 2 gives us the words of God the Father to His Son just prior to Jesus' earthly birth: "You are My Son, today I have begotten You" (v. 7). In the midst of such prophecies, the psalms give us the heart and soul of the writer, whether David or others. We feel passion and fear: "Arise, O LORD; save me, O my God!" (3:7). And, "By Your abundant loving-kindness I will enter Your house" (5:7).

As mentioned, many psalms seem to have been written by David but sung by a choir under the direction of a chorus leader (Psalms 8, 9). Both of these psalms are prophetic, describing the glory of the Son of Man (8:4) and the future "throne for judgment" God will some day set up (9:7). Besides the resurrection psalm (16), there is the psalm of the death of the Messiah (22). And who can read the cries of King David and not be moved as he shared with readers his sinfulness before the Lord: Turn to me and be gracious to me, for I am lonely and afflicted. The troubles of my heart are enlarged; bring me out of my distresses. Look upon my affliction and my trouble, and forgive all my sins (25:16–18).

Psalm 119 is the longest chapter of Scripture with 176 verses. All the verses are dedicated to some aspect and attribute of the Scriptures themselves. This psalm is a masterful work of poetic and doctrinal art that has never been duplicated in literature. It is divided into twenty-two segments, each starting with a word related to a letter in the Hebrew alphabet. Our English translations have divided the poetic paragraphs into eight verses each. This psalm is a crowning achievement in its dedication to the greatness of God's Word. In describing Scripture, the psalmist used in every verse a synonym such as:

- *Commandments*
- *Judgments*
- *Laws*
- *Ordinances*
- *Precepts*
- *Statutes*
- *Testimonies*
- *Ways*
- *Word*
- *Words*

From David's point of reference, these descriptives would refer to the Torah (Law of Moses) and the historical books of Samuel, Kings, and Chronicles.

In Psalm 119, David gave descriptions that make the reader believe he understood the inerrancy of the Word of God. He wrote:

- *"Your ordinances are good" (v. 39).*
- *"Your salvation [is] according to Your word" (v. 41).*
- *"I trust in Your word" (v. 42).*
- *"Your word is settled in heaven" (v. 89).*
- *"You Yourself have taught me [from Your ordinances]" (v. 102).*
- *"I esteem [as] right all Your precepts concerning everything, [in contrast] I hate every false way" (v. 128).*
- *"Your word is very pure" (v. 140).*
- *"Your law is truth" (v. 142).*
- *"Your testimonies are righteous forever" (v. 144).*
- *"The sum of Your word is truth, and every one of Your righteous ordinances is everlasting" (v. 160).*
- *"All Your commandments are righteousness" (v. 172).*

It must be remembered again that the burden of disproof rests with the critic. If the psalms are not inspired and thus errant, doubters must establish that as so. One simply has to deny the entire Word of God in order to attack the Psalms and their messages. Interestingly, Webster's defines errant as "deviating from an accepted pattern or standard." The Psalms have all the marks of the standard of inspiration. Few have attempted to prove them as false.

Proverbs

Some may argue with sarcasm, How could the Book of Proverbs be inspired or inerrant? Isn't the book just a collection of human sayings and practical wisdom? The answer to this charge is not as simple as might be expected. Some proverbs are profound, demonstrating that the wise thoughts truly are direct from the Lord. But it is also true that the bulk of the proverbs are wise concepts that anyone could invent and use for wise living.

It must be remembered that in the selection and collection of wisdom verses to be included in Scripture, the Holy Spirit was active in this process as well. God gave us in His Word just what He wants us to know. And there can be wise sayings, learned through experience, that are worthy to be part of the canon.

Thus, to prove the inspiration and inerrancy of the Book of Proverbs may be a difficult task. But again, the burden of proof that Proverbs is not to be taken as the Word of God lies with the doubter.

Wisdom Literature

Rabbi Cohen comments:

> The Bible supplies evidence that three classes of teachers existed in
> ancient Israel. They are mentioned in Jeremiah xviii.18:
> "Instruction shall not perish from the priest, nor counsel from the
> wise (*chacham*), nor the word from the prophet;" and in Ezekiel vii.
> 26: "They shall seek a vision of the prophet, and instruction shall
> perish from the priest, and counsel from the elders (*zekenim*)." The
> priest had the duty of providing the community with instruction
> (Torah) in the practices of religion, in the narrower connotation of
> the term . . . ; the function of the prophet was to communicate to
> the people the Divine word or vision which he had received; and in
> addition there were the "wise" or "elders" who imparted counsel,
> guidance in the secular affairs of life.[7]

Besides Solomon, the Proverbs are ascribed to a certain Agur
(30:1–33) and a King Lemuel (31:1–9), about whom nothing is known.
But again, almost since the days of Solomon, these wise sayings have
been an important part of the Scriptures of Israel. Bullock writes:

> The basic nature of wisdom as viewed by the author of Proverbs is
> summed up in his statement, "The fear of the Lord is the beginning
> of knowledge" (1:7; cf. 9:10). That is, the fundamental nature of
> wisdom was theological. Thus in Proverbs the underlying basis of
> life is one's relationship to God. Out of that relationship grow moral
> understanding and the ability to judge what is right (2:6–22).[8]

And Bullock adds to that:

> The book then purports to be a primer of right conduct and essen-
> tial attitudes toward life, aimed at producing lives in conformity to
> the divine will. The immediate object was to train and educate for
> the preservation of the family unit, and social stability of the socie-
> ty as a whole. Therefore, prominent in wisdom was the recognition
> that fulfillment of God's will is actualized in the personal and social
> conduct and institutions of His people.[9]

The Personification of Wisdom

From chapters 1:20 through 4:27, the author encouraged the reader to
acquire wisdom. Sometimes wisdom is personified as female: "Do not forsake her [wisdom], and she will guard you; love her, and she will watch

over you. The beginning of wisdom is: Acquire wisdom; and with all your acquiring, get understanding" (4:6–7). The same thing is done to instruction. "Take hold of instruction; do not let go. Guard her, for she is your life" (v. 13). The pronoun "her" is used because the noun *wisdom* is feminine. But what is most important is that repeatedly in this section, "wisdom" is actually God's wisdom. It comes directly from Him, as the writer noted: "For the LORD gives wisdom; from His mouth come knowledge and understanding. He stores up sound wisdom for the upright" (2:6–7).

This association then, demonstrates inspiration and inerrancy. These proverbs ultimately were from God, no matter who the human instruments were.

Personification was used to assist the reader in understanding the Lord by setting forth one of His attributes (wisdom) and endowing it with personality. The author showed that wisdom is a divine attribute eternally related to Him, understood only in relation to Him, and is an extension of His dynamic Being to mankind.[10]

> The method of personification is the means by which the practical perspective of wisdom is connected to God. It is the closest thing wisdom has to the prophetic formula "Thus says the Lord." By means of personified wisdom, the knowledge of God's nature is delivered to and integrated with the everyday life of men and women.[11]

Ecclesiastes

The Hebrew word *Qōhelet* ("Preacher") means "the one who speaks" with the idea of "before an assembly." In fact, the word comes from the idea of "assembly." The author called himself "the son of David, king in Jerusalem" (1:1). From this, most have assumed the writer is Solomon. In fact, few conservative scholars would challenge this theory.

On the purpose of the book, Leupold writes:

> The book is written primarily for the godly in Israel. They are the only ones, as usual, who would give attention to a book such as this. Since the times are evil and the godly suffer much, this is primarily a book of comfort. It shows God's people how to meet their difficult problems.

> By teaching with tremendous emphasis the vanity of all earthly things, the author first disillusions his hearers. For men will have at least some expectation of the comfort and the solace that are to be derived from the possession of earthly goods. As long as they are

thus minded, they are preparing the way for added sorrows. Especially in evil times men should stake no hope on earthly goods and treasures. The best service that can be rendered a man is to divorce him from the things of this world as completely as possible. We call that disillusionment.[12]

With this in mind, the author began by crying, "'Vanity of vanities,' says the Preacher, 'Vanity of vanities! All is vanity'" (1:2) or, "emptiness of emptiness." Looking at the book through modern glasses, Solomon was criticizing at what we would call the philosophies of existentialism, humanism, and materialism. He asked, "What advantage does man have in all his work which he does under the sun?" (v. 3). In other words, if a person just does external works in this life, what satisfaction does that bring? The physical world will not give fulfillment or spiritual meaning. Achievements will not bring happiness. Only relating to God brings peace.

Is Ecclesiastes inspired and inerrant Scripture? First, the issue of Solomonic authorship is extremely important to this issue. If Solomon is the prime contributor to Proverbs, this would place his work in the camp of the inspired. Though some may take this argument as circular, it really is not. Solomon was not only mightily used of God in his life but also through what he wrote.

Ecclesiastes 1:12–18 almost completely settles the issue of Solomon as author of this work. As one reads the words of these verses, no other name comes to mind. The writer said he was king over Israel in Jerusalem (v. 12) and that he set his mind to explore things by wisdom (v. 13). He admitted that he had "magnified and increased wisdom more than all who were over Jerusalem before me; and my mind has observed a wealth of wisdom and knowledge" (v. 16). He finally admitted that he crossed the line to "know madness and folly" (v. 17) and with this, his much sought-after wisdom turned to grief (v. 18).

Rabbi Reichert notes:

> The experiences of Solomon, as recorded in I Kings, are the same as those ascribed to himself by Koheleth [*Qōhelet*]. The luxury of his household, his numerous wives, the buildings he erected, his reputation for outstanding wisdom—all these foundations upon which the king's fame rested find reflection in the person of Koheleth as delineated in the Book. Likewise the follies to which he became addicted later in his reign find a parallel there. Koheleth depicts the

conditions of life in the country as unsettled and the people as existing under hardships; here too confirmation may be found in the history of Solomon.[13]

Second, the final words of Ecclesiastes show all the earmarks of inspired Scripture. The author concludes, "In addition to being a wise man, the Preacher also taught the people knowledge; and he pondered, searched out and arranged many proverbs" (12:9). This places him in the category of a teaching elder and priest of the people. He adds "The words of wise men are like goads, and [the words of] masters of these collections [of sayings] are like well-driven nails; they are given by one Shepherd [God]" (12:11).

Third, it may be pointed out that the theology of Ecclesiastes conforms to the rest of the Old Testament. There are no surprises in reference to the doctrine of God or the depravity of man. The teachings of the book relate perfectly to truth given in all the other works of Scripture, both Old and New Testaments.

Finally, the argument of disproof comes into play. One must show that Ecclesiastes is not inspired and then not inerrant. Gill summarizes:

> This book has been universally received into the canon of the Scriptures by Jews and Christians. The former, indeed, had once some controversy about it; and they thought to have hid it, or put it among the apocryphal books; because at first sight, some things seemed contradictory to each other, and to incline to heresy, atheism, and epicurism, and to assert the eternity of the world: but they better considered of it; and when they observed those passages were capable of a good sense, and that the whole agreed with the law of God, they changed their minds. . . . The book carries in it such internal evidence of a divine original, as cannot well be denied; it delivers out and inculcates such divine instructions, concerning the duties of men to God, and one another; concerning the contempt of the world, and the carnal pleasures of it; the fear and worship of God, and a future judgment; as none but the wisdom of God could suggest.[14]

Song of Solomon

The "Song of Songs, which is Solomon's" (1:1) is one of the most misunderstood books of Scripture. But it was not so with early Jewish rabbis. In the Septuagint, the book was simply called "The Song" whereas the

Syriac versions called it "the Wisdom of Wisdoms of the same Solomon." In old English, it was also titled "the Canticles."

The ancient Jews received and esteemed the book as a valuable part of the Scriptures. There was never any controversy over its inclusion in the canon. Though sometimes calling the book "the Holy of Holies," the orthodox Jews forbade their youngsters from reading the book because of its sublimity and the sexual nature of the text. When their children were of age, they could then explore its mysteries.

The early church fathers and councils also accepted the Song as part of the ancient canon of inspired writings. Basically, Christians in all generations have accepted the book as authentic and inspired of the Lord. Gill summarizes:

> This book of Canticles [Song of Solomon] has plain marks of a divine origin, and proofs of its being of divine inspiration: it was written by one that was inspired of God, as appears by the books of Proverbs and Ecclesiastes, written by him; the greatness of the matter contained in it, the dignity, sublimity, and majesty of its style, shew it to be no human composure; the power and efficacy which it has had over the hearts of men in reading it, and hearing it explained, is another evidence of its being the word of God, . . .[15]

How is the book controversial? The church began to look at the book allegorically in order to diffuse the sexual nature of the poem. The theme of the book is basically how a married couple gives to one another in true marital intimacy. In poetic fashion, the book can be explicit in its love descriptions. Some of this material is subtle and requires some knowledge of rural and pastoral mentality. The question must be asked, Why is God not interested in the expression of physical and emotional love in the realm of marriage? To many, until recently, even marital love was a taboo subject. But the evangelical church, for the most part, has returned to what it believes is the original intent of the Holy Spirit in the composition of this wonderful little book, and that is, it is a pattern for romance among married couples.

A Compelling Argument

The Hebrew poetical books blend into the fabric of the entire Old Testament and its overall claim of inspiration with the resulting doctrine of inerrancy. Tradition plays a large part in this issue, because it must be remembered that these books were accepted as from God many centuries back. Those far-off generations examined the books, argued over them, pondered and prayed, and came to a firm conviction that they ultimately were from the Lord. Because those days are so far past us does not negate the truth of the doctrine of inspiration. Tradition then becomes a compelling argument.

In this study, internal evidence for inerrancy is not as strong as in the prophetic books. And so we must rely on other sources, such as tradition, to confirm the integrity of these writings.

Finally, how was the entire Old Testament understood in the days of Christ and the apostles? What did Paul mean when he gave us the classic passage "All Scripture is inspired by God [God-breathed]" (2 Tim. 3:16)?[16]

By all Scripture, Paul had in mind the entire accepted canon of the Old Testament, including the poetical books that were well established as the Word of God. Neither Christ nor the apostles gave any disclaimers, warning us not to read these books. The issue had long ago been settled in heaven and then on earth.

Gaussen wraps up the issue by noting:

> First of all, all the Scriptures are without distinction called The Word of God. This title is sufficient of itself to demonstrate to us, that if Isaiah began [for example] his prophecies by inviting the heavens and the earth to give ear because the Lord had spoken, the same summons ought to come forth for us from all the books of the Bible, for they are all called "The Word of God." "Hear, O heavens, and give ear, O earth; for the Lord hath spoken!"
>
> Nowhere shall we find a single passage that permits us to detach one single part of it as less divine than all the rest. When we say that this whole book is the Word of God, do we not attest that the very phrases of which it is composed have been given by Him?[17]

FOR DISCUSSION

1. What is outstanding about the Book of Job?

2. Is there prophecy in the Book of Job?

3. Can we know for certain if Job was the author of the book that bears his name?

4. How many prophets and teachers contributed to the Psalms?

5. What is important about Psalm 119?

6. If some proverbs were collected from other sources, does this invalidate the concept of inspiration and inerrancy?

7. Why is Ecclesiastes 12:9 an important verse?

For Further Study

Bible Introduction

Bullock, C. Hassell. *An Introduction to the Old Testament Poetic Books*. Chicago: Moody, 1988.

Unger, Merrill F. *Introductory Guide to the Old Testament*. Grand Rapids: Zondervan, 1978.

Bibliology Texts

Gaussen, Louis. *The Inspiration of the Holy Scriptures*. Chicago: Moody, n.d.

Warfield, Benjamin Breckinridge. *The Inspiration and Authority of the Bible*. Philadelphia: Presbyterian and Reformed, 1948.

Commentaries

Cohen, A. *Proverbs*. New York: Soncino, 1985.

Leupold, H. C. *Exposition of Ecclesiastes*. Grand Rapids: Baker, 1987.

Reichert, Victor E. "Ecclesiastes" in *The Five Megilloth*, ed. A. Cohen. London: Soncino, 1974.

Reichert, Victor E. *Job*. New York: Soncino, 1985.

Smick, Elmer B. "Job" in *The Expositor's Bible Commentary, Volume 4: 1 Kings-Job*, edited by Frank E. Gaebelein. Grand Rapids: Zondervan, 1988.

Unger, Merrill F. *Unger's Commentary on the Old Testament*. Reprint. Chattanooga, Tenn.: AMG, 2002.

Chapter Thirteen

Inerrancy of the Major Prophets

*T*he Major Prophets with their many predictions become significant sources in the discussion of the inspiration and inerrancy of the Bible.

God alone can declare the end from the beginning. The dumb idols of the heathen know nothing concerning the future, and man himself is powerless to find out things to come. However, the Lord, who made this challenge, has demonstrated his power to predict. None of the "sacred books" of the nations contains predictions of the future. If the authors of these writings had attempted to foretell the future, they would have furnished the strongest evidence of their deception. But the Bible is pre-eminently a book of prophecy. These predictions are declared to be the utterances of the Lord; they show that the Bible is a supernatural book, the revelation of God.[1]

Thus, the inspiration and inerrancy of the Major Prophets is a key factor of concern in affirming the inerrancy of the entire Bible. And the issue of the inerrancy of Scripture is a foundational belief of the Christian dogma.

God's written revelation came in inerrant form, free from discrepancies or contradictions, and this inerrancy contributes to its achieving its saving purpose. If there were genuine mistakes of any sort in the original manuscripts, it would mean, obviously, that the Bible contains error along with truth. As such it would become subject to human judgment, just like any other religious document. The validity of such judgment, of course, depends upon the judge's

189

own knowledge and wisdom. If he rejects the truth of the scriptural record simply because it seems to him to be unlikely or improbable, then he is in danger of eternal loss. The charge of scriptural self-contradiction or factual error is to be taken quite seriously; it cannot be brushed off as a matter of minor consequence. At stake is the credibility and reliability of the Bible as authentic revelation from God.[2]

The presentation of inerrancy as formulated by evangelicals has generally been grounded on several lines of argumentation. The first one is to show deductively that inerrancy flows naturally from the character of God. Since God cannot lie (Rom. 3:4) and the Bible has its source in God (2 Tim. 3:16), then the Scriptures cannot have errors. This line of arguing may not convince someone who does not accept the particular statements used from the Bible as reliable.[3] However, it does demonstrate that it is impossible to accept the complete biblical view of God and reject inerrancy simultaneously. For the sake of discussion about the Major Prophets, this deductive argument is assumed in this chapter.

The second way of reasoning one's way to the doctrine of inerrancy is to show the self-attestation of Scripture.[4] A proponent of inerrancy will often marshal the internal evidence in a portion of Scripture that suggests its divine origin.[5] The end result is a catalog of internal information showing such things as authorial claims for divine inspiration, compositional formulas asserting divine origin, and various special occurrences such as predictive language that can be verified as directly fulfilled.[6]

Two areas of internal evidence will be singled out as special cases. One is the occurrence of prophecy while the second is the harmony of Scripture. The harmony of Scripture can be dealt with at several levels such as the unity of the book in question or across historical and authorial boundaries in the canon. The focus of this chapter in this particular area will be on alleged discrepancies that have been asserted about the book under consideration.

A final way that the doctrine of inerrancy is strengthened is by an appeal to the witness of the rest of Scripture to the divine origin of the text being studied. This line of reasoning in light of the progress of revelation solidifies the nature of self-attestation. This is especially true since, from a human perspective, the Bible is a collection of writings by forty or so authors spanning some sixteen centuries. This fact and those above provide a cumulative case for an incontrovertible doctrine of inerrancy.

The Book of Isaiah

The marvelous intertwining of historical narrative and prophecy that is the Book of Isaiah has been the center of controversy on several fronts. It is of special interest since it may be the most quoted book in the New Testament. Our discussion will review the book's picture of itself, a sampling of fulfilled prophecies, a sampling of alleged discrepancies, and other biblical references to Isaiah.

Self-Attestation of the Book of Isaiah

Eleven times in Isaiah the word *oracle* (Hebrew, *maśśā'*) is used to describe words given in the book (13:1; 14:28; 15:1; 17:1; 19:1; 21:1, 11, 13; 22:1; 23:1; 30:6). The word comes from the Hebrew verb that means "to be carried." The prophet was carried along as God gave him the message. This concept is analogous to the teaching of Peter in 2 Peter 1:19–21 concerning the giving of Scripture as men were "moved" or "borne along" by the Holy Spirit. The word is commonly used by the Old Testament prophets (see Jer. 23:33–38; Ezek. 12:10; Nah. 1:1; Hab. 1:1; Zech. 9:1; 12:1; Mal. 1:1), but Isaiah appears to use it most frequently.

The oracle concerning the wilderness of the sea (Isa. 21:1–10) especially helps the reader to see Isaiah's understanding of the divine origin of his words. The historical context was when Babylon rebelled against Assyria which was the dominant power in the eighth century B.C.[7] Israel hoped Babylon would end the growing Assyrian dominance. God told Isaiah to station a sentry to await news of the outcome ("thus the Lord says to me," v. 6). The crushing news came that the Assyrians defeated Babylon. Lest anyone doubt the news, Isaiah commented, "What I have heard from the LORD of hosts, the God of Israel, I make known to you" (v. 10).

Isaiah 41:21–24 also provides insight into how the Book of Isaiah viewed its words. The particular words of the section were indeed those that "the LORD" said (v. 21). God challenged the heathen gods to predict the future, something only God himself can do: "Declare the things that are going to come afterward, that we may know that you are gods" (v. 23). The wording is strong as Leupold suggests: "It must be said at the outset that there is more involved here than just ability to foretell the future. The Lord can indeed do that. But at the same time he also has control of all the issues that the future may bring."[8] The ready deduction from this and similar passages in Isaiah is that the book itself claims divine origin for its words.

Fulfilled Prophecies in the Book of Isaiah

Among the clearest fulfillments of prior predictions in Holy Writ are the pronouncements based on Isaiah 52:13—53:12, the account of the suffering servant as illustrated in the table below:[9]

Isaiah Passage	Passage Showing Fulfillment	Nature of the Fulfillment
Isaiah 53:1	John 12:37–38	Jesus was rejected by many in spite of his miracles.
Isaiah 53:3	Luke 23:18; John 1:11	Jesus was rejected by his own people, the Jews.
Isaiah 53:5	Romans 5:6–8; 2 Cor. 5:21	Jesus became our vicarious sacrifice on the cross.
Isaiah 53:7	Mark 15:4–5	Jesus was silent before His accusers.
Isaiah 53:9	Matt. 27:57–60	Jesus was buried with the rich.
Isaiah 53:12	Mark 15:27–28	Jesus was crucified with two thieves.

An honest reader must observe that these kinds of correlations are compelling evidence that Jesus was indeed the fulfillment of predictions in Isaiah. This supernatural character of the book reinforces the concept of inerrancy as applied to it.

A second example passage is the section introduced by the first oracle statement (Isa. 13:1—14:27). It is momentous because it introduces a divine prediction concerning the future destruction of Babylon.

> This section (13:1—14:27) is ascribed to Isaiah son of Amoz . . . This is significant in view of the fact that it is clearly prophecy spoken *before* the fall of Babylon. This is important for many believe that Isaiah 40—66 could not have been written by Isaiah son of Amoz because he could not have prophesied about something yet future. The passage in 13:1—14:27 shows that Isaiah's writing about events *before* they happened *was* possible.[10]

The most controversial passage in Isaiah has been 7:14, the famous virgin birth passage. Conservative, as well as liberal scholars, have been divided on how Matthew 1:23 uses the Isaiah statement. John Willis cites at least nine different logical ways that Matthew's use of Isaiah can be explained.[11] It is out of the scope of this chapter to deal with the intricacies of the entire debate. A few comments will suffice. Young appeals

to the mysterious character of prophecy and distinguishes the direct prediction of Isaiah 7:14 (which is directly fulfilled in Christ's virgin birth)
from the following verses which appear to localize the prophecy's fulfillment to Isaiah's time.[12] Many conservative interpreters prefer to see a
near and far fulfillment usually expressed in terms of typology.[13] The
localized account of a child becomes a type of the Christ child to come in
the future, and a legitimate expansion of the language allows for a miraculous virgin birth. Regardless of how one views the fulfillment, there
appears to be adequate reason to see the Isaiah passage as opening up the
world of supernatural prediction at some level. This can only enhance
one's understanding of the character of the book itself.

A Sampling of Alleged Discrepancies in the Book of Isaiah

Critics have suggested several discrepancies in the Book of Isaiah. Many
times a shallow reading of the text creates the alleged contradiction. For
example, the Bible says in Isaiah 1:11 that God does not desire sacrifices
and burnt offerings. This supposedly contradicts many passages such as
Leviticus 1:9 where the Lord *does* desire sacrifices and offerings. After all,
they are commanded throughout the Old Testament. Could the writer of
the Book of Isaiah miss such a clear point and plainly contradict it? The
answer is given in the context. The issue is not whether God desires a
sacrifice but whether the worshiper brings a *meaningful* sacrifice. Verse 13
commanded, "Stop bringing meaningless offerings!" (NIV) As one writer
notes concerning Isaiah's statements in this section, "He [Isaiah] merely
expresses the great additional truth that sacrificial worship, if not pro-
ceeding from a believing heart, is offensive in His (God's) sight."[14]

A second example of a supposed discrepancy is the declaration of the
coming Messiah as the Prince of Peace from Isaiah 9:6. This appears to be
at odds with Jesus' warning in Matthew 10:34: "Do not think that I came
to bring peace on the earth; I did not come to bring peace, but a sword."
In what way, then, can Isaiah call Jesus the Prince of Peace? It is important to note that in the Gospel account Jesus warned that families would
be divided because of Him. He was not speaking of war in the conven-
tional sense but a lack of harmony. This may have suggested the trouble
that believers, especially the disciples, were to endure.[15] However, the
interpreter can also point out that the Isaiah passage is dealing with the
coming eschatological age associated with the second coming of Christ.[16]
Isaiah 9:7 predicts the future time of peace during the Messiah's government or coming kingdom. The Matthew passage is dealing with the first
advent, so there is no contradiction.

The final and perhaps most significant area to discuss is the statement by Yahweh in Isaiah 45:7, "I make peace, and create evil" (KJV). If evil is taken in a moral sense, then there is a theological contradiction between this passage and the many passages that affirm God's holiness, and His separateness from sin. The Hebrew word for *evil* is *ra'*, which is the general word for evil in a moral context throughout the Old Testament. Young takes the word to mean precisely that in this passage but tries to assert on the basis of systematic theology that this is an example of a great mystery (like the sovereignty of God versus human responsibility) that humans cannot harmonize completely.[17] Thus, it is a divine paradox and not actually a theological contradiction. A better way to approach the question may be to understand that the word in context can easily mean "disaster" (NIV) or "calamity" (NASB, NKJV) which refers to the coming of judgment. G. W. Grogan comments: "So the God who created the darkness that is not itself evil—though it is sometimes used to symbolize it—and who brings disaster as a punishment for sin, is supreme over all."[18] One should view God as the Lord over life who puts structure to human actions rather than as the author of sin.[19]

Other Biblical References to Isaiah

References to the name *Isaiah* in the Old Testament outside of the book itself are confined to the historical books of 2 Kings and 2 Chronicles. In all these cases, Isaiah was the person in view. He was referred to as the son of Amoz at least six times (2 Kgs. 19:2, 20; 20:1; 2 Chr. 26:22; 32:20, 32). He was called a prophet at least four times in these historical works (2 Kgs. 19:2; 20:14; 2 Chr. 26:22; 32:32). In addition, he *acted* like a prophet. He pronounced "thus says the LORD" to the fearful people (2 Kgs. 19:6). On another occasion, the text says, "The word of the LORD came to him, saying" (2 Kgs. 20:4). Isaiah made the rather brash presumption that the Lord would give Hezekiah a sign by moving the shadows backwards in a miraculous show of power (2 Kgs. 20:9). King Hezekiah even recognized that Isaiah's words were God's words when he announced, "the word of the LORD which you have spoken is good" (2 Kgs. 20:19).

Perhaps the most enlightening Old Testament verses for our purposes are 2 Chronicles 26:22 and 32:32. In both these passages, Isaiah was called a writer, not just a speaker. In 26:22 Isaiah was simply the chronicler of all of the acts of the king. In 32:32 the text reveals, "The rest of the acts of Hezekiah and his deeds of devotion, behold, they are written in the vision of Isaiah the prophet, the son of Amoz, in the Book of the Kings of Judah and Israel." Again, Isaiah was a writer who recorded his vision or message from God. This is also compared to the other chronicles found in the Book of the Kings of Judah and Israel, which related to the information found in 1 and 2 Kings and 1 and 2 Chronicles. Thus, the non-Isaiah Old Testament references to the name *Isaiah* also demonstrated an awareness of his writings, which were taken as prophetic writings within the orbit of the canon. The attitudes of the average Jew would be to accept them at face value.

The New Testament referred to the name *Isaiah* at least twenty-two times in the Gospels, Acts, and Romans.[20] In every case, it was the Old Testament Book of Isaiah that was in mind, although most of the time the language of Isaiah "speaking" was used to introduce that book. In addition, Isaiah was almost always introduced as the "prophet" and assumed to be the author of the book that bears his name. All four Gospels quoted from Isaiah in general and cited in particular the quotation from Isaiah 40:3 while identifying John the Baptist as the fulfillment of the prophecy about the one preparing the way (Matt. 3:3; Mark 1:2; Luke 3:4; John 1:23).

Beyond these facts, three specific New Testament examples stand out. First, the consequential passage found in Luke 4:17–21 showed the attitude of Jesus Christ to the scroll of Isaiah. Jesus was handed the scroll of Isaiah (4:17) who was called a prophet. Verses 18–19 quote from Isaiah 61:1–2, "The Spirit of the LORD is upon Me, because He anointed Me to preach the gospel to the poor." What is fascinating was Christ's comment when he finished reading. He remarked, "Today this Scripture has been fulfilled in your hearing" (Luke 4:21). By the term *Scripture*, Jesus declared that the scroll of Isaiah was a divine document. Furthermore, this document made predictions about the future that came true. Jesus saw the fulfillment of one of the passages in Himself on that occasion. For those who accept the authority of Christ, this is a conclusive use of Isaiah. It is especially noteworthy that the passage in Isaiah came from the so-called Deutero-Isaiah or second part of Isaiah (chaps. 40—66) whose genuineness has often been challenged.[21]

A second example demonstrates the understanding of the nature of Isaiah as understood in the Book of Acts. In the story of Philip witnessing to the searching Ethiopian eunuch (8:26–40), the eunuch sat in his chariot as he read from the Book of Isaiah (v. 28). He was reading Isaiah 53:7–8, which was referred to as "the passage of Scripture" (v. 32). Philip assisted him in his understanding by beginning at "this Scripture" (v. 35) with his explanation that Jesus was the Messiah the eunuch had been reading about. The implication of this wording is the acceptance by Luke, the author of Acts (and by the eunuch and Philip) of the truth of Isaiah as part of a supernatural Bible that predicted the future, whose fulfillment can be measured in Jesus Christ. With respect to this passage's use of Isaiah, F. F. Bruce makes the intriguing comment that

> There is no evidence that between the time of the prophet and the time of Christ anyone had identified the Suffering Servant of Isaiah 53 with the Davidic Messiah of Isaiah 11 or with the "one like unto a son of man" of Daniel 7:13. But Jesus identified them and fulfills them in his own person and by His own act, thus confirming the identification.[22]

A third significant example is the standard Pauline affirmation of the divine origin of the Book of Isaiah. This is especially clear in Romans. Paul quoted from Isaiah 10:22 (Rom. 9:27) and from Isaiah 1:9 (Rom. 9:29) while indicating that these were the words of Isaiah ("Isaiah cries out"; "as Isaiah foretold"). These two quotes are part of a string of Old Testament references in the chapter. The previous quote is from Hosea and is prefaced with the words, "As He says also in Hosea" (Rom. 9:25). The "He" is God (see vv. 23–24). Consequently, Paul's thought was that Isaiah's words were God's words. In the next chapter, Paul introduced Isaiah 28:16 as Scripture (Rom. 10:11) and prefaced Isaiah 52:7 with the formulaic words "as it is written" (Rom. 10:15). Later in the chapter, Paul put Isaiah in the same company with Moses. Moses says (Rom. 10:19), but Isaiah "is very bold and says" (Rom. 10:20). The end result of this survey of Paul's use of Isaiah shows that he had an extremely high view of the written words of the book and considered it of divine origin.

The Books of Jeremiah and Lamentations[23]

The discussion below will give a brief overview of the witness of the Book of Jeremiah to itself, a condensed statement about fulfilled prophecy in the book, a review of two alleged discrepancies found in Jeremiah, and a survey of the attitudes of other biblical authors to Jeremiah.

Self-Attestation of the Books of Jeremiah and Lamentations

In the Book of Jeremiah, a pattern is set which will be seen again in Ezekiel. The name *Jeremiah* occurred 131 times. The phrase, "The word of the LORD came to me [or to Jeremiah]" occurred twenty-one times (e.g., 1:2, 4; 13:3; 18:5; 35:12). The introductory formula, "Thus says the LORD," occurred 150 times. The word *oracle* (like Isaiah) was used nine times to emphasize the divine origin of Jeremiah's words. In addition, there were variations on all the above phrases. Eight times Jeremiah was said to be "prophesying," and the word *prophesy* was used fourteen times. In a practical way, the entire book was covered with these terms of self-attestation, which show its internal witness to its divine origin.

Fulfilled Prophecies in the Books of Jeremiah and Lamentations

The most famous fulfilled prophecy in Jeremiah was the prediction that the Babylonians would take Judah captive for seventy years (Jer. 25:11; cf. Dan. 9:2). That Jeremiah could predict the future was clearly shown by all the detailed oracles he gave concerning the detailed history of his time.

> The times of Jeremiah are among the most important in Old Testament history; thus details are essential. Because of their great significance, they are the best-documented times in all of Israel's history. The Book of Jeremiah is so filled with historical, biographical, and autobiographical material that his life can be synchronized with dates and known events to a degree unparalleled in the writings of the other prophets.[24]

Consequently, the book shows such an awareness of the historical times it proclaimed to be part of, it is virtually impossible to relegate its composition to a time after the events. Predictions such as the seventy years of captivity and others throughout the book add to the supernatural understanding of its writings. This enhances the ideas of inspiration and inerrancy for the Book of Jeremiah.

A Sampling of Alleged Discrepancies in Jeremiah and Lamentations

One alleged discrepancy in the Book of Jeremiah is found in Jeremiah 36:30. Jehoiakim, due to his sin of rejecting the prophecies of Jeremiah (even burning the scroll with them on it), was judged by the declaration that he would not have a son to sit on the throne of David. This, on the surface, seems to contradict the historical records (e.g., 2 Chr. 36:8–9), which show that his son Jehoiachin took his place as king. Archer remarks that the point of the Jeremiah passage "was that he (Jehoiakim) would have no dynasty to succeed him."[25] In the historical account, his son Jehoiachin was only in charge of Jerusalem for three months during the siege of the Babylonians. After the Babylonians took the city, Jehoiachin was removed and none of his descendants ever had kingship status in specific fulfillment of the prophecy of Jeremiah.[26]

A second supposed disparity in the biblical record of Jeremiah is God's statement given in Jeremiah 7:22–23: "For I did not speak to your fathers, or command them in the day that I brought them out of the land of Egypt, concerning burnt offerings and sacrifices. But this is what I commanded them, saying, Obey My voice, and I will be your God, and you will be My people." On the face of it, some have seen a contradiction between this and the Exodus account. As Archer notes, "Liberal scholars invariably point to the Jeremiah passage as proving that the sacrificial regulations of the Mosaic Code were unknown in the seventh century B.C. as having any sanction from God or from Moses himself."[27] However, there is no contradiction whatever. The Jeremiah passage precisely echoes Exodus 19:5 and illustrates the spirit with which sacrifices should be undertaken (see the discussion of Isa. 1:11 above). Archer correctly concludes: "It should be carefully observed that the whole thrust of Jeremiah 7 is to the effect that for sacrificial worship to be acceptable to God, worshipers must come to the altar with yielded and believing hearts, with a sincere purpose to do God's will."[28]

Other Biblical References to the Books of Jeremiah and Lamentations

The name *Jeremiah* occurred sixteen times in the Old Testament outside the Book of Jeremiah. About ten of those times, Jeremiah was just a name in a list or references to someone else with that name. The other six times are revealing in how Jeremiah is pictured. In 2 Chronicles 35:25, he chanted a lament at the death of Josiah. In 2 Chronicles 36:12, the young king Zedekiah "did not humble himself before Jeremiah the prophet who spoke for the LORD." The author implied that Jeremiah should be respected and listened to because his words came from God. A similar attitude was shown in the two passages 2 Chronicles 36:21–22 and Ezra 1:1. Three times in these passages the text used the words "to fulfill" or "in order to fulfill the word of the LORD by the mouth of Jeremiah." The teaching in view was the length of the captivity so the land could rest and the proclamation by Cyrus to permit a return to the land and the building of the Jewish temple.

Perhaps one of the most significant uses of Jeremiah is found in Daniel 9:2. During the Babylonian captivity, Daniel discovered the length of the captivity based on Jeremiah's prophecy (given in Jer. 25:11). The text says that Daniel observed in the "books" or scrolls and asserted that revelation was given as "the word of the LORD to Jeremiah the prophet." In this way, Daniel confirmed that the words of Jeremiah were the words of the Lord. Consequently, the passages in the Old

Testament outside of Jeremiah that spoke of him lead one to conclude that those writers had a high view of Jeremiah's written prophecies and considered them true in every respect.

In the New Testament, two passages in Matthew quoted from Jeremiah. Both introduced the citation similarly, that the prophecy "spoken through Jeremiah the prophet was fulfilled." In the first passage, there appeared to be analogous fulfillment in the weeping of Rachel over the death of the children in Bethlehem (Matt. 2:17; cf. Jer. 3:15). The second passage, however, showed direct fulfillment as Judas betrayed Jesus for thirty pieces of silver but had a conflated citation using Zechariah (Matt. 27:9; cf. Jer. 19:1–13; Zech. 11:12–13).[29] A final passage in Matthew (16:14) reveals the high regard the Jews held for Jeremiah as a prophet. He along with Elijah and John the Baptist were viewed as possible identifications for Jesus. Finally, the writer to the Hebrews quoted from the new covenant passage in Jeremiah 31:31–34 (Heb. 8:8–12; 10:16–17) in his argument to show that Jesus was superior to the old covenant, since it had been replaced.

The Book of Ezekiel

The review below will begin with the Book of Ezekiel's self-understanding, continue with a discussion of fulfilled prophecies given in the book, proceed with a review of one alleged discrepancy often cited in the book, and finish with an extremely brief overview of the use of Ezekiel in other parts of the Bible. On this last score, it must be admitted that there is little material.

Self-Attestation of the Book of Ezekiel

The phrase "thus says the LORD" occurred in the Book of Ezekiel 126 times. In this way the book highlighted the belief that these words were from God. Nearly the entire book of Ezekiel was introduced in this fashion. The verb *prophesy* was used thirty-one times, most often in the context of a command from God to Ezekiel (e.g., Ezek. 4:7; 6:2; 11:4). The phrase, "The word of the LORD came to me" was used forty-six times (e.g., Ezek. 21:18; 28:20; 29:1; 30:1; 34:1). This phrase is reminiscent of the oracles of Isaiah since it frequently introduced a specific section, giving a future prophecy of judgment against certain cities or peoples.

Since Ezekiel just recounted the words that God gave, the Book of Ezekiel testifies to its divine origin. The Spirit of Yahweh was mentioned two times as the agent producing the vision. In 11:5, the Spirit of the

Lord fell on Ezekiel so he could give the words of God. In 37:1, the Spirit actually transported Ezekiel in his vision to the valley of dry bones so he could witness what God wanted him to see and record. The summary of this induction from the text leads to the testimony that Ezekiel believed that the words he recorded in the book came from a divine, supernatural source. This internal evidence reinforced the conclusion of inerrancy.

Fulfilled Prophecies in the Book of Ezekiel

Most of the key prophecies in the Book of Ezekiel are yet to be fulfilled, according to evangelical premillennialists. These include the battle of Gog and Magog from Ezekiel 38—39, the millennial predictions, the building of a Jewish temple, and the parceling out of the land in fulfillment of God's previous promises to the nation of Israel (Ezek. 40—48). There is also the question of whether the formation of the modern state of Israel beginning in 1948 is a fulfillment of the coming to life of the nation cited in Ezekiel 37. In addition, debate exists over the promises of a spiritual renewal of the Jews (Ezek. 36) and whether this finds any fulfillment in the church today.[30]

However, one clear example of past fulfillment, not without its controversies, is Ezekiel's prediction that the city of Tyre would be completely destroyed (Ezek. 26:1–21). Ezekiel gave a number of dire predictions that began with Nebuchadnezzar's siege of the mainland part of Tyre (v. 7ff). It was not until two centuries later under Alexander the Great that the taking of the island part of the city fulfilled verses 13–14. Archer comments:

> History tells us that after Alexander's naval forces proved incapable of storming the island (due to the determined resistance of the superior Tyrian fleet), he resorted to an ambitious engineering effort, consisting of a mile-long mole built out from shore to the east wall of the island. In order to get material for this causeway, the Greek invaders used every movable piece of rock or stone to cast into the sea, until after several months of strenuous endeavor the wall was reached, broken through, and the city sacked. Exasperated by the long delay in his invasion schedule, Alexander resolved to make a fearsome example of Tyre; so he had the island city totally destroyed so that it should never be rebuilt (v. 14).[31]

In this way, Ezekiel's prophecy demonstrated supernatural ability to predict the future, a trait that once again reinforces the doctrines of inspiration and inerrancy.

A Sampling of Alleged Discrepancies in the Book of Ezekiel

One example of a supposed problem in the Book of Ezekiel begins with the statement in 18:20: "The person who sins will die. The son will not bear the punishment for the father's iniquity, nor will the father bear the punishment for the son's iniquity; the righteousness of the righteous will be upon himself, and the wickedness of the wicked will be upon himself." This rather individualistic emphasis is seen to be at odds with the corporate sense of sin taught elsewhere in the Bible. For example, why do some Bible characters pray for forgiveness of the sins of others as if they were responsible (Dan. 9)? This concept seems related to the Hebrew idea of extended personality.[32] More striking is the statement from the Ten Commandments associated with the command to avoid idolatry: "You shall not worship them or serve them; for I, the LORD your God, am a jealous God, visiting the iniquity of the fathers on the children, on the third and the fourth generations of those who hate me; but showing lovingkindness to thousands, to those who love Me and keep My commandments" (Ex. 20:5–6). These passages do not seem, on the surface at least, to be compatible.

However, one must not perform a mere casual reading of the text. The Exodus passage cited a general principle without specifying how descendants would bear the iniquity of their fathers. It also did not address the possibility or the impossibility of a son breaking the sequence by a righteous response to God. Keil remarks that "the words neither affirm that sinning fathers remain unpunished, nor that the sins of fathers are punished in their children and grandchildren without any fault of their own."[33] The Ezekiel passage was more specific. It dealt in context with the situation of a young son who saw the sins of his father and refused to repeat them (Ezek. 18:14–20). The son's rewards were his own, which was also true of the father's punishments. There really is no contradiction. The Ezekiel account in the progress of revelation simply added more details to how the general principle of Exodus 20:5–6 might be worked out in real life.

Other Biblical References to Ezekiel

No specific references to Ezekiel the prophet occurred outside the book itself. Allusions to various events or imagery can be found. In 2 Corinthians 6:16, the apostle Paul appeared to quote from Ezekiel 37:27 when he taught the Corinthians, "I will dwell in them and walk among them; and I will be their God, and they shall be My people." It is true that similar statements occurred elsewhere in Scripture (Ex. 29:45; Lev. 26:12). However, Paul's quote most completely followed the verse from Ezekiel. The introduction of this verse from Ezekiel with the words "just as God said" demonstrates Paul's belief that the Book of Ezekiel had been supernaturally given by God. Ezekiel's words are in fact God's words.[34]

A second example can be found in Revelation 6:8. The account of the fourth seal that will be unleashed on earth revealed a "pale" horse (KJV) on which sat Death and Hades. The statement follows that "authority was given to them over a fourth of the earth, to kill with sword and with famine and with pestilence and by the wild beasts of the earth." This language comes from Ezekiel 5:12, 17 and 14:21. The section from Revelation serves as a kind of fulfillment of at least the latter passage from Ezekiel.[35]

The Book of Daniel

Perhaps no other book in the Bible other than Genesis has been criticized more than the Book of Daniel. The reason for such carping is that the precise prophecies in the book challenge the presuppositions of anti-supernaturalists. Daniel's prophecies were not vague for they gave historical detail that can be verified. If it can be shown that the book was written before the fulfillment of many of the prophecies, then belief in the supernatural character of the book is bolstered. It would be a small step, in that case, to affirm the inerrancy of the text of Daniel. As Merrill notes,

> One of the most ancient and potent weapons in the armory of biblical polemics is that of fulfilled prophecy. If it can be demonstrated conclusively that a biblical prediction has come to pass in the time and manner intended by its author, such a correspondence carries ipso facto evidence of something beyond natural happenstance; indeed, it is an argument for Divine revelation, inspiration, and inerrancy.[36]

The book was generally written over a seventy-year period in the sixth century B.C. and contains historical material and prophecies dating from the time of Nebuchadnezzar's first victory over Jerusalem in 605 B.C. until the third year of Cyrus the Persian king in 535 B.C. The discussion of the book below will follow several tracks including the dating of the book, the past fulfillment of prophecies, and the authority of Christ.[37]

Prophecy and the Date of the Book of Daniel

Scholars have given two main opinions as to the date of the Book of Daniel. The first is the traditional view that sees Daniel as written during the sixth century B.C., most likely by Daniel himself as an eyewitness of historical events and seer of the prophecies pronounced. The second view is called the Maccabean thesis, which claims that the Book of Daniel was written in the second century B.C., most likely by a Hasidic Jew. This would place a number of the prophecies after the fact rather than as predictive oracles. In the process of deciding which view is correct, one cannot underestimate the influence of one's presuppositions about supernaturalism. The conservative Miller comments:

> For almost 1,800 years the traditional view went virtually unchallenged within both Judaism and Christianity. Porphyry (c. A.D. 232–303) was an exception. Eissfeldt explains: "The Neo-Platonist Porphyry . . . in the twelfth book of his polemical work 'Against the Christians' indicated the second century B.C. as the actual date of the book's composition and described the greater part of its 'prophecies' as *vaticinia ex eventu*," that is, prophecies or predictions made after the event. His polemic "Against the Christians" has been lost, but its argument is preserved in Jerome's commentary on Daniel. Porphyry reasoned "from the *a priori* assumption that there could be no predictive element in prophecy." According to Jerome, Porphyry "claims that the person who composed the book under the name of Daniel made it all up in order to revive the hopes of his countrymen. Not that he was able to foreknow all of future history, but rather he records events that had already taken place.
>
> The church condemned Porphyry's work, and B. Croke relates, "The ultimate condemnation of the notorious Arian heretics was for them to be officially referred to as 'Porphyrians.'" In spite of its origins, the Maccabean thesis has become popular today.[38]

Although it is necessary to avoid a kind of historical-root fallacy argument (the late date is wrong simply because enemies of Christianity originated it long ago), believers should note the origin of the view and place the modern historical debate in proper perspective. At least, this information forces one to reexamine presuppositions that are held. Neither the faith of the faithful nor the rationalism of unbelievers validates or falsifies the various positions. Miller further summarizes the issue:

One's overall view of Scripture generally and prophecy in particular will dramatically affect the decision concerning the late date of the book. Porphyry denied predictive prophecy, and so for him it was not possible for a Daniel of the sixth century B.C. to have written events four hundred years later in the Maccabean period. Those concurring with Porphyry's antisupernatural presuppositions will of course accept the Maccabean thesis. Some scholars who support the late date while not rejecting the possibility of miraculous prediction nevertheless argue, "It is not the nature of biblical prophecy to give a literal account of events before they take place."[39]

Which presupposition does the evidence warrant? There are several significant indications that the early date for Daniel is correct.

There is the surprising lack of any mention of the main figures of the Maccabean period (e.g., Judas Maccabeus). This would be unlikely for a writer who is writing after the Jewish victory.[40]

Persian words in Daniel (which mostly give government terms) fit the time of the sixth century B.C. better than the second century B.C.[41]

Greek loan words are scarce in the Aramaic portions of Daniel. In fact, only three can be found,[42] and one of the three goes back to the time of Homer.[43] This sparse number would be highly unlikely if the book had been written during the Greek period.

The Aramaic of Daniel (2:4—7:28) has more affinities with sixth century B.C. Aramaic than with second century B.C. Aramaic.[44]

The Hebrew of Daniel fits the Hebrew style of Ezekiel more than the later Qumran texts.[45]

First Maccabees cites history from the Book of Daniel in such a way as to indicate that it occurred in the distant past.[46] Since this apocryphal book is considered relatively good historical material by liberals and conservatives (in spite of its noncanonical status), a late date for Daniel would entail a major criticism of one of the mainstay historical works for the Maccabean period.

The presence of Daniel in the Septuagint makes it difficult to hold to the late date since more time may have been necessary for the book to circulate and be recognized as canonical by the Jewish community. As one author noted, traditions take time to develop.[47] In addition, the Septuagint translation shows evidence that the translators did not have access to the meanings of some Persian words. This would be a strange occurrence if the translators were translating a relatively recent document.[48]

The circulation problem for the Book of Daniel, which is cited above for the Septuagint, can be repeated for the collection of canonical books at Qumran. In fact, Daniel's circulation and inclusion in the canon would have occurred within fifty years of the original writing if the late date is held. Such an occurrence is a possible but unlikely event.[49] The fact that the Qumran community may not represent mainstream Judaism complicates the discussion of this problem for those who hold a late date. Walvoord made the interesting observation almost thirty years ago, "Strangely, liberal critics have been slow to publish and comment upon the Qumran fragments of Daniel which seem to indicate a pre-Maccabean authorship."[50]

Whitcomb summarizes some problems with the late date theory in the following way:

> Jews living in the inter-testamental period, especially in Palestine, would never have accepted as canonical a book "hot off the press" that claimed to be over 350 years old and that was supposedly filled with historical blunders. Jewish scholars of that period had access to numerous historical records of the Neo-Babylonian, Medo-Persian, and Hellenistic periods (e.g., the writings of Herodotus, Ctesias, Xenophon, Megasthenes, Berossus, Alexander Polyhistor, Polybius, Diodorus Siculus, and at least thirty other historians referred to by Josephus, most of whose books are now lost to us). Even more important, inter-testamental Jews were keenly aware of the identity and boundary lines of their own sacred canon of Scripture and thus did not hesitate to exclude from their canon such books as Tobit, Judith, and even First Maccabees. Would Jews who were dying for their God-given faith and their God-given Scriptures have looked for encouragement to fictional characters and events in a pseudograph?[51]

The Past Fulfillment of Prophecies

Perhaps the most incredible prophecy in the entire Bible is the prophecy of Daniel's seventy weeks (9:24–27). While futurist premillennialists see the seventieth week as still to be fulfilled in the coming seven-year tribulation period, there is general agreement that the first sixty-nine weeks (weeks of seven years) found fulfillment in the first advent. Sir Robert Anderson formulated in detail the mathematical calculations.[52] Daniel's prophecy gives as a starting point the going forth to rebuild Jerusalem. It also gives as an ending point "Messiah the prince." Anderson used the date of March 14, 445 B.C. as the beginning point based on a tedious study of the chronological options given in the Bible. Then using the Jewish reckoning for 360–day years (lunar years) and making the appropriate calculations, he saw that the sixty-nine weeks of years would take 173,880 days.

According to Anderson's studies, this takes the prophecy up to the triumphal entry on April 6, 32 A.D. Although not every evangelical is going to accept this exact chronology, it is fascinating that the prophecy is in the ballpark for the ministry of Christ in His first coming. With our own lack of certainty of calendars and chronology, we could never disprove the general aim of the prophecy. Furthermore, in light of these very particular calculations, the detailed fulfillment of the prophecy is more than likely.

A second area of fulfillment seen in Daniel is especially troublesome to those who reject inerrancy. The prophecies in Daniel 2 and 7 both described the four world kingdoms in relation to Israel that outline biblical and world history. These prophecies were given, of course, during the Babylonian captivity. In chapter 2, the four world kingdoms were seen through the image of a statue. Chapter 7 reviewed the same predicted history with an image of an animal for each kingdom. This flow of history occurred so precisely as laid out that antisupernaturalists must date the text after the fact. The table below shows the kingdoms:

Kingdoms	*DANIEL 2—Statue*	*DANIEL 7—Animals*
Babylon	*Head of gold*	*Lion with wings of an eagle*
Medo-Persia	*Chest and arms of silver*	*Bear*
Greece	*Belly and thighs of bronze*	*Leopard with four wings and four heads*
Rome	*Legs of iron; feet of iron and clay*	*Dreadful beast with large iron teeth*

Other details could be pointed out as well. Chapter 8 and its prediction of Antiochus Epiphanes gives details corroborated in later history related to the Maccabean period. Chapter 11 predicts details from the Persian period down through the Greek period. Any standard commentary on Daniel can show the correlation. In the end, if the early date for Daniel is correct, the book supernaturally predicts detailed historical accounts. This leads easily to the conclusion that the book was supernaturally inspired and inerrant in its presentation.

Other Biblical References to Daniel

From a conservative point of view, the fact that the name *Daniel* is used for two sons among postexilic Jews (Ezra 8:2; Neh. 10:6) may point to the hero status of Daniel among them.[53] It certainly does nothing to detract from the Book of Daniel as a genuine exilic work. In addition, the references to Daniel in the exilic Book of Ezekiel provide insight into the heroic standing of Daniel when he is listed with Noah and Job (Ezek. 14:14, 20).

Ezekiel 28:3 furthermore highlights the king of Tyre's prideful attempt to know more than Daniel. These references from Ezra, Nehemiah, and Ezekiel speak more of the person of Daniel rather than the writing that bears his name. One could easily question, however, how the high reverence that is seen could exist apart from an exilic belief in the legitimacy of the historical events, including the supernatural revelatory abilities of Daniel, which are recorded in the book.

The Authority of Christ

Most disturbing of all for the genuine evangelical is the critic's discounting of the prophecies in the Book of Daniel in spite of the teachings of Jesus Christ on the matter. The Olivet Discourse gives the words of Jesus that appeal to Daniel 9 as prophetically accurate:

> Therefore when you shall see the abomination of desolation which was spoken of through Daniel the prophet, standing in the holy place (let the reader understand), then those who are in Judea must flee to the mountains. Whoever is on the housetop must not come down to get the things out that are in his house. Whoever is in the field must not turn back to get his cloak. But woe to those who are pregnant and to those who are nursing babies in those days! But pray that your flight will not be in the winter, or on a Sabbath. For then there will be a great tribulation, such as has not occurred since the beginning of the world until now, nor ever will. (Matt. 24:15–21; cf. Mark 13)

In this section, Jesus emphasized several things: 1) Daniel was a genuine prophet whose words should be heeded; 2) the Book of Daniel was a Jewish canonical writing which should be read and understood; 3) the abomination of desolation from Daniel 9:27 and 12:11 is a future event that will happen just like the Book of Daniel outlines; 4) a time of horrible tribulation will occur (v. 21), which is described in the language of Daniel 12:1.

The fact that Jesus viewed these events from the Book of Daniel as pointing to the future precludes any belief in the Maccabean thesis, which sees all the events (such as the abomination of desolation) as fulfilled in the time of Antiochus Epiphanes in the second century B.C. In other words, Jesus accepted the Book of Daniel as true at face value. Therefore, if a critic denies the inerrancy of the Book of Daniel, he is simultaneously denying the teaching of Christ. In this way, the inerrancy of Daniel, including its prophetic portions, is wrapped up with a denial of the Gospel accounts and the authority of Christ.[54]

The Supernatural Character of the Books

The discussions above only serve to highlight some issues involved in the inerrancy debate in the Major Prophets and are certainly not exhaustive. However, each book of the Major Prophets was shown to possess internal evidence that reinforced the idea of inspiration and inerrancy. In most cases, each book's self-understanding was that of divine origin.[55] Furthermore, other books in the collection of the canon supported that testimony concerning the book. The special cases of past-fulfilled prophecy throughout may be the strongest evidence of the supernatural nature of the books.

In the case of Daniel, the evidence is so precise and correct historically that the dating of the book becomes the most important issue to discuss. Finally, the fact that rational explanations exist for the cited samples of alleged discrepancies help to show that the books are in harmony with themselves, with the rest of Scripture, and with reality. In the end, there is no adequate reason to reject the inspiration and inerrancy of the Major Prophets. The one True and Living God has given them to us.

FOR DISCUSSION

1. How strong is the evidence for the inspiration and inerrancy of the Book of Isaiah?

2. Why is Isaiah an important book concerning the person of Christ?

3. Internally in the Old Testament, is Isaiah well attested as a major book of prophecy?

4. How are the prophecies of Isaiah quoted in the New Testament?

5. Why is the Book of Daniel important to the overall message of the entire Bible?

6. Why are Daniel 2 and Daniel 7 important to the prophetic unfolding of Scripture?

For Further Study

Apologetics

Machen, J. Gresham. *The Virgin Birth of Christ*. Grand Rapids: Baker, 1930.

Bibliology Texts

Archer, Gleason L. "Alleged Errors and Discrepancies in the Original Manuscripts of the Bible." In *Inerrancy*, edited by Norman L. Geisler. Grand Rapids: Zondervan, 1980.

Archer, Gleason L. *Encyclopedia of Bible Difficulties*. Grand Rapids: Zondervan, 1982.

Arndt, W. *Does the Bible Contradict Itself?* Reprint. St. Louis: Concordia, 1955.

Helm, Paul. "Faith, Evidence, and the Scriptures." In *Scripture and Truth*, edited by D. A. Carson and John D. Woodbridge. Grand Rapids: Zondervan, 1983.

Wenham, John. "Christ's View of Scripture." In *Inerrancy*, edited by Norman Geisler. Grand Rapids: Zondervan, 1980.

Commentaries

Bruce, F. F. *The Book of Acts*. Vol. 5 of *The New International Commentary on the New Testament*. Grand Rapids: Eerdmans, 1977.

Bultema, Harry. *Commentary on Daniel*. Grand Rapids: Kregel, 1988.

Delitzsch, F. and C. F. Keil. Vol. 1 of *Commentary on the Old Testament*. Reprint. Grand Rapids: Eerdmans, 1980.

Feinberg, Charles. "Jeremiah" in *The Expositor's Bible Commentary, Volume 6: Isaiah-Ezekiel*. Edited by Frank E. Gaebelein. Grand Rapids: Zondervan, 1986.

————. "Lamentations" in *The Expositor's Bible Commentary, Volume 6: Isaiah-Ezekiel*. Edited by Frank E. Gaebelein. Grand Rapids: Zondervan, 1986.

Goldingay J. E. *Daniel*. Vol. 30 of the *Word Biblical Commentary*. Dallas: Word, 1989.

Grogan, G. W. "Isaiah" in *The Expositor's Bible Commentary, Volume 6: Isaiah-Ezekiel*. Edited by Frank E. Gaebelein. Grand Rapids: Zondervan, 1986.

Leupold, H. C. *Exposition of Isaiah*. 2 vols. Reprint. Grand Rapids: Baker, 1971.

Martin, John A. "Isaiah." In *The Bible Knowledge Commentary: Old Testament*. Edited by John F. Walvoord and Roy B. Zuck. Wheaton, Ill.: Victor Books, 1985.

Miller, Stephen R. *Daniel*. Vol. 18 of *the New American Commentary*. Nashville: Broadman and Holman, 1994.

Walvoord, John F. *Daniel: The Key to Prophetic Revelation*. Chicago: Moody, 1971.

Whitcomb, John C. *Daniel*. From the *Everyman's Bible Commentary*. Chicago: Moody, 1985.

Young, Edward J. *The Book of Isaiah*. 3 vols. Reprint. Grand Rapids: Eerdmans, 1996.

Related Articles

Merrill, Eugene. "Internal Evidence for the Inerrancy of the Pentateuch." *The Conservative Theological Journal*, June 1998.

Willis, John T. "The Meaning of Isaiah 7:14 and Its Application in Matthew 1:23." *Restoration Quarterly* 21, 1978.

Prophecy

Anderson, Sir Robert. *The Coming Prince*. Reprint. Grand Rapids: Kregel, 1957.

Gaebelein, Arno C. "Fulfilled Prophecy a Potent Argument for the Bible." In *The Fundamentals*. Edited by R. A. Torrey. Reprint. Grand Rapids: Kregel, 1990.

Theology

Erickson, Millard. *God in Three Persons: A Contemporary Interpretation of the Trinity*. Grand Rapids: Baker, 1995.

Chapter Fourteen

Inerrancy of the Minor Prophets

*T*he second division of the Hebrew canon is called "The Twelve" or "The Book of The Twelve Prophets" or simply the "Minor Prophets." From the time of Augustine, the Latin church used the title "Minor Prophets" because of its brevity when comparing the "Major Prophets." "The order in the Hebrew Canon is apparently partly chronological but other now-unknown factors account for the final arrangement."[1]

The Book of Hosea

Hosea (Hebrew *hôshēaʻ*, "salvation"), a southern prophet, ministered from about the time of King Uzziah (767 B.C.) to the beginning of the reign of Hezekiah (711 B.C.). The Lord used the prophet to teach the nation about the unfaithfulness of Israel to her God. God instructed Hosea to marry a prostitute to illustrate spiritual unfaithfulness. Because of this unusual event, some have felt the book was without inspiration. But Orthodox Judaism understands the dynamics of what was happening.

> God spoke to [Hosea] once and his task was clear. Even when bidden to marry Gomer, he understood; for there is no reason why this incident should not be interpreted literally. The unhappy experience that touched his personal life so intimately taught him in the most realistic manner to appreciate the disloyalty of Israel and the compassion of God.[2]

Many verses indicate the doctrine of the inspiration of Scripture: "The word of the LORD which came to Hosea" (1:1); "Then the LORD said to me" (3:1); "Listen to the word of the LORD, O sons of Israel"

211

(4:1); "Hear this, O priests! Give heed, O house of Israel! Listen, O house of the king!" (5:1). Because this is God's Word given through the prophet, it is truthful, must be obeyed, and is without error. The final verse in the book states this:

> Whoever is wise, let him understand these things; whoever is discerning, let him know them. For the ways of the LORD are right, and the righteous will walk in them (14:9).

Cohen rightly concludes:

> Hosea does not begin with words of rebuke and threat of retribution, but with the extraordinary command given him by God, which was to be symbolical of Israel's waywardness. The opening phrase (1:1) indicates that Hosea's message had Divine authority.[3]

The Book of Joel

Joel (Hebrew *yô'ēl*, "Yahweh is God") probably wrote and ministered during the reign of young King Joash (Jehoash) (835–796 B.C.). The child king took the throne when he was seven (2 Kgs. 11:21) and was placed under the regency of priests. The subject of the book is the day of the Lord, with many prophetic references that take us far into the future and the tribulation period. Joel comes to us with the stamp of the highest authority from the Lord Himself. The book was quoted often. The apostle Peter especially drew on its unequaled prophetic reliability when he quoted the book (chapter 2) before the crowd in Jerusalem (Acts 2). Cohen again notes: "The prophet came to the people with a mandate direct from God. His credentials lend authority to his message and demand that his words be treated seriously."[4]

Inspiration is attested throughout the book: "The word of the LORD that came to Joel" (1:1); "Hear this, O elders" (v. 2); "You will know that I am in the midst of Israel, and that I am the LORD your God" (2:27); "The LORD has spoken. ' Proclaim this among the nations'" (3:8–9); "You will know that I am the LORD your God" (v. 17).

Because much future prophecy is in the book, the writing automatically demands a hearing. And what is said must happen historically or the prophet and his message are placed in doubt. The writing ends with great hope for the restoration of the nation. Joel said, "Judah will be inhabited forever and Jerusalem for all generations" (3:20). The world and the Jews wait for this day.

The Book of Amos

Amos (Hebrew *'āmôs*, "burden") was one of the greatest personalities in biblical literature. He was a prophet with a lofty concept of the Lord. He pictured God defending the oppressed, coming against injustice, and setting forth right conduct. "The contents of the Book also reveal God's power in the course of human history, since everything is due to His omniscience, omnipresence, and omnipotence."[5]

Amos was not a professional prophet. He was a herdsman who was used of the Lord to prophecy around 760–755 B.C. during the reign of Uzziah king of Judah and Jeroboam king of Israel. He exposed the pagan worship of the people.

Many verses attest inspiration: "Thus says the LORD" is used throughout the book. The prophet followed with: "Declares the LORD" (2:16); "Hear this word which the LORD has spoken against you" (3:1); "Thus the Lord GOD showed me" is also used in the writing (7:1; 8:1). The book closes with a strong future prophetic message about the restoration of Israel: The Lord "will raise up the fallen booth [tent] of David" and "raise up its ruins" (9:11). Amos added these words from the Lord: "I will also plant them on their land, and they will not again be rooted out from their land which I have given them" (v. 15).

Again, with such a strong prophetic forecast, what was said must happen. These are the promises of God, not simply the thoughts of Amos.

The Book of Obadiah

Obadiah (Hebrew *'ōbadyāh*, "The servant of Jehovah") is the shortest prophecy and the smallest book in the Old Testament. Written probably around 848 B.C. during the reign of Jehoram, the southern king, the book denounced the people of Edom for their mistreatment of their own brothers of Judah. The writing held out for a final day of salvation for Judah in the ultimate day of the Lord.

Obadiah was extensively quoted by Amos and the prophet Jeremiah (49:7–22), who quoted almost all of Obadiah 1:1–6. This in itself shows how important the book was to later prophets who clearly viewed the book as inspired of the Lord.

At the very beginning, Obadiah showed his message was from Jehovah when he wrote: "The vision of Obadiah. ' Thus says the Lord GOD'" (v. 1). In verses that follow, the claim was further made: "I will make you [Edom] small among the nations" (v. 2); "declares the LORD" (v. 8); "For the LORD has spoken" (v. 18). The book was also quoted or alluded to in many other books of Scripture, including Revelation 11:15: "The kingdom of the world has become the kingdom of our Lord."

Though this prophecy is not long (twenty-one verses), it stands tall in the way it was quoted or indirectly referred to in many other prophecies. Its place in the canon as part of the Word of God is assured.

The Book of Jonah

Jonah (Hebrew *yônāh*, "Dove") is the story of the reluctant prophet whom the Lord used to speak to the pagan city of Nineveh. It was written probably during the time of Jeroboam II around 782–753 B.C. The book is extremely honest in how it reveals the prejudice of this Jewish prophet against an unbelieving city of Gentiles. All the way through the book, Jonah remained bitter. But the writing shows the incredible mercy of God toward a sinful nation. Why Nineveh was given a chance to repent was not revealed.

Though some have counted the story as myth because of Jonah being swallowed by a large fish, the narration stands in full view of what can certainly be accounted as true. All the data surrounding the story falls into the guidelines of a genuine happening. There is not a trace of what could be claimed as false.

> In addition, the period of Jonah coincides admirably with historical conditions at Nineveh. Under Semiramis, the queen regent and her son Adad-Niari III (810–782), there was an approach to monotheism under the god Nebo somewhat comparable to the earlier monotheistic reforms of Amenophis IV in Egypt. Either in the closing years of this reign or early in the reign of Assurdan III (771–754), Jonah appeared at Nineveh.[6]

Through Jonah the Lord could have been giving this people an opportunity to believe in the one true God rather than a fictional version that may have had some vestiges of truth but still did not represent the full nature of the Lord Himself. Jonah was mentioned in 2 Kings 14:25 as a prophet who lived in the reign of Jeroboam II. "If, then, the Book is history, the events recorded therein took place early in the eight century."[7]

Since the book is a narration, its style and internal evidence of inspiration is focused a little differently than the average prophetic writing. But the story has the evident marks of the Lord dealing specifically with the prophet, as Jonah himself told us what happened. He said, "The word of the LORD came to Jonah" (1:1); "The word of the LORD came to Jonah the second time" (3:1); "The LORD said" (4:4); "The Lord GOD appointed" (4:6); "God appointed" (4:6–8); "Then God said" (v. 9); "Then the LORD said" (v. 10).

The New Testament placed its stamp of approval on the book's inspiration and inerrancy or accuracy. Christ quoted the prophecy in Matthew 12:39–41 and Luke 11:30. The prophets Nahum and Zephaniah also mentioned the fact that Nineveh had an opportunity to hear the truth but turned from it. The city therefore was cursed (Nah. 1–3; Zeph. 2:13–15).

The Book of Micah

Micah (Hebrew *miykāh*, "Who is like Jehovah?") was active as a prophet around the time of King Jotham (740–735 B.C.), King Ahaz (735–715 B.C.), and King Hezekiah (715–687 B.C.). "Like Amos he was a simple villager and espoused the cause of the poor" that cried for social justice.[8] Micah is full of messianic and prophetic overtones. This prophet gave some of the most outstanding prophetic verses to us.

In Matthew the priests and scribes quoted 5:2 when they told Herod where the Messiah would be born (Matt. 2:5–6). Jesus quoted 7:6 when He commissioned the disciples (Matt. 10:35–36). Chapter 4 of Micah gives one of the most important descriptions in Scripture of the future millennial glory of the nation of Israel. And Micah 6:8 is one of the most quoted passages in the Old Testament: "What does the LORD require of you but to do justice, to love kindness, and to walk humbly with your God?"

Inspiration is assured by many passages: "Hear, O peoples, all of you; listen, O earth and all it contains, and let the Lord GOD be a witness against you" (1:2); "Thus says the LORD" (2:3); "Thus says the LORD concerning the prophets" (3:5); "'In that day,' declares the LORD" (4:6); "From you [Bethlehem] One will go forth for Me to be ruler in Israel" (5:2); "Declares the LORD" (5:10); "Answer Me" (6:3).

The Book of Nahum

Nahum (Hebrew *nahûm*, "comforter") was an Elkoshite of the town of Elkosh. His prophetic ministry was between 661–612 B.C. His one subject was the destruction of the city of Nineveh. C.H.H. Wright notes, "The descriptions given by Nahum [of the destruction of Nineveh] are exceedingly fine and vivid, and the book is deservedly classed among the finest productions of Old Testament literature."[9]

> [Nahum] came to his people with the Divine assurance that the dreaded specter of their mightiest foe will soon cease to stalk the

earth. It would be true to say that the Book contains no superfluous word, and that a noble and mighty passion suffuses all that the
prophet says. The vigor of his style and the realism of his prophecy
lift the Book out of the commonplace and set it on the topmost
rung of sublime literature.[10]

The prophet spoke for the Lord, who gave him "The oracle of
[about] Nineveh" (1:1). But he also said, "Thus says the LORD" (v. 12).
He told the people, "The LORD has issued a command concerning you"
(v. 14). God as well spoke directly and said: "I am against you
[Nineveh]" (2:13; 3:5). There is an allusion to 1:5–6 in Revelation
6:14–17. Nahum reads, "Mountains quake because of Him and the hills
dissolve; indeed the earth is upheaved by His presence. . . . Who can
endure the burning of His anger? His wrath is poured out like fire."

The loftiness of this prophecy and the fact that it was so clearly
quoted by John the apostle assures the inspiration and inerrancy of the
message.

The Book of Habakkuk

Habakkuk (Hebrew $h^a ba'qq\hat{u}q$, "to embrace") is one of the least known
prophets. Some hints give us a small picture of him. He was referred to
as the "choir director" (3:19), and in the apocryphal *Legend of Bel and the
Dragon,* he was said to be "the son of Jesus of the tribe of Levi." Scholars
have assumed he was a prophet and a member of the temple choir, thus
a Levite. He probably wrote during the time of Manasseh (687–642
B.C.).

Habakkuk acted the part of the doubter in the book. He asked, Why
did God permit the increasing evil in Judah to go unpunished? and How
could a holy God justify using the Babylonians to punish the Jews? The
answers are given in 1:5–11 and 2:2–20. The Lord reminded the prophet
that the appointed time "will certainly come, it will not delay" (2:3).

In terms of inspiration and inerrancy, we read: "The oracle which
Habakkuk the prophet saw" from God (1:1). The Lord spoke directly
and said, "I am raising up the Chaldeans" for punishment (1:6). "The
LORD answered me and said, 'Record the vision'" (2:2).

The Book of Zephaniah

Zephaniah (Hebrew *ṣepanyāh*, "Jehovah hides, protects") prophesied
around 640–608 B.C. during the kingship of Josiah, the king in whose
reign the Law books were rediscovered. The prophet probably helped

bring about revival under Josiah. Without a doubt, the book speaks of far future calamity and tribulation that will fall on the earth (1:14–18). These thoughts are repeated in the Book of Revelation. Inspiration is set forth clearly in regard to the book: "The word of the Lord which came to Zephaniah" (1:1); "'Wait for Me,' declares the LORD" (3:8); "Behold, I am going to deal at that time with all your oppressors" (3:19). Referring to the millennium, Zephaniah said: "The King of Israel, the LORD, [will be] in your midst" (3:15) and "The LORD your God [will be] in your midst" (3:17).

The tone of Zephaniah, the scope of his prophetic visions, and the use of his quotes in other books speak clearly for the doctrines of inspiration and inerrancy in the details of fulfilled prophecy.

The Book of Haggai

Haggai (Hebrew *ḥaggay*, "Festal") was a "contemporary of Zechariah and labored with him to encourage the returned exiles to finish rebuilding the temple, which, though begun in the second year of Cyrus, 535 B.C., had been abandoned because of difficulties and opposition."[11]

Around the second year of Darius of Persia (520 B.C.), the prophet gave his four prophecies, portions of which are in his book. Because these addresses were written in shortened form, some have questioned the inspiration of the book. But Unger notes: "If Haggai wrote under inspiration, there is no reason why he might not have contented himself with short excerpts from his larger discourses, or used the third person."[12] It was quite common in ancient literature to write of oneself in the third person.

Haggai is full of markers that attest to its inspiration and inerrancy. The book is a masterpiece of writing and is one of the finest works among the Minor Prophets. Haggai addressed all the people to inspire them to rebuild the temple. And yet it also addressed the governor Zerubbabel who was assigned by Darius I to form the new province of Judah in Jerusalem.

Inspiration is keyed by these verses: "Thus says [or 'declares'] the LORD of hosts" or the Lord of the heavenly armies (1:2, 5, 7, 9; 2:4, 6–9, 23); "The word of the LORD came by Haggai the prophet, saying" (1:3; 2:1); "says the LORD" (1:8); "Then Zerubbabel . . . with all the remnant of the people, obeyed the voice of the LORD their God and the words of Haggai the prophet, as the LORD their God had sent him. And the people showed reverence for the LORD" (1:12); "Then Haggai, the messenger of the LORD, spoke by the commission of the LORD to the people saying"

(1:13); " 'Take courage, Zerubbabel,' declares the LORD" (2:4); "As for the promise which I made you when you came out of Egypt, My Spirit is abiding in your midst; do not fear!" (2:5); "Then the word of the LORD came a second time to Haggai" (2:20).

Finally, the book conveyed a direct message of encouragement and hope to the struggling community of returned exiles. It is furnished with dates throughout, and thus can easily be fitted into the historical circumstances of the time.[13]

The Book of Zechariah

Zechariah (Hebrew *zekaryāh*, "Yahweh remembers") and his preaching, along with that of Haggai, resulted in encouraging the people to complete the temple on their return from Babylon. Zechariah probably ministered for some forty-five or fifty years. His book explodes with messianic prophecies and promises and is replete with markers to the doctrine of inspiration. Its truthfulness also is easy to substantiate because of the large part the prophet and his utterances play in known historic events. This is one of the longest of the Minor Prophets (fourteen chapters), but it is also, in some places, one of the most difficult books to understand fully. Though the main characters in the book, Zerubbabel and Joshua, acted as anointed ones in the history of the return, they foreshadowed the future greater personality, Jesus, "who will make a triumphant entry into Jerusalem, and in his day the 'new Jerusalem' will arise as the capital of the Kingdom of God on earth, to which the nations of the world will flow and join themselves to the God of Israel and to His people."[14]

> Zechariah is rich in Messianism. The dominant note of Zechariah's prophecies is that of hope and joyful expectation. . . . The most characteristic feature of the prophecies of Zechariah is the visions. By them the prophet expresses the truths he received from God. They are personal revelations, and the prophet is taught to see in these images a Divine message, which he conveys to his people.[15]

In Zechariah and Ezekiel, angels played a part in imparting vivid prophetic visions. Though God does not need intermediate agencies, they still have a special place in this book. Some have suggested that angels were used to give the sense that the nation had failed, it was sinful, it was thrown into exile and now has returned, and the Lord held Himself one step away from dealing directly with even the holy prophets. This view has some inconsistencies and may not fully answer why such intermediate agencies were so used.

Zechariah's prophecies presupposed meaningful progress in the restoration of the city of Jerusalem and the temple. The prophecies assisted the book by historical retrospect and the glowing hopes of the messianic age to come. The prophetic visions also portrayed the restoration of the exiles and, announced the overthrow of pagan nations. They told of the new Jerusalem to come with the only wall being the Lord Himself. These visions clearly were the Word of the Lord and they are delivered plainly and with authority.

Because of its strong prophetic and messianic message, critics have attempted to tear the book from the canon of the Old Testament but without success. Zechariah stands firm as a cornerstone of inspired prophecy and was authored by a great prophet. Unger concludes:

> In summary it may be said that to hold the unity of the prophecy of Zechariah is consonant with the highest scholarship and is in agreement with the internal evidence of the book itself, being witnessed to by both Jewish and Christian students from earliest times. The fact may be safely rested in that the book is not only an intrinsic part of God's inspired Word, but that it is throughout the work of the author whose name it bears.[16]

Many verses attest to the book's inspiration and inerrancy: "The word of the LORD came to Zechariah the prophet" (1:1); "Thus says the LORD of hosts" (1:3); "Declares the LORD of hosts" (1:3); "Did not My words . . . which I commanded My servants the prophets, overtake your fathers?" (1:6); "The angel who was speaking with me said to me, 'I will show you what these are'" (1:9); "Then the angel of the LORD said" (1:12).

Two interesting verses read: "The LORD answered the angel who was speaking with me with gracious words, comforting words" (1:13); "The angel who was speaking with me said to me, 'Proclaim, saying, "Thus says the LORD of hosts"'" (1:14). Zechariah also wrote: "I lifted up my eyes and looked" (1:18); "And he answered me" (1:19); 'Then the LORD showed me" (1:20).

Such statements were repeated over and over throughout the fourteen chapters of Zechariah, giving more detailed evidence for inspiration than any other Minor Prophet writing. These phrases make it clear that Zechariah is one of the outstanding books of the Old Testament. Its claim to inspiration is undaunting in its evidence. Interestingly, though Zechariah included himself as part of the sinning nation, he was still used of God to write this great prophecy. Though he had weaknesses, he was still one of the best of the Lord's messengers.

> The prophets are no more, but the words which those holy men of old spake as they were moved by the Holy [Spirit] are still with us, verifying themselves, and in spite of man's unbelief accomplishing, whether in judgment or in mercy, that whereunto they were sent. Oh, that men would take warning from the past history of Israel, and note the faithfulness of God in carrying out His threatenings as well as His promises![17]

The Book of Malachi

Malachi (Hebrew *mal'ākiy*, "My messenger") is the last of the Old Testament books and the final Minor Prophecy. The book was probably written around 433 B.C. The unity and authenticity of the book have never been seriously questioned. The canonical and doctrinal authority of the book is attested by New Testament citations (see Mal. 4:5–6 [Hebrew text 3:23–24] and Matt. 11:10, 14; 17:11–12; Mark 9:11–13; Luke 1:17. Compare Mal. 3:1 with Matt. 11:10; Mark 1:2 and Mal. 1:2–3 with Rom. 9:13).[18]

One of the great themes of Malachi is the day of the Lord. Though this writer disagrees with the Jewish Soncino commentary on its statement about the Gentiles not being judged on the day of the Lord, the quote is still worth sharing:

> [The day of the Lord] is to be a day of judgment, not for the Gentile world, but for Israel, when God will pass His people through the refiner's fire and remove the dross from the precious metal (iii. 2ff.). God will then bring to light the truly righteous, and the wicked will be consumed root and branch. It will be preceded by the advent of the prophet Elijah, whose mission will be to reconcile parents and children and turn the hearts of all to God, and will be followed by the dawn of the Messianic era.[19]

The doctrine of inspiration is strong in Malachi: "The oracle of the word of the LORD to Israel through Malachi" (1:1); "says the LORD of hosts to you" (1:6); "Behold, I am going to send My messenger, . . . says the LORD of hosts" (3:1); "A book of remembrance was written before Him for those who fear the LORD and who esteem His name" (3:16); "For behold, the day is coming, . . . says the LORD of hosts" (4:1).

Human Reason Incapable of Judging Scripture

The great Old Testament scholar Gleason L. Archer has some final thoughts on the infallibility of the Old Testament:

> It is a very difficult thing for human reason to attempt to pass judgment upon divine revelation as such, to determine its truth or falsity. For such judgments to be valid, they must proceed from a Judge who possesses knowledge of metaphysical truth that is superior to that of the revelation itself. In other words, man must know more about God and the soul and spiritual values than the Bible itself knows, if he is to pass valid judgment on the truth of the Bible.

> In the last analysis, then, every man must settle for one of two alternatives: the inerrancy of Holy Scripture, or the inerrancy of his own personal judgment. If the Bible contains errors in the autographs, then it requires an infallible human judgment to distinguish validly between the false and the true in Scripture.[20]

FOR DISCUSSION

1. Because the Minor Prophets are smaller books, does this mean that their message is less important than other books in the Old Testament?

2. On what grounds can we attest that the Book of Jonah is a historical account of what happened to this prophet?

3. What is significantly important about the Book of Micah?

4. In these Minor Prophets, what statements tell us they are the recorded words of the Lord Himself?

5. What makes Zechariah one of the most important of the Minor Prophets?

6. Has the authenticity of the Book of Malachi ever been seriously questioned?

For Further Study

Bible Introduction

Archer, Gleason L. *A Survey of Old Testament Introduction*. Chicago: Moody, 1994.

Unger, Merrill F. *Introductory Guide to the Old Testament*. Grand Rapids: Zondervan, 1981.

Commentaries

Baron, David. *Commentary on Zechariah*. Grand Rapids: Kregel, 1988.

Cohen, A., ed. *The Twelve Prophets*. London: Soncino, 1970.

Unger, Merrill F. *Zechariah*. Grand Rapids: Zondervan, 1963.

Chapter Fifteen

Inerrancy of the Gospels

*A*fter the death of the church father Justin (A.D. 165), an influential churchman named Tatian returned to his home in Assyria. There he edited a piece of literature concerning the Gospels called the Diatessaron that would last for centuries. *Diatessaron* is a musical term meaning the harmony of four. He created a continuous narrative in which he stitched the four Gospels together to form a chronology. The Gospels could then be viewed as a whole. The churches throughout the Bible world had already accepted the four Gospels as inspired and without error. These books were seen on an equal footing with the Old Testament prophets. Justin had earlier written that the apostolic memoirs were called Gospels, "and they are read in church along with the 'compositions of the prophets.'" These facts tell us the church had accepted the Gospels as the first part of the canon of the New Testament.

The issue of the inerrancy of the Gospels has been clouded by liberal attempts to say they are composed of a patchwork of myths, rumors, and traditions. Liberals argue for a two-document hypothesis and even up to a four-document hypothesis as the background of the Gospels. They contend for a very late writing of most of the books, although they argue for the primacy of Mark.

The Source of the Gospels

Form Criticism and the Gospels

To understand the view of inspiration in the Gospels, one has to address briefly the issue of form criticism. Even some evangelicals are currently embracing form criticism with its liberal bias. Evangelicals accepting at least some methods of form criticism still attempt to cling to inspiration and inerrancy, but as many observers argue, in time these doctrines will soon be jettisoned.

Farnell has an excellent discussion of form criticism in his coauthored book, *The Jesus Crisis*.[1] Citing F.F. Bruce, form criticism is an attempt to find the oral history of written sources and then to systematize that material by various "forms" or categories of narrative, discourse, etc.[2]

> The expression "Form Criticism" comes from the German word *Formgeschichte* (English, "form history"). The German name reveals its negative philosophical underpinnings through usage of the term *eschichte* instead of the *Historie*. *Historie* refers to objective facts of history (external and verifiable), while *Geschichte* dichotomizes the concept of history into interpretations of history, namely, history as significant, internal and nonverifiable. According to this distinction, that Jesus was a man who lived in the first century is an objective statement of historical fact, or *Historie*, that may be verified by canons of "historical reason." But, the assertion that Jesus was the Son of God is an interpretative statement and belongs to the realm of *Geschichte* in that an assumption of faith is its only verification. . . . The "Risen Christ" is a mythological concept of the early church that creatively thought of the dead Jesus as the risen "Son of Man."[3]

Kelber notes that form criticism actually had its origins in a supposed oral synoptic tradition that goes from a natural, evolutionary, biological process, or from simplicity to complexity, from an evolutionary transition from the pre-gospel stream of tradition to the written gospel. Without any proof, form criticism creates a huge scenario of how the stories of Jesus came about. The argument says the church went through an oral period of passing on traditions through teachers and storytellers. The assumption is that the Gospels were from the church, by the church, and for the church.[4] The church added fabrications and accretions, and the Gospels took on various fixed forms over time. The various Christian communities then locked in these forms. "Eventually, anonymous gospel writers collected and arranged the individual stories into written narratives that reflected the needs and interests of their particular communities."[5]

Rudolf Bultmann wanted to "modernize" the Gospels by demythologizing them. He felt they were outdated with popular but unscientific ideas. Miraculous thoughts of the divine, the Son of God, demon possession, angels, resurrection, voices from heaven, and so on "are first-century man's primitive understanding of the world that needs to be demythologized and put in twentieth century terms."[6]

Farnell maintains:

> Form Criticism has a predilection toward allowing for errors in the
> Gospels; grammatico-historical exegesis presupposes inerrancy and
> has for centuries supplied genre descriptions without negative con-
> clusions regarding historicity and the miraculous therein.[7]

He then writes:

> One can learn what Jesus taught and understand the Gospels with-
> out Form Criticism, for the Gospels are not reinterpretations of the
> life of Christ to fit later historical circumstances in the Christian
> community. They present one life situation, that of Jesus Himself.
> To go beyond that and hypothesize an additional one impugns the
> text and courts hermeneutical disaster.[8]

As one can see, it is a small leap from a naturalistic, evolutionary
application in history to a denial of the doctrines of inspiration and
inerrancy. Many evangelical schools are progressively making the move.
These biblical institutions do not suddenly publish a denial of the inspiration and inerrancy doctrines, but the shift is there. The final results will
be seen down the road in a younger group of scholars.

The Arguments of Harrison

Everett F. Harrison produced an excellent standard work, *Introduction
To The New Testament*.[9] For years he was the senior conservative New
Testament professor at Fuller Seminary. What he writes about the synoptic Gospel problem is worth quoting at length. Concerning Mark being
the first Gospel, he says:

> It may well be that the Synoptic Criticism has too readily relegat-
> ed Matthew and Luke to the position of editors who are at times
> quite unimaginatively dull in their following of sources, at other
> times quite perverse in their attempted originality. [The disciples]
> ought rather to be thought of as men who had a keen interest in
> the material that passed through their hands and a full knowledge
> of the extent of the tradition, from which they were drawing what
> served their purpose to best advantage.[10]

Form criticism either forgets or minimizes the regulating influence of
the apostles and other witnesses of the life of Jesus. In their desire to
honor the Lord, the apostles would not ascribe words to Jesus that did
not originate with him at all.[11]

The notion that much of the material in the Gospels is the result of random selection of isolated bits of tradition does not satisfy. It ignores the existence of the Gospel pattern with its common outline running through all the accounts.[12]

It is utterly fanciful to see in the choice of materials for our Gospels simply those things that had an existential interest for Christians. Jesus Himself was the greatest interest they had, as the Acts and the Epistles abundantly attest.[13]

The prologue of Luke's Gospel does not substantiate the liberal theory of form criticism. This theory makes the community of churches the creator, custodian, and transmitter of the tradition. Individual authorship and influence on the tradition are reduced almost to the vanishing point as factors to be considered. But in Luke's opening words, we find there was a certain group, much smaller than the church as a whole, which preserved the truth about the life of Christ and made it available as testimony.[14]

The Aramaic Matthew

There are various false theories as to how Matthew came about. For example, the Q theory argues that various stories outside the Gospels about the life of Christ were collected to create our present Gospel accounts. Besides the Q theory, there is the M document theory and the Ur-Markus theory. These theories argue that the Gospels were penned much later than we think. They maintain the writers drew from early oracles or "notes" and then compiled their own books by picking and choosing what they wanted to highlight.

Another theory called the Logia approach has to do with Matthew specifically. This theory is based on two statements made by the church fathers Papias and Irenaeus. Papias wrote, "Matthew composed the Logia in the Hebrew tongue; and each one interpreted them as he was able." (Most believe "Hebrew tongue" refers to the Aramaic language that is related to Hebrew.) Irenaeus said, "Matthew also issues a written Gospel among the Hebrews in their own dialect."[15] Irenaeus' statement carries weight because he knew Polycarp in his early age, and Polycarp said he taught what he had learned from the apostles.

Several questions arise: 1) Did Matthew first write an Aramaic version and then translate it into Greek? 2) Did Matthew write a Greek version apart from the Aramaic copy?

Other questions: 1) Does *Logia* mean the "sayings" of Jesus or "oracles?" If *Logia* means "sayings," it could simply refer to a collection of what Jesus said and not the complete Gospel of Matthew. If it means "oracles," as it does in almost all of its New Testament usage, then it may refer to Matthew's Gospel.

If there was an entire edition of Matthew's Gospel in Aramaic, it is never again referred to. The only edition that the early church acknowledged and that has come down to us in history is the Greek version. Since Matthew was a multilingual government official, he would have no problem in producing both versions. He would not have had to translate what he previously wrote in the way we normally think. In fact, many argue it would have been easier for him to simply write both versions independently, though it is not necessary to maintain a strong view of inspiration. "It is evident that when the Greek Matthew had once become current in the Church, the Aramaic edition of it dropped out. . . . Without the assistance of Greek writers, Matthew reproduced his Gospel in Greek."[16]

From all the evidence, including important internal statements, inspiration and inerrancy is a sovereign work of God's Spirit. Matthew wrote his Gospel to meet a need. Thus, "he formed a definite purpose for his Gospel; and that he [then] selected his materials, under the guidance of the Holy Spirit, with that object in view."[17]

The Gospel of Matthew

As already shown, inerrancy implies that inspiration extends to every sentence and every word in Scripture. The Holy Spirit inspired each word. One of the tests for the inspiration and inerrancy of Matthew would be his extensive quoting from the Old Testament. Did he do this with accuracy?

The Book of Matthew teaches that the life of Christ was a detailed fulfillment of prophecies made in the past. Seventeen times the apostle Matthew wrote, "It is fulfilled" or "fulfills." Nine times he said Christ fulfilled what "is written." Fifty-nine times Matthew wrote about other fulfillments without using "written" or "fulfilled" to introduce the Old Testament quote. Matthew took for granted that his reading audience knew from what book in the Old Testament he was quoting. Dozens of allusions point back to other ancient prophecies.

It is not an overstatement to say that Matthew the apostle wove verses in prophetic fulfillment throughout this Gospel. In fact, the very framework of this writing was based on Old Testament prophecies. Many argue that some of Matthew's quotes were only a parable or illustration fulfillment. In other words, he simply reached back into the Old

Testament and tried to make some event in Christ's life be a fulfillment
of prophecy. Thus, Matthew is accused of forcing an interpretation. But
this is not true.

Two of the most cited Old Testament quotes for this accusation are
Matthew 2:15 and 2:18. The first quotes Hosea 11:1, "Out of Egypt I
called My Son." The second quotes Jeremiah 31:15, "A voice was heard
in Ramah, weeping and great mourning, Rachel weeping for her children; and she refused to be comforted, because they were no more."

First, the 2:18 passage: Right off, it must be noted that Rachel
stands as a figure of Jewish motherhood. Rachel was the beloved wife
of Jacob who bore his favorite sons Joseph and Benjamin (Gen. 35:24).
But Matthew cited the story as a historic event. The argument, even
by conservative scholars, is that "the voice . . . heard in Ramah, . . .
Rachel weeping" has to do with the Babylonian captivity. Jewish mothers were crying for their dead children as they left a place called Ramah
for exile in Babylon. Ramah was a staging area used by the Babylonians for deportation, five miles north of Jerusalem. This seems to be
confirmed by Jeremiah 40:1: "Nebuzaradan captain of the bodyguard
had released him [Jeremiah] from Ramah, when he had taken him
bound in chains among all the exiles of Jerusalem and Judah who were
being exiled to Babylon."

In rabbinical hermeneutics, a passage "fulfilled" could be seen as 1) a
literal fulfillment, 2) a parallel circumstance, or 3) a type that illustrates
a specific idea or passage. Herod's slaying of the children as recorded in
Matthew would be either 2) or 3). This in no way destroys Matthew's use
of the word "fulfilled." Matthew the apostle understood how he was using
the Jeremiah 31:15 passage. And Jewish readers also understood how he
was quoting the passage.

> Here again we have an example of St. Matthew's application of a
> passage that had a direct bearing upon the events of the time when
> it was delivered to those that his narrative had brought before him.[18]

Matthew felt for the mothers of Jeremiah's day as children were
dragged away to death.

> St. Matthew felt history had been reproduced once again. The tomb
> of Rachel was as familiar to the people of Bethlehem (it stands
> about one mile to the north of the town) as it had been in the time
> of Jeremiah, and the imagery was therefore as natural in the one
> case as the other.[19]

Matthew 2:15 is a partial quote of Hosea 11:1: "When Israel was a youth I loved him, and out of Egypt I called My son." Matthew probably used this passage as a type of Joseph, Mary, and Jesus coming from their stay in Egypt. An angel had instructed Joseph to take the family there because of the intense searching of Herod who wanted the Messiah killed (Matt. 2:13). Herod died a year later. "This was to fulfill what had been spoken by the Lord through the prophet: 'Out of Egypt I called My Son' " (2:15).

Israel was called God's son (Ex. 4:22–23). Collectively as a people, they were called forth from the Egyptian sojourn. Matthew saw a higher representative in the person of the only begotten Son. He went from the more common meaning to the higher application given to Christ as the Son of God. Again, was Matthew simply inaccurate in his interpretations, or did he not know what he was doing? And, did his readers understand? It is easy to judge far-off history and assume that no one caught an error.

> What God said about the nation of Israel in Hosea was brought to a more complete realization through Messiah, who typically represented all that the nation was to God. Along this same line of reasoning, Jesus referred to Himself as the "true vine" (John 15:1), whereas that analogy was used of Israel in Isaiah 5:1–7.[20]

We can trust the doctrines of inspiration and inerrancy of Scripture. Over and over in his narration, Matthew made historic and chronological references that can be trusted. Though the book is not always written chronologically, Matthew placed the stamp of accurate history on the events surrounding the life of Jesus. He made it clear that he described events as they happened. He used such phrases as: "now after," "now when," "and having heard," "then when," "but when," "now in those days," "while He was saying," "and behold," "now there was," "then He began," "at that time," etc.

As with other books of the Bible, the burden of proving the Scriptures wrong or in error lies with the doubter, and that doubt must be proven objectively. So far, those who deny inspiration and inerrancy use naturalistic theories in their attempts to destroy the Bible.

The early church accepted Matthew as the first Gospel and never challenged its truthfulness. It stands supreme and foremost in the New Testament.

The Gospel of Mark

As we continue to look at the doctrine of inspiration and the resultant doctrine of inerrancy, we must note that the early church for centuries thereafter saw the four Gospels as given from God. The writers were on the same par as the Old Testament prophets. This point was not disputed in the early church, and the accuracy of the apostles' work was rarely questioned.

Eusebius (263–339), the great early church scholar, quoted Papias (circa 140), bishop of Hierapolis, who in quoting John the apostle gave a strong endorsement of Mark and its accuracy. He wrote:

> The elder [John] said this also: Mark, who became Peter's inter-preter, wrote accurately, though not in order, all that he remem-bered of the things said or done by the Lord. For he had neither heard the Lord nor had been one of his followers, but afterwards, as I said, he had followed Peter, who used to compose his discours-es with a view to the needs of his hearers, but not as though he were drawing up a connected account of the Lord's sayings. So Mark made no mistake in thus recording some things just as he remembered them. For he was careful of this one thing, to omit none of the things he had heard and to make no untrue statements therein.[21]

Some have rightly noted that the Papias tradition, with its insistence on the apostolic eyewitness source of Mark's Gospel, runs counter to lib-eral criticism as to how the Gospels came about. Another important tra-dition is the Anti-Marcionite Prologue to Mark (A.D. 160–80) that men-tioned Mark as a Gospel writer and connected him with Peter. It noted, "He was Peter's interpreter. After the death of Peter, Mark wrote down this same gospel in the regions of Italy." On this Bruce adds:

> On Mark's record Papias speaks somewhat defensively, as though he knew of criticisms that had been voiced against it, especially on the ground that its order was defective. To this Papias replies that Mark did not set out to write an orderly account: his aim was to record in writing whatever Peter had to tell of the works and words of Jesus; and Peter simply mentioned from time to time those things which the circumstances of the moment required. In what he wrote down Mark made no mistake: in order, as in matter, he adhered to what Peter said.[22]

Finally, "The tradition of the Markan authorship, though called in question from time to time, remains secure."[23]

The Gospel of Luke and the Book of Acts

Luke and Acts are often seen as two parts of one book. Most believe that the apostle Luke wrote the life of Christ and then penned the story of the early church in the volume we call "the *Acts* of the apostles." Both books begin with almost the same wording. But as well, the opening verses place the accuracy of the writer Luke on the line. And as we've already shown, the burden of denial of the doctrine of inerrancy lies with those who attempt to destroy the Bible.

Luke's Prologues

The prologues to Luke's two books are extremely strong. They tie the work of the Holy Spirit in the life of Christ together with the apostles. Though Luke and Acts have not escaped the spotlights of the humanistic literary critics, these books have a certain stamp on them that cannot be denied. Though certain details have been raised about the Gospel of Luke, these have not brought into question Luke's authorship.

> Inasmuch as many have undertaken to compile an account of the things accomplished among us, just as they were handed down to us by those who from the beginning were eyewitnesses and servants of the word, it seemed fitting for me as well, having investigated everything carefully from the beginning, to write it out for you in consecutive order, most excellent Theophilus; so that you may know the exact truth about the things you have been taught. (Luke 1:1–4)

> The first account I composed, Theophilus, about all that Jesus began to do and teach, until the day when He was taken up to heaven, after He had by the Holy Spirit given orders to the apostles whom He had chosen. To these He also presented Himself alive after His suffering, by many convincing proofs, appearing to them over a period of forty days and speaking of the things concerning the kingdom of God. (Acts 1:1–3)

Because Luke was a close follower of Paul, Irenaeus believed when Paul said "my gospel" in Romans 2:16, he had in mind Luke's Gospel account. This view was also widely believed by many church fathers, though more than likely Paul was simply referring to the doctrine of the gospel as he presented it. But the fact that Irenaeus made this statement shows us how early Christians respected the Gospel of Luke.

Both Origen and Jerome believed Paul's statement about a certain brother "whose fame in the things of the gospel has spread through all the churches" (2 Cor. 8:18) was written to praise Luke's Gospel account. Harrison adds:

> The Lukan writings themselves contain no explicit statement of authorship, yet they are not completely anonymous, for the writer refers to himself in the Prologue ("it seemed good to me also") and at the beginning of the Acts ("in the former treatise I made"). It is understood that he must have been known therefore to others as well. This conclusion is strengthened by the circumstance that the patristic writers make much of apostolicity as the criterion for the reception of books. In view of this tendency, the very fact that the third Gospel bears the name of Luke rather than some apostolic figure in the stricter sense speaks eloquently in favor of tradition.[24]

In the prologue (1:1–4) of the Gospel, there are strong, historic indicators that are compelling. For example, the apostle wrote that he had "undertaken to compile an account of the things accomplished among us" (v. 1). By this he might have meant he was an observer on the side, or the "us" could simply refer to the larger body of apostles before Luke arrived on the scene. Either way, it elucidates that what he was writing was confirmed by a group and not simply by an individual. In addition, "They [the facts] were handed down to us by those who from the beginning were eyewitnesses and servants of the word" (v. 2).

Luke noted that he "investigated everything carefully from the beginning" (v. 3). This would mean that he interviewed many witnesses. He apparently compared stories, notes, and experiences. If Luke had inaccuracies in his compiled work, someone could have objected and called the account untrue. Thus, there were many checks and balances in what Luke set forth for examination.

Luke further said that "it seemed fitting to write it out . . . in consecutive order" or chronologically (v. 3). He did it so Theophilus would "know the exact truth about the things you have been taught" (v. 4). Some speculate that Theophilus may have assisted in the publication of Luke's work. Only the truth would be adequate. To falsify information about Jesus the Messiah would be virtually impossible.

The Muratorian Canon

Written around A.D. 170, this gives one of the first references to the tradition of Lukan authorship. It reads:

> The third book of the Gospel: According to Luke. This Luke was a physician. After the ascension of Christ, when Paul had taken him along with him as one devoted to letters, he wrote it under his own name from hearsay. For he himself has not seen the Lord in person, but, insofar as he was able to allow [it all], he thus began his account with the birth of John.[25]

The second and third centuries produced a long list of endorsements for the Book of Luke. There was little question about Luke until the destructive work of form criticism began to doubt it. Sir William Ramsay, the great Oxford scholar, opposed with factual accuracy the critical Tubingen school of criticism. After careful investigation, he found the legendary historical and geographical data in Luke-Acts proved factual over and over again. He concluded:

> [Luke's] statements of fact [are] trustworthy; he is possessed of the true historic sense; he fixes his mind on the idea and plan that rules in the evolution of history, and proportions the scale of his treatment to the importance of each incident. He seizes the important and critical events and shows their true nature at greater length, while he touches lightly or omits entirely much that was valueless for his purpose.[26]

The Gospel of John

Many scholars believe that the four Gospels were named after their authors early in history. Also, early on, they were bound together and circulated as a "four-chapter" book. One of the earliest fragments of John was dated around A.D. 130, with a few words from chapter 18. Beginning in the third century, all four books were discovered bound together along with the Book of Acts. One can well argue that the early church viewed these volumes as a unit. Together they painted a full picture of the ministry of Christ, the coming of the Holy Spirit, and the birth of the church.

The first unambiguous quotation from the fourth Gospel ascribed to John comes from a Theophilus of Antioch (A.D. 181). But before this there were other quotes from Tatian (a student of Justin), Claudius Apollinaris (bishop of Hierapolis), and Athenagoras.

This pushed us back to Polycarp and Papias, information about whom derives primarily from Irenaeus (end of the second century) and Eusebius historian of the early church (fourth century). Polycarp was martyred in A.D. 156 at the age of eighty-six. There is no reason therefore to deny the truth of the claims that he associated with the apostles in Asia (John, Andrew, Philip) and was "entrusted with the oversight of the Church in Smyrna by those who were eye-witnesses and ministers of the Lord."[27]

Irenaeus adds that the author of the fourth Gospel is "John the disciple of the Lord, who leaned back on His breast, published the Gospel while he was resident at Ephesus in Asia."[28] Another statement, which cannot be substantiated, is that Papias, one of John's closest disciples, wrote this Gospel at John's dictation. One of Papias' works survived into the Middle Ages but was later lost to history. Clement of Alexandria in the second century wrote:

> But that John, last of all, conscious that the outward facts had been set forth in the Gospels (the three synoptics), was urged on by his disciples, and, divinely moved by the Spirit, composed a spiritual Gospel.[29]

By "spiritual" he probably meant that John's work dealt with deeper meaning rather than just historical facts. The early church recognized this in his work. As well, the church recognized that the book did not follow the same detailed chronology as the other Gospels. Its outline follows the sayings of the Lord and, with great sensitivity, notes the spiritual reaction of people around Him.

> Certainly from the end of the second century on, there is virtual agreement in the church as to the authority, canonicity and authorship of the Gospel of John. An argument from silence in this case proves impressive. "It is most significant that Eusebius, who had access to many works which are now lost, speaks without reserve of the fourth Gospel as the unquestioned work of St. John." . . . The silence is "most significant" precisely because it was Eusebius' concern to discuss the doubtful cases [in his writings].[30]

The argument of silence is compelling, and it is a good argument. The great literary thinkers of those early centuries surely had the opportunity to raise questions about John if they had reasons to do so. They were closer to the events, and they knew people who knew people.

The last chapter of John has some interesting statements that catch our attention. Christ's statement to Peter about John, "If I want him to remain until I come, what is that to you?" (21:22), became a much-discussed saying. John then commented on a historic fact: "Therefore this saying went out among the brethren that that disciple would not die" (v. 23). Some believe the Ephesian elders added verse 24 in order to place a stamp of authenticity and accuracy on this Gospel. Since John spent his last years at Ephesus, it may be that the elders wrote this verse in his Gospel: This is the disciple [who has written this Gospel] who is testifying to these things and wrote these things, and we know that his testimony is true (v. 24).

No one could make this claim unless living witnesses could vouch for his honesty and that what he wrote was factual. As this Gospel was copied and passed about, this next-to-the-last verse was like a guarantee of authenticity. Readers who knew John or at least knew of him could also verify the final verse of the book (v. 25). He wrote:

> And there are also many other things which Jesus did, which if they were written in detail, I suppose that even the world itself would not contain the books that would be written.

FOR DISCUSSION

1. What is the Diatessaron?

2. Explain form criticism.

3. Summarize the issue of the Aramaic Matthew.

4. What is important about the prologue statements in Luke 1:1–4 and Acts 1:1–3?

5. What is the Muratorian Canon?

6. What is important about Irenaeus's statement in regard to the Book of John?

For Further Study

Bible Introduction

Harrison, Everett F. *Introduction to the New Testament*. Grand Rapids: Eerdmans, 1974.

Thiessen, Henry Clarence. *Introduction to the New Testament*. Grand Rapids: Eerdmans, 1958.

Bibliology Texts

Bruce, F.F. *The Canon of Scripture*. Downers Grove, Ill.: InterVarsity, 1988.

Commentaries

Carson, D.A. *The Gospel According to John*. Grand Rapids: Eerdmans, 1991.

Ellicott, Charles John. "Matthew" in vol. 6 of *Ellicott's Commentary on the Whole Bible*. Grand Rapids: Zondervan, 1959.

Carson, D.A. "Matthew" in in *The Expositor's Bible Commentary, Volume 8: Matthew, Mark, & Luke*. Edited by Frank E. Gaebelein. Grand Rapids: Zondervan, 1984.

Glasscock, Ed. *Matthew*. Chicago: Moody, 1997.

Pate, C. Marvin. *Luke*. Chicago: Moody, 1995.

Textual Criticism

Thomas, Robert L. and F. David Farnell. *The Jesus Crisis*. Grand Rapids: Kregel, 1998.

Chapter Sixteen

Inerrancy of the Pauline Epistles

*T*he apostle Paul wrote thirteen letters that were providentially kept for the guiding of the future church. Though he may have written other documents, these were preserved for our spiritual benefit by the divine superintendence of the Spirit of God. By what Paul said within these letters and by the external confirmation of the church, there is no doubt that they constitute the Word of God.

Letting history speak for itself and not imposing speculative theories on his work, Paul became an outstanding authority on the entire corpus of New Testament truth and revelation. Showing his apostleship was an important step in demonstrating his spiritual authority as a spokesman and prophet of the Lord. He would then be representing the Lord, and his message would be an authentic revelation from God.

Paul's Calling and Apostleship

When looking at the doctrines of inspiration and inerrancy and the apostolic authority of Paul, two sources of testimony come into play. The first is the external witness of those who knew the apostle and could clearly verify that he was indeed called of God to be an instrument of revelation to the world and the church. Many believed he was marked by the Lord to transmit inspired knowledge. They saw Paul's conversion, testified to his dramatic change, and realized that God had His hand on his ministry.

The second witness is Paul himself. With unflinching conviction, he claimed to have the same apostolic authority as the most eminent of the twelve disciples. The question is, was he lying, or was he telling the truth about his appointment as an apostle? And can the truthfulness of his message be substantiated?

Paul the Man

We are not sure of Paul's date of birth, but church tradition said he was born around the second year after Christ's birth. A tradition attributed to Chrysostom said that he died around A.D. 66 at age sixty-eight. That would mean he was born in 2 B.C. Paul possessed an important heritage as the son of a respected Pharisee of the tribe of Benjamin, a Hebrew of the dispersion (Phil. 3:5). As a young man, he had the privilege of studying the Law, like most Jewish men, especially those from wealthy families. Raised in Tarsus, Paul understood the Greek mind-set.

Tarsus was the capital of Cilicia, a city founded by the Assyrians and an important crossroads during the first century. Not only did he have access to Greek and Hebrew culture, but he was also born a Roman citizen (Acts 22:25–28). In his zealousness for Judaism, he approved of and possibly participated in the murder of Stephen (7:58; 8:1), at least by vocal consent. On his way to capture and put in prison the early Christians, he encountered the Lord Jesus Himself on the Damascus road (9:1–6). "But little did he know that this journey would end his life as he knew it."[1]

External Testimonies to Paul's Calling and Apostleship

1. When Paul (Saul) was struck down on the Damascus road, his traveling companions heard the voice of the Lord. They must have realized that a miracle had occurred because they "stood speechless" but saw no one (Acts 9:7). We don't know who these men were nor whether later they came to a saving knowledge of Jesus. But they were the first witnesses to the fact that God had begun a dramatic work in this man.

2. Ananias became the next important witness to verify the calling of Paul. The Lord spoke directly to him about Paul and said, "He is a chosen instrument of Mine, to bear My name before the Gentiles and kings and the sons of Israel" (9:15). Ananias shared this dramatic message with Luke, the author of Acts or perhaps with others who told Luke later of what actually happened. Ananias shared the words of the Lord with Paul shortly after the Damascus road incident happened. He told him that his blindness would be lifted (vv. 17–18), and he certainly made it clear that he believed the genuine calling of Paul as a chosen vessel.

3. For some days, the Christian disciples in Damascus took care of Paul while he rested from his emotional and physical ordeal

(9:19). They even helped him escape from Jews who were plotting to arrest him (vv. 23–24). By so doing, they proved they were convinced that Paul's selection by the Lord was real. Later, the Jerusalem disciples were afraid of him, fearing he was only an imposter (v. 26).

4. Barnabas, an early disciple who was confirmed and trusted by the apostles (4:36), believed the dramatic calling of Paul (9:27–30). He brought the new convert to Jerusalem and told the apostles how Paul spoke out boldly about Jesus in Damascus (v. 27). While in Jerusalem, Paul put his life at risk by preaching Christ to the Hellenistic Jews (v. 29). He was rushed out of town and sent home to Tarsus, probably to rescue his life from those who would kill him (v. 30).

5. By Paul's second missionary journey (15:36–18:23) it was clear that the Lord had placed Paul on center stage to be one of the most important voices for the gospel. As far as we can tell, his ministry eclipsed that of the other apostles in terms of its doctrinal and geographical scope. This does not mean that other outstanding apostles, such as Peter, John, and James were competing. But it does mean that Paul became the most significant figure used by the Lord to reach the Greek and Roman world.

6. Luke described how miraculously God worked through Paul by noting how "God was performing extraordinary miracles by the hands of Paul" so that even evil spirits went out of those possessed (19:11–12). Paul was clearly marked as one who was central in the Lord's work.

7. Even the evil spirit that Paul encountered recognized the apostle and his unique power. The spirit said, "I recognize Jesus, and I know about Paul" (19:15). Because Paul's authority was so evident to the crowds who saw what was happening, "the name of the Lord Jesus was being magnified" (v. 17), and "the word of the Lord was growing mightily and prevailing" (v. 20).

8. Peter gave one of the most powerful testimonies as to the apostolic authority of Paul. His statement also placed the writings of Paul on the same level as the authoritative revelations of the Old Testament prophets. Peter noted that the Lord gave wisdom to Paul, who also had previously written to those addressed in Peter's letter. "As also in all [Paul's] letters, speaking in them of

these things, in which are some things hard to understand, which the untaught and unstable distort *as they do also the rest of the Scriptures, to their own destruction*" (2 Pet. 3:16, emphasis added). Paul's revelations came to him by the wisdom and work of the Holy Spirit. "He had not this of himself naturally, nor did he learn it at Gamaliel's feet, but it was what was given to him; it came from above, from God who gives it liberally, . . . by the revelation of Christ."[2] As Lenski correctly notes:

> Peter is acquainted with Paul's letters, and his readers are acquainted with them. All that Paul had written up to this time, and all that Peter now writes are in complete agreement.
>
> This is said so that Peter's readers may be certain and may stand firm when the heretics arrive. . . . The point that Peter makes is the fact that some people, namely the ignorant and unstable, wrest these difficult things in Paul's letters, "torture" them, "put them on the rack."
>
> . . . These ignorant persons do not stop with certain things in Paul's letters; they do the same with the rest of the Scriptures; they would be compelled to because all inspired writing speaks the same thing with the same wisdom. But those who wrest such writings do it "to their own perdition."[3]

Paul's Testimony as to His Calling, Apostleship, and Authority

Since Paul was personally commissioned by the Lord Jesus and was clearly authorized to speak for Him, he exercised this right in carrying the gospel far into the Roman and Greek culture. There is overwhelming evidence to support the fact that he was inspired from above to represent the Lord in this new dispensation of the church. Below is a list of indicators the apostle enumerated to substantiate his position:

1. He said he was set apart for serving the Lord "even from my mother's womb and called me through His grace" (Gal. 1:15).

2. The clearness of the gospel he received came from no one "but through a revelation of Jesus Christ" Himself (1:12).

3. After fourteen years, by revelation the Lord led him to Jerusalem to be examined by the apostles, "those who were of reputation" (2:2), so that his message might be confirmed.

4. As the Lord entrusted Peter with taking the gospel to the Jews, so He commissioned Paul to carry it to the Gentiles. God "effectually worked" Paul's apostleship as He in like manner "worked" the apostleship of Peter (2:8).

5. Paul heard the voice of the Lord in his Damascus experience (Acts 9:4, 27), though he did not say where or when this took place. He told us that he also saw Jesus (1 Cor. 9:1).

6. Paul related how Ananias was used of the Lord to bring back his sight following his conversion. Ananias said, "The God of our fathers has appointed you to know His will and to see the Righteous One and to hear an utterance from His mouth. For you will be a witness for Him to all men of what you have seen and heard" (Acts 22:14–15).

7. After Paul had gone to Jerusalem the first time, while praying he fell into a trance and heard the voice of the Lord again saying, "Make haste, and get out of Jerusalem quickly, because they will not accept your testimony about Me" (22:18).

8. Later, Christ spoke again to Paul and said, "Take courage; for as you have solemnly witnessed to My cause at Jerusalem, so you must witness at Rome also" (23:11).

9. One of the greatest miracles happened to Paul exclusively: God took him into His very presence in the third heaven. Whether this happened bodily or not, Paul "was caught up into Paradise and heard inexpressible words, which a man is not permitted to speak" (2 Cor. 12:4). To Paul this became a special stamp of approval and verification as to his unique mission on earth as an anointed ambassador of the Lord.

Paul Answers His Opposition

In his second letter to the Corinthians, Paul felt compelled to defend his apostleship against apparently growing opposition. Some were saying of him, "His letters are weighty and strong, but his personal presence is unimpressive and his speech contemptible" (10:10). But the apostle stood his ground. His human limitations, if they were obvious, did not bother him in the least. "We will not boast beyond our measure," he wrote (v. 13). He remained firm and continued, "For it is not he who commends himself that is approved, but he whom the Lord commends" (v. 18).

Taking the offensive against those who seemed to hate him and questioned his apostolic calling, Paul twice wrote, "I consider myself not in the least inferior to the most eminent apostles . . . even though I am a nobody" (11:5; 12:11). Continuing on, he wrote, "The signs of a true apostle were performed among you with all perseverance, by signs and wonders and miracles" (12:12). His success came only from "the grace that was given me from God" (Rom. 15:15). He operated "in the power of signs and wonders, in the power of the Spirit" (Rom. 15:19). Finally, after describing for the Corinthian church all the terrible things that had happened to him for the sake of Christ, he added that "the God and Father of the Lord Jesus . . . knows that I am not lying" (2 Cor. 11:31).

All that is quoted above is to demonstrate that Paul was a special chosen instrument of the Lord Jesus. Paul's testimony was even inspired by the Holy Spirit. And if inspired, his words would therefore be inerrant.

The Epistle to the Romans

Probably written at the end of A.D. 55 or the beginning of A.D. 56, this book stands as the hallmark among the writings of Paul. Romans has been called a legal brief and the most astute presentation of justification by faith found in the New Testament. With clear and logical precision, Paul argued for human depravity and the fact that salvation by faith is the only way of redeeming the lost world.

The apostle began his letter with a reminder that he was a bond-servant of Christ and was "called as an apostle, set apart for the gospel of God" (1:1). In reminding his Gentile readers how the Lord sidetracked the nation of Israel and brought salvation to the pagan world, he said, "I am speaking to you who are Gentiles. Inasmuch then as I am an apostle of Gentiles, I magnify my ministry" (11:13). In setting forth his many arguments, he further informed them that he could speak strong words of rebuke "through the grace given to me" (12:3). He did not simply chide and correct his audience with his own thoughts, but instead, he represented the Lord Himself.

As Paul closed this letter, he seemed to address again some who doubted his apostolic calling and mission. He admitted that he wrote to them boldly "on some points" to remind them anew "of the grace that was given me from God" (15:15). Because of this grace, he became a minister of Christ, "ministering as a priest the gospel of God, . . . sanctified by the Holy Spirit" (v. 16). With forceful words, he concluded his argument about his predestined role by adding:

Therefore in Christ Jesus I have found reason for boasting in things pertaining to God. For I will not presume to speak of anything except what Christ has accomplished through me, resulting in the obedience of the Gentiles by word and deed, in the power of signs and wonders, in the power of the Spirit. (15:17–19)

The Two Epistles to the Corinthians

Both letters were written months apart, probably in the year A.D. 55. The Corinthian church was in the eye of the moral and spiritual storm of the Greek and Roman world. A cosmopolitan city with mixed races and cultures, the area spawned gross sin and wicked heathenism. The city bragged of its outdoor theater that held twenty thousand spectators. The temple of Aphrodite was a pagan religious center with one thousand prostitutes sexually serving the transient and permanent population of this vast metroplex. The Greek word *Korinthiazomai* expressed the immoral condition of the city, literally "to act as a Corinthian" or to "practice fornication."

The believers in Corinth waged a terrible spiritual struggle to break the chains of this sinful environment. This is why it is possible that there were no spiritual leaders in the local assembly. Paul had to act as a distant elder in correcting their behavior.

In the beginning of Paul's first letter, he had to strongly defend his apostleship. He wrote, "Let a man regard us in this manner, as servants of Christ and stewards of the mysteries of God" (1 Cor. 4:1). He added, "It is a very small thing that I may be examined by you. . . . I am conscious of nothing against myself, . . . but the one who examines me is the Lord" (vv. 3–4). Though he realized he was not one of the original twelve apostles, he reminded his readers, "God has exhibited us apostles last of all" (v. 9). Setting forth his authority, he further stated, "I became your father through the gospel" (v. 15). He reminded them that he could wield this authority and judge them from a distance "as though I were present. . . . In the name of our Lord Jesus, . . . with the power of our Lord Jesus" (5:3–4). When the issue of incest in the assembly was brought up, Paul strongly exercised his authority. Having such an awesome right to represent Christ, he "decided to deliver such a one to Satan for the destruction of his flesh" (v. 5).

Though we believe Paul's writings were inspired of the Holy Spirit, this does not mean that he was perfect in all his ways. Inspiration only extends to the Spirit's safeguarding the truthfulness of the facts and the message of the writings that have been so profoundly marked out and preserved. However, inspiration probably also spilled over into his verbal apostolic teaching ministry, since so much that he said was tightly tied to what he wrote. But again, caution must be applied when advocating this as a possibility. Yet there is no doubt that Paul walked with far greater spiritual maturity than most believers. This is why he could boldly write, "Be imitators of me, just as I also am of Christ" (11:1). Because of his earlier mistreatment of the early Christians, he remained humble so that the Lord would use him in the ministry. He wrote, "I am the least of the apostles, and not fit to be called an apostle, because I persecuted the church of God. But by the grace of God I am what I am, and His grace toward me did not prove vain" (15:9–10).

We previously looked at other statements in the Corinthian letters that illustrate his divine calling as least of all of the apostles, yet "as to one untimely born, He appeared to me also" (15:8). Because of all this evidence, we conclude with certainty that he wrote as an apostle under the inspiration of the Holy Spirit. Thus, these letters, though directed to the Corinthian congregation, were protected from error so they could instruct later generations of believers with truth.

The Epistle to the Galatians

Some believe this was Paul's first letter and was written around A.D. 49. Whatever, it contains much historical evidence that supplements and adds to the history of the Book of Acts. Showing righteous indignation, Paul was greatly concerned about the distortion of the gospel. He criticized Judaizers and anyone who mixed error with the free grace of God found in simply trusting Christ. He also made it clear that his calling was to be "an apostle (not sent from men nor through the agency of man, but through Jesus Christ and God the Father, who raised Him from the dead)" (1:1). With more strong words, he told his readers to accept no other gospel "contrary to what we have preached to you" (v. 8).

To make his point about the purity of the gospel he was given from the Lord, in 2:11–16 he shared with his readers the incident with Peter (Cephas) in Antioch. He told how both Peter and Barnabas became hypocritical about the doctrine of justification by faith alone, apart from the works of the law. He argued, "They were not straightforward about the truth of the gospel" (v. 14). He asked Peter, "How is it that you compel the Gentiles to live like Jews?" (v. 14). With strong apostolic authority, he told the Galatians, "I have confidence in you in the Lord that you will adopt no other view; but the one who is disturbing you will bear his judgment, whoever he is" (5:10).

Paul had full confidence in his understanding of the gospel, and he was not afraid to write it down because it was the message the Lord had given him.

The Epistle to the Ephesians

Again, though this letter was written to a specific group of Christians in the city of Ephesus, the writing was preserved by the Holy Spirit for all future posterity to read. Though our preserved manuscripts show that it was sent to Ephesus, there is strong evidence that it was also a circular letter that was passed on to other congregations. Many believe this church epistle was penned around A.D. 60 from prison in Rome. In fact, this letter, along with Philippians, Colossians, and Philemon, are considered Prison Epistles.

As he did in 2 Corinthians, Paul reminded the readers of his apostolic authority by writing, "Paul, an apostle of Christ Jesus by the will of God" (1:1). In chapter 3 he pointed out that he was given a special revelation about the mystery of Christ. This "stewardship" or dispensation was given to him by the grace of God (3:2–9). The special revelation was that the Gentiles would become fellow heirs of salvation and members of the body of Christ. By special calling, the apostle Paul "was made a minister, according to the gift of God's grace which was given to me according to the working of His power" (v. 7). He was called to preach to these Gentiles "and to bring to light what is the administration [dispensation] of the mystery which for ages had been hidden in God" (v. 9).

Even when confined in jail, he asked his readers to pray for him that he might speak "with boldness the mystery of the gospel, for which I am an ambassador in chains; that in proclaiming it I may speak boldly, as I ought to speak" (6:19–20). Though Paul had his critics, for the most part the majority in the churches realized he was authorized as an apostolic ambassador to represent the Lord Jesus. By inspiration of the Holy Spirit, he revealed the mystery of the church (Jew and Gentile forming the one body of Christ) and the mystery of the rapture of the church. Since the revelation of these facts came by the superintending and guidance of the Spirit of God, it is truth inspired, preserved, and inerrant.

The Epistle to the Philippians

Both of these letters probably were written at the middle and at the end of A.D. 60. In the Philippian letter, Paul gave the great doctrine of the *kenosis* of the Lord Jesus Christ. This truth had to come by inspiration of the Spirit of God. No human being alone could figure out the mysterious nature of the eternal Son of God as He came to earth and walked in flesh. By the kenosis, the "emptying" of Christ, He de-focused His deity and took the form of a bond-servant, while made in the likeness of humanity (2:7). Yet He still existed in the same form (*morphē*) as God and "did not regard equality with God a thing to be grasped" (v. 6). Revealed by inspiration of the Holy Spirit, Paul wrote of this complicated doctrine, giving the perfect balance concerning the nature of Christ on earth. Any natural human argument could not explain the mysterious nature of the incarnation of the Lord Jesus Christ.

Though this book does not have an overwhelming number of apostolic markers, Paul wrote with the same authority that is shown in his other letters. Few would argue against its inspiration and inerrancy.

The Epistle to the Colossians

Written to the church in Colossae approximately A.D. 60–61, the theme of this letter is about the supremacy and sufficiency of Christ. Up front, Paul reminded the readers that he was an apostle "of Jesus Christ by the will of God" (1:1). For the benefit of the church, he said he "was made a minister according to the stewardship (dispensation) from God bestowed" on him from God (1:25). He added that he was given this mystery about the church from the Lord, willed by God, "the hope of glory" (v. 27). He was appointed to give this revelation "according to His power, which mightily works within me" (v. 29).

Because of that divine power and authority, the apostle could close this letter by reminding them to have his letter "read in the church of the Laodiceans," and to read his letter to the congregation "that is coming from Laodicea" (4:16).

The Two Epistles to the Thessalonians

Both these letters could have been written within months of each other (circa A.D. 51). Some feel that they may have been Paul's first letters. These writings bear evidence that critics were following Paul from city to city, attempting to discredit him and his message about Christ. They made it sound as if Paul was a cult leader who was not only advocating a false religion but also bilking the gullible of their money. Besides answering questions about the resurrection, the rapture, and the day of the Lord, he felt compelled to defend his authority also. Apparently responding to false charges, he wrote, "We did not act in an undisciplined manner among you, nor did we eat anyone's bread without paying for it" (2 Thess. 3:7–8). In both letters Paul stood his ground as an inspired apostle.

The apostle reminded the Thessalonians that his gospel came in the power of the Holy Spirit (1 Thess. 1:5), and it was received with the "joy of the Holy Spirit" (v. 6). In addition, he noted that when he proclaimed the gospel, it was the Word of God being sounded forth. He added, "Our exhortation does not come from error or impurity or by way of deceit; but just as we have been approved by God to be entrusted with the gospel, so we speak, not as pleasing men, but God" (2:3–4).

Paul reminded the church that he could have exercised his apostolic rights, but he proved to "be gentile among you, as a nursing mother" (v. 7). He wrote, "As apostles of Christ we might have asserted our authority" (v. 6). He also said that he gave them living instructions "by the authority of the Lord Jesus" (4:2). Finally, in his second letter, he gave the apostolic salutation because he was the representative of the Lord Himself: "Grace to you and peace from God the Father and the Lord Jesus Christ" (2 Thess. 1:2).

The Two Epistles to Timothy and the Epistle to Titus

Many conjecture 1 Timothy and Titus were written somewhere around A.D. 62 and 2 Timothy late in A.D. 64. These letters are called the pastorals because they contain detailed instructions about handling church affairs. Paul also gave directives to the elders who were the pastors and leaders of the assemblies with which Timothy and Titus may have been working. He also enumerated the specific qualifications for both the elders and church deacons.

In 1 Timothy, the elder statesman Paul set forth again his calling as an apostle by writing, "Paul, an apostle of Christ Jesus according to the commandment of God our Savior, and of Christ Jesus, who is our hope" (1:1). Notice how strongly Paul made this declaration, stating that both God and Jesus had established his apostolic authority. The apostle was not bragging but simply mentioning the fact that Christ found him faithful for his task as an apostle. "I thank Christ Jesus our Lord, who has strengthened me, because He considered me faithful, putting me into service" (v. 12). For the sake of the gospel, Paul was given a special mandate: "I was appointed a preacher and an apostle (I am telling the truth, I am not lying) as a teacher of the Gentiles in faith and truth" (2:7). Notice that he says "in faith and truth." The thought was that he became a teacher of the Gentiles and an apostle "to the objective truth of the doctrine he delivered."[4]

In a similar manner, Paul began 2 Timothy by writing, "Paul, an apostle of Christ Jesus by the will of God" (1:1). He repeated some of the comments he made in the first letter: "I was appointed a preacher and an apostle and a teacher" (1:11). By using the definite article before each word, he is differentiating between the three words. *Preacher* (*kērux*) emphasized his role as a proclaimer of the gospel and of truth, *apostle* (*apostolos*) stressed his unique and authoritative office, and *teacher* (*didaskalos*) focused on his activity of setting forth the objective facts of the revelation of salvation in Christ (1 Tim. 2:7).

Though Paul believed God could deliver him from more trials that seemed certain, he saw how the hand of the Lord had already providentially worked in his apostolic ministry. He wrote, "The Lord stood with me and strengthened me, so that through me the proclamation might be fully accomplished, and that all the Gentiles might hear" (2 Tim. 4:17). Paul certainly did not know then how true that statement would turn out to be. Following his death, his letters were preserved, along with the writings of the other authors of New Testament literature. Quickly, his words and teachings would dramatically affect the entire world, especially the world of Western civilization. The writings of this apostle would stand as the iron-hardened core of truth and doctrine for the church. And as well, the writings of Paul would be seen as what they are, the inspired and inerrant Word of God, given through the dynamic work of God's Holy Spirit.

Though the process was often painful and argumentative, the early church groped forward to discover for certain the books of the New Testament that would be considered canonical. In the broad sense, various bishops and church leaders considered only the books that clearly stood the test of apostleship and showed all the signs of inspiration by the Holy Spirit. The idea of inerrancy was not so much discussed separately. They considered inspiration, truthfulness, and accuracy all in the same context. Bruce puts the issue in proper perspective in this excellent paragraph concerning canonicity and the whole of the New Testament:

> Certainly, as one looks back on the process of canonization in early Christian centuries, and remembers some of the ideas of which certain church writers of that period were capable, it is easy to conclude that in reaching a conclusion on the limits of the canon they were directed by a wisdom higher than their own. It may be that

those whose minds have been largely formed by scripture as canonized find it natural to make a judgment of this kind. But it is not mere hindsight to say, with William Barclay, that "the New Testament books became canonical because no one could stop them doing so" or even, in the exaggerated language of Oscar Cullmann, that "the books which were to form the future canon forced themselves on the Church by their intrinsic apostolic authority, as they do still, because the . . . Christ speaks in them."[5]

The Epistle to Philemon

In the letter to Philemon, Paul pleaded for the good treatment and even restoration of a runaway slave named Onesimus. The apostle led him to Christ and now asked that all be forgiven him. Two statements point to Paul's authority: He began by writing that he was "a prisoner of Christ Jesus," incarcerated as a special minister of the Lord (v. 1). Secondly, he sent an apostolic greeting similar to what was found in other letters: "Grace to you and peace from God our Father and the Lord Jesus Christ" (v. 3). Again, this was not simply a polite salutation but an authoritative pronouncement from one who represented the Lord to people.

By the way Paul wrote and pleaded in this small letter, there is no doubt that, because of his apostolic position, he was diplomatically arguing for grace in the matter of Onesimus. Yet no one could accuse Paul here of an unfair advantage. He was understanding and was not asserting his authority in Philemon's personal affairs in an unjust manner. This is an important letter, though short, because it revealed the heart and soul of the great apostle. He spoke for the Lord, but he was also compassionate in his human dealings.

FOR DISCUSSION

1. What is important about Paul's calling and his testimony about his apostleship?

2. What can be learned from Paul's statements to those who were opposing his ministry?

3. What makes the Book of Galatians an important letter?

4. How strongly did Paul state his apostolic authority in the Galatian and the Thessalonian letters?

5. What does it mean to the doctrine of inspiration when Paul, in almost all his letters, began by writing, "Paul, an apostle by the will of God"?

For Further Study

Commentaries

Bruce, F.F. *The Canon of Scripture*. Downers Grove, Ill.: InterVarsity, 1988.

Couch, Mal. *A Bible Handbook to the Acts of the Apostles*. Grand Rapids: Kregel, 1999.

Gill, John. *Expositions on the Old and New Testaments*. 7 vols. Grand Rapids: Baker, 1980.

Lenski, C. H. *The Interpretation of 1 and 2 Epistles of Peter*. Minneapolis: Augsburg, 1966.

Nicoll, W. Robertson. *The Expositor's Greek Testament*. 5 vols. Grand Rapids: Eerdmans, 1988.

Chapter Seventeen

Inerrancy of the Epistle to the Hebrews

*T*he Book of Hebrews contains a number of unusual features that are readily noticeable by those studying the book. For example: 1) It is not a letter or epistle in the normal sense, but it reads like a legal brief or a doctrinal treatise containing specific arguments about the person of Christ. 2) It was written specifically to prove to Jewish readers who Jesus was. 3) It quoted extensively from the often imperfect Greek translation of the Old Testament called the Septuagint. 4) It was sent to believers who apparently were well known by the author and was probably meant to be an evangelistic and apologetic tool. 5) It was penned by an author unknown by us today, though it is certain that those living at the time of its composition knew him well. Some but not all of the points will be taken up below.

The Date of Hebrews

Most scholars agree the Book of Hebrews was written before the destruction of the temple (A.D. 70). The author wrote as if the temple were still standing. If the temple and Jerusalem had been destroyed by the time of this writing, more than likely this terrible event would have been mentioned. Since Jewish resistance to the gospel was increasing and persecution was on the rise, more than likely the book was written before A.D. 64.

Not Written as an Epistle

The author in chapter 1 immediately began with the issue of how God spoke to the ancient Jewish fathers. Verse 2 moved directly to the importance of the coming of His Son to speak to that generation. "In these last days [God] has spoken to us in His Son, whom He appointed heir of all things."

The book can be called an exhortation (13:22), to understand the nature of Christ, His work on the cross, and His present intercessory ministry in heaven. But the arguments are more like a doctrinal treaty rather than the normal letter of encouragement written by Paul. It is true, however, that Hebrews closed with a benediction addressed to certain ones the author knew in an intimate way. But for the most part, the book is not an epistle.

Written to Jewish Readers

Hebrews may have been written to prove to the Jews who Jesus really was. This is not the view of most interpreters of Hebrews, but it seems this is most plausible when all the facts are considered. Some scholars seem to agree and note that it was a homily written to skeptical Jews who were well aware of the coming of Jesus but who had not yet arrived at a decision about Him. Most have thought that Hebrews was a Christian epistle like the letters of Paul because of the reference to believers at the end of the book. Obviously, the book was sent to Christians so they could use it in answering the doubts of the Jewish communities. Nicoll quotes Reuss who says it "is not a letter properly so called written in view of a local necessity; and the few personal and circumstantial details added on the last page were certainly not the reasons which prompted the author to write."[1]

Extensive Quotes from the Septuagint

Nicoll agrees and suggests that the author of this treatise was writing to the Christian community that was in conflict with the Jews who lived in Rome. The writer seemed to be saying in 13:24 that Roman Christians with him were sending greetings *back to Italy* (*probably Rome*). These facts explain why the Septuagint, the translation of the Hebrew of the Old Testament into Greek, was quoted so often in Hebrews. Jews outside the Holy Land used the Septuagint almost exclusively. Few of them would have known the Hebrew language or even the related Aramaic that was the popular dialect spoken in the land at the time of Christ.

The Septuagint is an imperfect translation with license taken in explaining the Hebrew text, and yet it is quoted in the inspired Book of Hebrews. Does this fact violate the concept of inspiration and inerrancy? The answer is no. Several important reasons can explain why this does not adversely affect these important doctrines.

First, one rule of inspiration is that what the authors of Scripture may cite or quote from other sources is left in its natural condition. We can also observe that the authors of the Bible had different levels of literary skills. Some had great linguistic abilities, and others wrote with simple vocabulary and grammatical styles. The case of Peter may prove the point. He was a fisherman who had limited writing abilities and probably dictated his thoughts which a scribe wrote down in more sophisticated Greek. The imperfections in the Septuagint do not rescind the fact that the Septuagint was quoted in an inspired book like Hebrews.

Second, the author of Hebrews was extremely well educated in Old Testament doctrinal matters. His Greek was almost classical. He was a master logician who fine-tuned his arguments. He certainly believed the Old Testament Hebrew text was inspired. He also knew the imperfections of the Septuagint but quoted from it because his audience was familiar with it.

The Author of Hebrews

A well-known saying goes, "Only God knows who wrote Hebrews." Eusebius said:

> Paul's fourteen epistles are well known and undisputed. It is indeed right to overlook the fact that some have rejected the Epistle to the Hebrews, saying that it is disputed by the Church of Rome on the ground that it was not written by Paul.[2]

Several early church fathers rejected the Pauline authorship, such as the elder Caius, Photius, and Hippolytus. The old Latin version also omitted the book from the Pauline list. The Eastern and Syrian churches accepted the authorship of Paul. Others followed suit in Alexandria. Augustine often showed confusion on the subject. Sometimes he ascribed Hebrews to Paul; at other times he did not. Other authors suggested were Luke, Clement of Rome, Apollos, and Barnabas. To this writer, the last two men seem to be likely candidates.

No doubt, the name of the author of Hebrews was known in the early years after its composition. In the last few verses of the book (13:19–25), the author showed great closeness to the Christian community who received this work. He used the first person pronoun *I* often in this section and spoke of some form of restoration with those to whom he is writing (v. 19). He used such personal language as: "I urge you," "brethren," "I have written to you," "our brother Timothy," "I will see you," "those from Italy greet you," "Grace [from me] be with you all."

External Acceptance into the Canon

Generally speaking, Hebrews was well accepted and was usually attributed to Paul. Origen wrote, "Men of old time have handed it down as Paul's."[3] However, many early writers who mentioned the book recognized that its language was not typically Pauline. In many cases, one doubt about the book was that it was too Jewish or Hebraic in its message. And, of course, that was precisely why the book was written—to convey to Jewish people that Jesus was indeed their Messiah.

Origen offered another theory about how the book came to be written. Quoting Origen, Eusebius said, "The thoughts are the thoughts of the apostle [Paul], but the language and its composition that of one who recalled from memory and, as it were, made notes of what was said by [Paul] the master."[4] This is a compelling argument, but time has erased any evidence that might give credence to this view.

For the most part, Hebrews was well accepted in the New Testament canon. As the book is studied today, few would doubt its rightful place as part of the inspired and inerrant Word of God. Ellicott writes:

> At the close of the third century it would seem, as far as we may judge from extant Christian literature, that the Epistle was known and received by the churches of Alexandria, Syria, Rome, and Asia Minor.

> The influence of Jerome and Augustine ultimately prevailed in the West: neither of these eminent Fathers appears really to have regarded the Epistle as St. Paul's, but they agree in the expression of a strong conviction of its canonical authority.[5]

Despite the ongoing argument about its authorship, Hebrews holds a vital position in the canon of the New Testament. Thiessen quotes Westcott's *Epistle to the Hebrews*, "If we hold that the judgment of the Spirit makes itself felt through the consciousness of the Christian society, no book of the Bible is more completely recognized by universal consent as giving a divine view of the facts of the Gospel, full of lessons for all time, than the Epistle to the Hebrews."[6]

Internal Evidence of Inspiration and Inerrancy

Going back to what we have already said about 13:19–25, the author of this book wrote with a certain apostolic acceptance as one who was recognized as a spiritual leader in the early church community.

With strong authority, the author warned his readers: "See to it that you do not refuse Him who is speaking [right now to you]" (12:25). Though he included himself later in this warning by adding *we*, the context appears to show that he was referring to the entire Jewish nation, and thus the "brothers" he addressed were national blood relations. Such corporate warnings are found throughout Hebrews.

Additional evidence of the writer's authority is found in the way he quoted the Old Testament. He was not writing as a bystander but as one who held a commission from God to express grand spiritual ideas. The church fathers commenting on the book later also saw these important factors in the same light.

As already pointed out (but worth repeating), the author wrote with absolute apostolic authority. He made doctrinal connections not found anywhere else in the New Testament.

The author gave a strong salvation warning worthy of one having importance (2:3–4). He pointed out that he learned from those who had directly seen the Lord, and he was confirming and passing on what he had heard (v. 3). He added that those who knew Jesus had been witnessed to "by signs and wonders and by various miracles and by gifts of the Holy Spirit" (v. 4). He might be saying that this confirmation from the original apostles and passed down to him was "according to [God's] own will" (v. 4). In other words, it seems as if the witness of Christ came down through the apostles directly to this individual, though some have interpreted his statements to mean that he was *there* as Christ spoke and ministered when he said, "We must pay much closer attention to what we have heard" (2:1).

To his readers, the author wrote: "Concerning [Christ] we have much to say" (5:11); "We are convinced of better things concerning you" (6:9); "though we are speaking in this way" (v. 9); "your work and the love which you have shown" (v. 10); "we desire that each one of you show the same" (v. 11).

FOR DISCUSSION

1. How is inspiration and inerrancy affected by the fact that the Greek Septuagint was quoted so often in Hebrews?

2. Since the author of Hebrews is not known, does this affect the doctrines of inspiration and inerrancy?

3. Is the internal evidence of authority in the Book of Hebrews equally as strong as in most of Paul's letters?

For Further Study

Bible Introduction

Thiessen, Henry Clarence. *Introduction to the New Testament*. Grand Rapids: Eerdmans, 1958.

Commentaries

Ellicott, Charles John. Vol. 4 of *A Commentary on the Whole Bible*. 4 vols. Grand Rapids: Zondervan, 1959.

Nicoll, W. Robertson. *The Expositor's Greek Testament*. 5 vols. Grand Rapids: Eerdmans, 1988.

Chapter Eighteen

Inerrancy of the General Epistles and Epistles of John

U sually, the General Epistles include the Book of Hebrews, but that book was dealt with in a separate chapter. Hebrews and the letters of John (1–3) are sometimes grouped together in what is called the Second Group of the General Epistles. However, in this chapter, we'll deal with the Books of James, 1 and 2 Peter, Jude, and 1, 2, and 3 John.

Many of these books went through a period of questioning by the early church fathers. The fathers were not attempting to declare the issue of their inspiration or force these books into an inspired mold. Instead, they were researching to ascertain if these books were indeed canonical Scripture. In other words, they were not necessarily attempting to force the issue but rather discover the truth. Probably many thousands of hours of debate, discussion, conferences, and letter writing transpired to settle the issue. Eusebius in his *Ecclesiastical History* (A.D. 324) labeled all but one of the General Epistles *Antilegomena* or the books that were disputed. His list included James, Jude, 2 Peter, 2 and 3 John, Hebrews, and Revelation.

But things began to change for these books. Much study, prayer, and thought brought about the belief that they were truly inspired writings. The early uncial document *Sinaiticus* (fourth century) included all of the General Epistles. *Vaticanus* (fourth century) included all but Revelation. But it was believed that the Book of Revelation had been damaged or lost and therefore was not available when the list was compiled. By the fifth century with the *Alexandrinus* collection, all the General Epistles were included as inspired.

It is not the purpose of this discourse to deal in detail with all the external evidence for the above writings but to look more at the internal evidence and internal cross-reference factors that show inspiration and affirm the inerrancy of these books.

The Epistle of James

Most scholars believe that James was written early, probably around A.D. 45–48. Though there are several theories as to who this James might be, Thiessen sets forth a compelling argument that he was the half-brother of Jesus who was mentioned often in the Gospels and Acts.[1] His evidence is quite convincing.

Though Eusebius classified James as *Antilegomena,* he nevertheless quoted 4:11 as Scripture. Origen recognized James as canonical, and so did the Third Council of Carthage in A.D. 397. Thiessen points out that the internal evidence for canonicity is stronger than the external.[2] One reason that James was probably rejected early on was the fact that it was so Jewish. Because the Jews had persecuted the beginning Christian church, many of the fathers wanted to repudiate anything with a strong Jewish flavor.

The author wrote with all the evidence of being an apostle in the early church. He wrote with authority and gave strong commands to those reading his letter. As well, he was a master at quoting the Old Testament but also alluded to parts of the New Testament. If his book was written early, as all the evidence seems to support, many would have been alive who could confirm the truthfulness and trustworthiness of what he said.

James 1:18 stands out as an important verse in that it appears to be a paraphrased quote of John 1:13. James alluded to the purpose of God who "brought us forth" by His will through the agency of "the word of truth." This last phrase is seen in John 1, but also Paul used it specifically in 2 Corinthians 6:7 and in part in Ephesians 1:13. This is not to say that these books were written before the Book of James. But the point is that such expressions and phrases were common and well known in the Christian community.

The writer James gave a sound theological discussion on the proper role of the Law. He uplifted the Law in value but then made an important contrast to something new—the perfect law of liberty. With cogent authority, the writer laid the Law down and picked up the new dynamic, which was "your faith in our glorious Lord Jesus Christ" (2:1). Chapter 2 is often misunderstood. James argued that as people see our Christian works carried out in human experience, we are "justified by works" (v. 21) before them. But concerning our salvation positionally, as with Abraham, our faith is reckoned as righteousness (v. 23). James clarified his point when he wrote that our faith works with our works, and by this, faith is perfected (matured, completed). Outwardly before other people, our faith is dead if they cannot see fruit or meaningful works (v. 26).

In the early church, this message was important for many Jews coming to Christ. Their background fostered law-keeping as a virtue and, for many, a way of salvation. James brought balance to the issue by telling his brothers to live as they believed; one can't believe one thing and say another. But at the same time, he was not advocating works-salvation, as many have misunderstood.

The Book of James contains some twenty-five commands, with many more in the third person as imperatives and translated, "Let him . . ." The author also gave authoritative orders concerning prayer for the sick and the calling of the elders (5:14). He disciplined the rich (v. 1) and commanded confession (v. 16). He criticized the hypocrisy of those who wanted to be teachers (3:1–12) and called his readers adulteresses (4:4) and murderers with the mouth (2:11). In 4:7–11 he gave a series of straightforward and heavy commands that indicated his right to chide with stinging authority: "Submit therefore to God"; "resist the devil"; "draw near to God"; "cleanse your hands, you sinners; and purify your hearts, you double-minded"; "be miserable and mourn and weep; let your laughter be turned into mourning and your joy to gloom"; "humble yourselves"; "do not speak against one another."

Though the Book of James is different than most New Testament writings, still the tone, along with strong circumstantial evidence, clearly indicates that it is an inspired work of the Holy Spirit. And if inspired, inerrancy follows.

Martin Luther had great problems with James because he felt the book contradicted Paul's doctrine of justification by faith. But a careful study does not indicate this. Luther was so zealous for justification by faith for salvation that he could not understand what James was teaching. Nothing within James contradicts or gives any indication that the book is not from the Lord. Thiessen summarizes the importance of James:

We must date [James] before A.D. 62 or 63, for according to Josephus that was the time when he was killed. The internal evidence points to a date still earlier than this. . . . There was apparently no very close [church] organization, for various members of the congregation put themselves forward as teachers. The believers still met in the "synagogue," one, of course, in which the Christians had control. All this points to a very early period in the history of the Church. . . . The question of the admission of the Gentiles seems not yet to have come to the fore. This indicates that the Epistle must have been written before the Jerusalem Council (A.D. 48 or 49), for that was the great question at that meeting. There is no contradiction between James and Paul. . . . There is a Judaic tone throughout. . . . James believes in saving faith just as well as Paul (see 2:1, 5, 22–24).[3]

The First Epistle of Peter

Origen distinguished the following books as *Homologoumena*, that is, books that were universally accepted in his day: the four Gospels, Paul's thirteen letters, 1 John, Acts, Revelation, and 1 Peter. Eusebius also considered 1 Peter canonical. In fact, no book had such early and strong attestation. First Peter was also quoted directly or alluded to by Hermas, Polycarp, Clement, Theophilus, Irenaeus, and Turtullian. Clement of Alexandria quoted the entire book. The internal evidence as well points to the genuineness of the letter and bears witness to its inspiration. It points also to the clear fact that the apostle Peter was the author.

Eusebius says that Peter was martyred during the thirteenth year of Nero's reign (A.D. 67–68), about the year Paul was beheaded by Nero though probably just before he was killed. The best date then for its composition is A.D. 65.

If any writers would be accepted as spokesmen for the Lord, even by the most vocal critics of the New Testament, it would be Matthew, John, Peter, and Paul, as well as James and Jude who were half-brothers of Christ. By the lofty nature of their Gospels and letters and by many statements they made, it is clear that the Holy Spirit inspired them. Their messages came from the Lord. Though early church fathers sometimes had difficulty in demonstrating the authenticity of the New Testament, they understood inspiration as a doctrine, though it was not formulated in any detail until years later. And inerrancy was part of the doctrine of inspiration. Inerrancy was simply accepted but not necessarily elaborated on.

The authority of the author of 1 Peter was stated in strong and virile terms. The book is personal, doctrinal, and apostolic. For example:

- *Peter claimed he was an apostle of the Lord (1:1).*
- *He virtually claimed inspiration when he wrote, "Through Silvanus [Silas], our faithful brother, . . . I have written to you briefly, exhorting and testifying that this is the true grace of God. Stand firm in it!" (5:12).*
- *With an overwhelming sense of authority, Peter gave specific commands to how wives and husbands are to relate to one another (3:1–12).*
- *He clarified in many verses the doctrine of salvation through faith. He wrote, "[You] are protected by the power of God through faith for a salvation ready to be revealed in the last time . . . obtaining as the outcome of your faith the salvation of your souls" (1:5, 9).*
- *Peter wrote with prophetic authority (4:7).*
- *Peter wrote with doctrinal authority (1:18; 2:1, 24).*
- *Peter called himself a fellow elder but one who was giving instruction to other elders (5:1). With great confidence and authority, he gave commands to these elders as to how they were to deal with the community of believers (5:2–9).*
- *Peter mentioned that he witnessed the sufferings of Christ (5:1).*
- *Peter alluded to the fact that he was at Christ's transfiguration and thus was "a partaker also of the glory that is to be revealed" (5:1; see Matt. 17:1–7).*
- *Peter was with Mark and Silas who were well-known early church personalities (5:12–13).*
- *Peter was well known by those to whom he was writing (5:12–14).*

In the opening greeting of 1 Peter 1:1, "The authoritative tone of this Epistle is shown at the outset. The writer assumes his full titles. . . . Observe also that while St. Paul constantly adds 'by the will of God,' or some similar phrase, by way of justifying his assumption of the title, St. Peter has no need to do more than mention it; his claim was never questioned. . . . Peter knows of no higher title to bestow on himself than that which he held in common with the other eleven—'an Apostle.' "[4]

The Second Epistle of Peter

Though 2 Peter was a disputed book, Origen said (A.D. 240), "Peter has left one acknowledged epistle, and perhaps a second; for it is disputed." Origen was one of the most thoughtful of the ancient critics, and this statement means that he was at least open to the book being canonical. He does not express what the issues were over 2 Peter. Though direct quotations are not there, the later noncanonical writings, the *Apocalypse of Peter, the Gospel of Peter, the Preaching of Peter,* and the *Acts of Peter,* seem to allude to 2 Peter. Eusebius said concerning the church father Clement, that in his "Outlines" he gave concise explanations of all canonical Scriptures and did not leave out any of the disputed books, which would have included 2 Peter.[5]

Critics want to place the date of the writing of 2 Peter into the second century but this is not a valid position and would destroy the Petrine authorship. The writing probably fell into the same time period of 1 Peter, around A.D. 64.

Around A.D. 330, Emperor Constantine requested that Eusebius produce fifty Bibles for the churches in Constantinople. The emperor would pay the cost and desired that they be elaborately bound. The work of Eusebius included our twenty-seven New Testament books, along with the disputed General Epistles.

By the fourth century, the issues of doubt surrounding 2 Peter seemed to be nearly over. The following New Testament collections or lists from church fathers include 2 Peter:

- *Sinaiticus (fourth century A.D.)*
- *Vaticanus (fourth century A.D.)*
- *Alexandrinus (fifth century A.D.)*
- *Athanasius (fourth century A.D.)*
- *Laodicea (fourth century A.D.)*
- *Epiphanius (fourth century A.D.)*
- *Chrysostom (fourth century A.D.)*

However, Theodore of Mopsuestia (died A.D. 428) rejected 2 Peter; in fact, he rejected all the General Epistles except 1 Peter and 1 John. By A.D. 508, the Syriac canon had included 2 Peter and the other General Epistles.

The doctrine of the inspiration of this book abounds in evidence. Peter put forth his apostolic office (1:1) and wrote with full apostolic authority (vv. 2–11). He reminded his readers that they had been "established in the truth" (v. 12) and that he wished to stir them up in remembrance of that position (v. 13). He said he knew "that the laying aside of my earthly dwelling [was] imminent" (v. 14). As in 1 Peter, the author reminded them that he was on the Mount of Transfiguration when "the Majestic Glory" gave His utterance in regard to Christ's deity: "This is My beloved Son with whom I am well-pleased" (v. 17).

Peter understood later how the Lord worked with him on the issue of prophetic inspiration. He wrote, "So we have the prophetic word made more sure, to which you do well to pay attention . . . in your hearts" (v. 19). In other words, You do well to heed what we saw and have written about. He reminded them that the prophetic message of the Old Testament Scriptures did not come by the self-interpretation of the prophets (v. 20), but they were borne along by the Holy Spirit and spoke from God (v. 21). In these two verses (vv. 20–21), Peter not only referred to the Old Testament Scriptures, but added his testimony as one who heard God the Father testify about Jesus. He seemed to put himself in the same camp as the prophets of old.

Second Peter 3 seems to be a key passage concerning the inspiration and inerrancy of this book. Peter pointed out that this was the second letter he had written to them. His purpose was "that you should remember the words spoken beforehand by the holy prophets and the commandment of the Lord and Savior spoken by your apostles" (v. 2). He implied by the verses that follow (vv. 3–12) that mockers denied those messages given by the older prophets, Christ, and the apostles, which included Peter himself. The rejecters turned against the message of Peter who was considered an inspired New Testament prophet.

Peter gave an important testimony about the inspired author Paul whom he called "our beloved brother" (v. 15). Paul, who wrote to the churches, he said, was granted wisdom from God. In his letters, "speaking in them of these things, in which are some things hard to understand, which the untaught and unstable distort, as they do also the rest of the Scriptures, to their own destruction" (v. 16). Peter thus viewed Paul's letters as being on the same level as the Old Testament.

There is no reason to deny 2 Peter in the lofty place of divinely inspired Scripture. In time the church came to that same conclusion:

> There was considerable hesitation about 2 Peter, but by the time of Athanasius it was no longer a disputed book in the Alexandrian church or in western Christendom. Its explicit claim to be the work of the apostle Peter was probably felt to be supported by the fact that it contained nothing unworthy of him.[6]

The Three Epistles of John

There was early on strong evidence for the acceptance of 1 John having been penned by the apostle John. In time, all three books were accepted as having been written by him. But 2 and 3 John took more time to be accepted, probably because they were short letters and therefore not universally circulated among all the churches. There is almost total agreement that these short epistles were written about the time of the composition of the Book of Revelation by John, around A.D. 85–91.

> The style and vocabulary of 2 John [and 3 John] are so much like that in the Gospel [of John] that the one who wrote the latter must also have written the former. Besides, there is no conceivable ground for forgery in this case; surely, a forger would have represented the writer as an apostle, and not as an elder.[7]

The first chapter of 1 John is loaded with authoritative and apostolic markers. John opened his first epistle with these words:

> What we have heard, what we have seen with our eyes, what we have looked at and touched with our hands, concerning the Word of Life—and the life was manifested, and we have seen and testify and proclaim to you the eternal life, which was with the Father and was manifested to us—what we have seen and heard we proclaim to you also, . . . These things we write. . . . This is the message we have heard from Him and announce to you. (1:1–5)

No New Testament letter contains more confirmation as to the authenticity of the writer, his spiritual authority, and the fact that he personally walked with the Lord Jesus. Over and over again he said "I am writing these things to you." He spoke as one representing Jesus and wrote with apostolic authority. In a most powerful verse, John wrote, "He who knows God listens to us; he who is not from God does not listen to us. By this we know the spirit of truth and the spirit of error" (4:6).

On this verse Kistemaker notes, "John stresses the first person plural in his use of pronoun and verbs to show (apostolic) authority."[8] Showing additional evidence of his apostleship, John added, "These things I have written to you who believe in the name of the Son of God, so that you may know that you have eternal life" (5:13).

Second John is the shortest epistle in the New Testament with just thirteen verses. The book has the same tone and language as 1 John. Grammatically, it also parallels the Gospel of John. In 2 John, the apostle wrote of himself as "the elder" (v. 1). This fits the fact that he was indeed the apostle of great age who had survived the persecutions and even martyrdom that fell earlier on the church and took the lives of all the apostles but himself. This also corresponds with the belief that these books, along with Revelation, were composed late. He added, "Though

I have many things to write to you, I do not want to do so with paper and ink; but I hope to come to you and speak face to face" (v. 12).

Third John is very similar to 2 John. The apostle in 3 John closed with the same thought of desiring not to write with pen and ink but to come to those he was addressing personally (v. 13). In this letter he also called himself "the elder" (v. 1) and mentioned that earlier he had written to the church (v. 9), probably where Gaius, to whom the letter was written, was a member.

All three letters carry apostolic and authoritative weight. They were addressed to personalities and spoke of a larger body of believers who knew and obviously respected the author as one speaking for the Lord.

The Epistle of Jude

In regard to Jude, Thiessen writes,

> Both 2 Peter and Jude deal with conditions to some extent already present in their day; but both are probably also to be regarded as predictions of the conditions that are to prevail in the last time. From this standpoint they are fitting introductions to the Apocalypse.[9]

Most scholars believe that all the evidence points to the fact that Jude was written after 2 Peter, probably around A.D. 75. This would put Jude as an older man, though many believe he was about ten years younger than Jesus. When Jude wrote, persecution against the early church was intensifying. The city of Jerusalem and the temple had been destroyed. In 2 Peter, the author seemed to have known some in his audience. But Jude appeared to be writing in a broader sweep, addressing Jewish believers in a wide circle. He repeated many things that Peter had written.

Peter and the other apostles (except John) had died, and this left Jude as a very important spokesman for the church. The consensus is that Jude, who said he was the brother of James (v. 1), was also a half-brother of the Lord. This would clearly identify him as part of the family of Christ, though he probably did not accept Jesus as the Messiah until after His resurrection. That he was a younger brother of Christ was mentioned in Matthew 13:55. Earlier he did not believe in the Lord (John 7:3–8), then he trusted in Him, was with the other brothers and Mary in the upper room after the ascension (Acts 1:14), and in later years, traveled with his wife for the sake of the gospel (1 Cor. 9:5).

The writer Hegesippus mentioned two grandsons of Jude, farmers who were brought before the Emperor Domitian (A.D. 95) and accused of being Christians and descendants of David. When the emperor saw they were simple laborers, he released them as harmless Jews.

Though Jude was not part of the inner circle of disciples and apostles, he was still considered an important witness in the wider sphere of early followers and leaders. As a brother of Jesus, he knew Him, saw His ministry (even as a skeptic), became a believer, and apparently became a strong influential spiritual force in the early church. Thus, when he wrote this small epistle, he confirmed the earlier message of Peter and placed his stamp on the prophetic ministry of the apostles.

A number of church fathers clearly alluded to and quoted the Book of Jude. Eusebius placed this book among the *Antilegomena* writings but not beside the more spurious letters. Jude thus had stronger external support than 2 Peter.

In verse 1 Jude wrote to his audience with certain apostolic authority. His words must have been heeded because he related how he was making every effort to communicate with them about their common salvation in Christ (v. 3). With bold authority, he warned them of the coming of false teachers (v. 4). He said that he wrote to "remind them" of the dangers of false prophets. He mentioned past events in the Old Testament Scriptures where error infected others (v. 5). He spoke of fallen angels (v. 6) and the sinful events of Sodom and Gomorrah (v. 7). In verse 11 Jude pronounced a woe on false teachers. In verse 17 he urged his readers to remember the words of the apostles of the Lord previously given to them specifically. He wrote that the apostles "were saying to you" (v. 18). This placed his audience and Jude himself close to the other writing apostles with whom they were associating or knew in an intimate way.

In verses 9–10 Jude quoted from the apocryphal books of 1 Enoch, the Testament of Moses, and possibly the writing called the Assumption of Moses. Because of this, some church fathers rejected Jude. But we should note some things about how Jude quoted these religious writings. First, he did not use any statements of authority in quoting, such as, "It is written" or, "the Word of God says." When he mentioned the rebuke against the devil, "The Lord rebuke you," he used this clause taken from Zechariah 3:2 as a principle way to refute Satan. Thus, his entire approach to these quotes was illustrative rather than authoritative.

By the fourth century, the church for the most part accepted Jude. By the fifth century, almost no one questioned the book's notable place in the New Testament canon.

The Stamp of Authority

These General Epistles all have the stamp of authority as canonical and inspired by the Holy Spirit. Up to the fourth century, the church wrestled with the arguments pro and con about some of them and their places in Scripture. However, this questioning does not mean that all scholars had doubts. We are incorrect to think that their research on this issue was primitive. By degree, the doubts faded, and scholars reached a measure of meaningful consensus. In time, the overwhelming conclusion from every aspect of examination put these letters as part of the written Word of God. No consequential objections denied them their places in the canon. They were accepted as the voice of God in written form. And since they are inspired, they are inerrant.

We must remember that when we speak of inspiration and inerrancy, we are referring to the original autographs or initial writings of the apostles, not later copies. Copy errors are continually being corrected even now, two thousand years after the time of the New Testament. Finally,

> In believing that the Bible is inspired and inerrant we hold that God divinely guided the apostles and prophets to write down exactly what He wanted, and that the Scriptures are totally without error and accurate. Evangelicals have historically held to this view, and it is often stated as a belief in verbal (the very words, not just thoughts and ideas), plenary (equally in every part of the Scriptures) inspiration. It should be stated, though, that only the original documents (. . . referred to as autographs) are free from error.[10]

FOR DISCUSSION

1. Why did Martin Luther have questions about the canonicity of the Book of James?

2. How do the straightforward commands and injunctions play on the authority of James and his letter?

3. Is there strong evidence for the inspiration and inerrancy of 1 and 2 Peter?

4. Because the Greek of 2 Peter is quite sophisticated and probably shows that Peter dictated this letter to a learned scribe, would this fact discredit the doctrine of inspiration? Why or why not?

5. Why were 2 and 3 John not widely accepted at first as canonical books?

6. Why did a long period pass before Jude was accepted as a canonical letter?

For Further Study

Bible Introduction

Bruce, F. F. *The Canon of Scripture*. Downers Grove, Ill.: InterVarsity, 1988.

Thiessen, Henry Clarence. *Introduction to the New Testament*. Grand Rapids: Eerdmans, 1958.

Bibliology Texts

Couch, Mal, ed. *An Introduction to Classical Evangelical Hermeneutics*. Grand Rapids: Kregel, 2000.

Harrison, Everett F. *Introduction to the New Testament*. Grand Rapids: Eerdmans, 1974.

Kistemaker, Simon J. *James and 1–3 John*. Grand Rapids: Baker, 1986.

Commentaries

A. J. Mason. "The First Epistle of St. Peter." In vol. 8 of *Commentary on the Whole Bible*. 8 vols. Edited by Charles John Ellicott. Grand Rapids: Zondervan, 1959)

Chapter Nineteen

Inerrancy of the Book of Revelation

*A*s the final book in the New Testament canon, Revelation stands out as the climax of all the Word of God teaches. Some distinct issues are worth noting about the Book of Revelation: 1) It contains more than 350 direct quotes, allusions, and indirect quotes from the Old Testament and even from the Gospels. 2) It speaks to the doctrine of the Trinity and the deity of Christ more than any other single source. 3) Its main thrusts are the events of the Tribulation. The happenings that close world history as we know it (the second coming of Christ, the millennial reign, the final judgment against Satan and the lost, and the beginning of the eternal state) are also salient features of Revelation. 4) If read in a normal fashion, the reader will obtain a premillennial understanding of end-time phenomena. Although it is full of illustration and comparative language, the Apocalypse can be properly exposited only by the utilization of plain interpretation.

The Value of the Book of Revelation

Many Christians have little idea of the value, purpose, and importance of the Book of Revelation. For some who try to read the apostle John's last letter to the church, the effort seems too great. Others make no attempt at grasping the message of the book. The word has already gone forth that "Revelation is too mysterious to try to understand."

Also, many are told that scholars themselves are woefully divided as to the meaning of this prophecy. And if godly men who study the Word cannot figure out its meaning, how can the average Christian? With such a comprehensive mountain to climb, this volume remains a closed book to most.

269

Consider the Books of Genesis and Revelation: They are bookends with the rest of Scripture in between. The Book of Revelation is necessary because it explains and summarizes how world history, God's history, will come to a conclusion. Revelation reveals the darkest times that will ever fall on humankind, but it also sheds light on how the redeemed have a final and glorious victory through the Lord Jesus Christ.

Revelation Is God's Word

Though most Christians struggle to understand the book, the average believer has no problem accepting it as one of the inspired books of Scripture. And for centuries Revelation has been accepted as part of the canon of the New Testament and as part of the Word of God. Perhaps more than any other book of Scripture, it contains overwhelming internal evidence of inspiration and inerrancy.

Although some questioned it for the first few hundred years of church history, later scholars almost universally accepted it as a unique feature of the inspired New Testament. They saw it as that final bookend of divine revelation. Walvoord writes:

> The revelation recorded by John the Apostle is presented as having a solid historical basis in his exile on the Isle of Patmos. In the literature of the second half of the second century, evidence begins to reveal wide circulation of the Apocalypse.[1]

Henry Thiessen notes

> the fact that the early church, in spite of certain objections, generally accepted the book of Revelation by the end of the second century and the Eastern Church soon followed suit. Among conservative scholars, there is little disposition to exclude the book of Revelation from the canon.[2]

Jesus Is the Divine Author

Though the Holy Spirit inspired the sacred writers of the Bible, the Book of Revelation has another important dimension to it. John the apostle was the human penman, but the message came directly from Jesus Christ Himself. The first line in the book reads, "The Revelation of [literally, 'from'] Jesus Christ" (1:1). Jesus passed on to His disciples a direct message from God the Father, who "communicated it by His angel to His bond-servant John."

Larkin writes,

Thus we see that the canon of Scripture would be incomplete without this message [of Revelation] from Jesus to His Church after His return to Heaven. While the Apostle John is the writer of the Book, he is not the author or composer. The author was the Lord Jesus Himself. The Apostle was only a "scribe."[3]

Daniel's Seventieth Week: Fulfilled in the Apocalypse

The phrase "seventieth week of Daniel" is found in Daniel 9:24–27.

Daniel was informed that God was going to have seventy weeks (490 years) of special dealings with Israel in order to accomplish six great purposes. The final week of seven years (the Seventieth Week) is yet future and is commonly called the Tribulation."[4]

When Daniel was praying for his people (Dan. 9), the angel Gabriel revealed that some 490 years would be "decreed for" Israel. Since a "week" was seven years, seventy "weeks" total 490 years. These would be special years in which God would deal with the nation. But Gabriel said that after the sixty-ninth "week" was finished and before that final seventh week took place, some important events would transpire.

The Messiah or promised King would be "cut off" or hindered from carrying out His great reign, and the temple of Jerusalem would be destroyed. Though risen from the dead and seated in heaven beside His Father, the Lord Jesus is not reigning now on His earthly Davidic throne. And as Daniel prophesied, the great temple was destroyed. This took place in A.D. 70.

Because of the intertwining of Daniel and Revelation, the inspiration of Scripture can be readily perceived.

Revelation Reveals the Second Coming of Christ

The Old Testament prophetic books were filled with descriptions of what we now know to be two comings of the One called the Anointed or the Messiah. His lineage, place of birth, nature of His birth (by a virgin), and His death for the sins of His people (Isa. 53) were all predicted and fulfilled in Christ's first coming.

Christ's second coming as King of Israel and the world is also clearly foretold. In fact, hundreds of verses describe this coming and its impact on the Jews, the Middle East, and all humanity. Whole chapters describe how the land will be changed, nature harnessed, evil punished, health increased, and the nations will truly know God and His Messiah. These themes occupy much of the content of the Major and Minor Prophets.

The Dating of Revelation

The debate regarding the integrity of the inspiration of Revelation is tied to the subject of its dating. If the book is dated late, the writing then is the literal conclusion of most of the inspired prophetic utterances of the Old Testament prophets. If the book was written before A.D. 70, it becomes meaningless and virtually unintelligible to the average thinking person. This conclusion is proven true by the teachings of amillennialists and preterists who rip the heart of its message from its pages.

The dating of the Book of Revelation has been used by amillennialists and preterists to spiritualize the idea of the kingdom and the second coming of Christ. For example, by dating the writing of the book just before A.D. 70, preterists claim that Christ came back in a spiritual sense at the fall of Jerusalem. This allows them to destroy any literal or normal interpretation of the book. They can then spiritualize away the main emphasis of its message, that is, the tribulation.

However, even the church historian and amillennialist Philip Schaff admits that only the later dating of the book makes sense from all we know of ecclesiastical history. He says, "The traditional date of composition at the end of Domitian's reign (95–96) rests on the clear and weighty testimony of Irenaeus, is confirmed by Eusebius and Jerome, and has still its learned defenders."[5]

Other writers attempt to sidestep the A.D. 96 dating by denying that the apostle John is the author. As Walvoord notes:

> It is most significant that in many cases the theological bias against the chiliastic teaching of the book of Revelation seems to be the actual motive in rejecting the apostolic authorship [and the late dating] of the book.[6]

Robertson adds:

> Based on . . . slim evidence some today argue that John did not live to the end of the century and so did not write any of the Johannine books. But a respectable number of modern scholars still hold to the ancient view that the Apocalypse of John is the work of the Apostle and Beloved Disciple, the son of Zebedee.[7]

Schaff points out that strong tradition held that John was the apostle of Christ and that he taught that the antichrist would come after the destruction of the Roman Empire. Christ will then appear visibly, bind Satan, reign in the rebuilt city of Jerusalem, and celebrate the millennial

Sabbath that subsequently prepares the saints for eternal glory. After a temporary liberation of Satan, a final resurrection will follow, the lost will be judged, and the consummation of the universe will take place, with the new heavens and new earth coming after.[8]

This, of course, is what premillennialists teach today. We seem to be in the good company of the most outstanding teachers among the early fathers. Too, such statements by the church fathers give credence to the inspiration of the Scriptures. The church fathers verify that John was giving truth that was inspired by the Holy Spirit.

The Inspiration and Inerrancy of Revelation

Many internal markers point to these important doctrines. For example:

- *John recorded the words, it was "said unto me" fifty-two times.*
- *Jesus was the first author of the book (1:1).*
- *Christ "sent and communicated it by His angel" (1:1).*
- *The message was handed over to the bond-servant John (1:1).*
- *The message was to be transmitted to His bond-servants (1:1).*
- *The message of the book was given to Christ to reveal (1:1–3).*
- *John "testified to the word of God and to the testimony of Jesus Christ" (1:2). This declaration more than likely refers to the beginning of Christ's ministry when John first met and traveled with Him.*
- *A special blessing comes to those who read, hear, and heed the words of Revelation (1:3; cf. 22:7). The plural "words" suggests that each word of the Apocalypse is inspired, not simply the large ideas of the book.*
- *John was told to write his words "in a book" (1:11).*
- *John was told to write the things he had seen, "and the things which are, and the things which will take place after these things" (1:19).*
- *In Revelation 2—3 Jesus said, "He who has an ear, let him hear what the Spirit says."*
- *John was shown "what must take place after these things" (4:1).*
- *Revelation 11:15–19 was written like a prophetic proclamation. God will reward His "bond-servants the prophets" (v. 18). "The mystery of God is finished, as He preached to His servants the prophets" (10:7).*
- *"For the testimony of Jesus is the spirit of Prophecy" (19:10). This means that the very nature or purpose of prophecy is to testify of and bring glory to Him. The disciples were merely vehicles of Jesus' words.*
- *The angel speaking to John said that he was only "a fellow-servant of yours [John's] and of your brethren the prophets and of those who heed the words of this book" (22:9).*

Seven times in Revelation 22, John referred to "this book," "the words of this book," and "the words of this prophecy of this book" (vv. 7, 9–10, 18 [twice], 19 [twice]). The idea conveyed is that this work has great spiritual authority because God Himself and His Son authored it.

With these references, John presented a sober warning: Do not tamper with these words! "I testify to everyone who hears the words of the prophecy of this book: if anyone adds to them, God will add to him the plagues which are written in this book; and if anyone takes away from the words of the book of this prophecy, God will take away his part from the tree of life and from the holy city, which are written in this book" (22:18–19).

In addition to warning against adding or subtracting from the Book of Revelation, it may also speak against adding any new "revelation" to the entire New Testament. Anyone claiming to present new revelation as if it were from God will be condemned. What a solemn warning this is to critics who have tampered with this book and other portions of Scripture in the belief that they are equipped intellectually to determine what is true and what is not true in the Word of God.

Thomas believes the admonition in these verses verifies the close of the New Testament canon:

> This is a warning not just to the would-be prophets themselves, who might try to continue prophetic ministries beyond the time of Revelation's writing, but also to "everyone who hears," i.e., those in the churches who needed to refuse any authority that challenged the divine authority, accuracy, and finality of this prophecy. The observation is true that this warning applies specifically to the book of Revelation only, but by extension it entails the termination of the gift of prophecy and the NT canon also.[9]

Allusions to the Old Testament

The Apocalypse, perhaps more than any other book of Holy Writ, is packed with numerous references to the important subjects of inspiration and inerrancy. Scores of allusions to the Old Testament weave a tapestry of divine revelation that make this book a summary of a vast storehouse of ancient prophetic utterances. The Bible would be woefully incomplete without the insights of the inspired final "chapter" of Scripture, the Apocalypse.

Why do the critics work so hard to discredit the Book of Revelation? LaHaye gives an insightful answer:

No book in the Bible has been more discredited than Revelation except for its counterpart in the Old Testament, the book of Daniel. Because Revelation deals predominantly with prophecy and the future, and because it exposes Satan as a deceptive fraud, the arch-enemy of man has tried his hardest to discredit the book. The last thing he wants is for people to become aware of Christ's majesty, Satan's treachery, and the Christian's final trump when this old world system ultimately fails.[10]

Fulfilled Prophecy

A compelling force in this subject of inerrancy is fulfilled prophecy. If a prediction is made hundreds or thousands of years in advance and then happens with astonishing accuracy, such a prophecy had its source in God.

On the doctrine of inerrancy, the quotes below have stood the test of critical scrutiny for generations:

> The Scriptures contain no error; they are written throughout by inspi-ration of God. . . . We are called to respect them and to study them, even to their smallest iota and their slightest jot: for "this Scripture is pure, like silver refined seven times: it is perfect." – *Louis Gaussen*

> You know that in the Scriptures there has not been written any-thing that is unrighteous or counterfeit. – *Clement*

> There is no discrepancy in the facts recorded. The prophets com-piled accurately the history of their own time. – *Josephus*

> The very phrases of Holy Scripture are the result of Inspiration. – *Tertullian*

> We trace the accuracy of the Spirit in detail to each separate stroke and letter; for it is blasphemous to suppose that exact pains were bestowed by the compilers of the Books, or even the smallest let-ters, without design. – *Gregory of Nazianzus*

> There is divergence in the historical narratives of the Gospels, but there is no contradiction. – *Chrysostom*

> Every phrase or syllable or point in Holy Scripture is full of meaning. – *Jerome*

> God bade the prophets to write, as though they were His own very words. – *Augustine*

The Scriptures have never erred. — *Luther*

If we consider how slippery is the human mind, how prone to all kinds of error, we can perceive how necessary is such a repository of heavenly doctrine [in the Bible], that it will neither perish by forgetfulness, nor vanish in error, nor be corrupted by the audacity of men. — *Calvin*

The Scripture is the only infallible rule of faith and practice. — *Westminster Confession*

If Jesus spoke erroneously at the beginning or mingled the true with the false, what could we think of Him? With our eternal salvation standing or falling on it, what certainty could we find in a revelation like that? — *Pache*

A few years ago Lindsell wrote a sober warning to us today:

In recent years evangelical Christianity has been infiltrated by people who do not believe in inerrancy. This penetration into the evangelical spectrum is my deep concern. Having laid a foundation to demonstrate that the church historically has been committed to biblical inerrancy, I must now show that among evangelicals who have carried on this long tradition there are evidences of concessions and departures that require attention. So I now will paint the picture of what has happened among denominations and parachurch groups that long have been committed to evangelical truth and biblical infallibility but who now have begun to stray from that viewpoint.[11]

FOR DISCUSSION

1. Why is the Book of Revelation important to the canon of the New Testament?

2. Why is the authorship, or the way the book was transmitted, complicated and different than any other book of Scripture?

3. Why is the issue of the dating of Revelation vital to its purpose and message?

4. How strong is the internal evidence for the doctrine of inspiration?

5. What reason can be offered as to why Revelation has been discredited as a part of the divine message from God?

For Further Study

Bibliology Texts

Lindsell, Harold. *The Battle for the Bible*. Grand Rapids: Zondervan, 1976.

Commentaries

Hindson, Edward. *The Book of Revelation: Unlocking the Future*. Chattanooga, Tenn.: AMG Publishers, 2002.

LaHaye, Tim. Foreword to *Revelation: Illustrated and Made Plain*. Grand Rapids: Zondervan, 1980.

Robertson, A. T. *Word Pictures in the New Testament*. Nashville: Broadman, 1933.

Thomas, Robert L. *Revelation 8—22: An Exegetical Commentary*. Chicago: Moody, 1992.

Walvoord, John F. *The Revelation of Jesus Christ*. Chicago: Moody, 1966.

History

Schaff, Philip. *History of the Christian Church*. 8 vols. Grand Rapids: Eerdmans, 1991.

Prophecy

Benware, Paul N. *Understanding End Times Prophecy*. Chicago: Moody, 1995.

Appendix

The Sufficiency of Scripture for Christian Living

S ome Christians want to help God out in their spiritual experience. They apply this desire to please God with human effort and self-generated energy to both salvation and sanctification. Some feel they must add works, church membership, baptism, and financial contributions to make God accept them for salvation. Others believe the Word of God is not enough for living the Christian life. They have to apply human effort to keep their salvation or to mature spiritually.

The underlying principles of their belief is that the Bible is not adequate for Christian living, the sacrifice of Christ was not adequate to completely save and deliver them, and their faith is not strong enough for living the Christian life. Because of this, there is a growing tendency among Christians to try to overcome the obstacles and questions in their life without using the Scriptures.

Christ's Sacrifice Is Sufficient to Save

Many do not consider the sacrifice of Christ sufficient for complete salvation. But the apostle Peter said that Christ "died for sins once for all, the just for the unjust, so that He might bring us to God" (1 Pet. 3:18). What the Lord did on the cross is sufficient enough to save.

But humans like to add personal efforts to their redemption. The Scriptures, however, do not allow this. In fact, the New Testament pictures salvation as a free and unearned gift that does not leave room for human efforts. Paul said we are "justified as a gift by His grace through the redemption which is in Christ Jesus" (Rom. 3:24).

God's grace is sufficient, and Christ's work on the cross was so great, that our salvation is complete. The apostle Paul added, "For by grace you have been saved through faith; and that not of yourselves, it is the gift of God" (Eph. 2:8). But what if we are accused as sinners, and someone brings a charge against us? (Rom. 8:33).

> It makes no difference what the answer is. It makes no difference who in all the universe may try to charge us with whatever. It makes no difference as long as it is not God who charges us. And God does not. In fact, He has already announced the verdict in all instances when we are and will be charged. And that verdict is "not guilty." Paul answers his own question about who will charge God's elect by simply saying, "God is the one who justifies" (v. 33). Every single time we sin, a charge can be legitimately leveled at us. But whenever that happens, whoever brings the accusation finds that the case has already been decided and the verdict rendered, "Not guilty."[1]

Faith Is Sufficient to Save

Some say faith is not sufficient to save. As mentioned, many attempt to add some form of human assistance to the salvation process. "Oh, yes," they argue, "we are saved by faith, but also by . . ." Many denominations add to faith: water baptism, church membership, taking of the Lord's Supper, abstaining from certain foods and dress, taking pilgrimages, etc. While the Bible mentions some of these things, it never pictures them as "additional" requirements for salvation. The Lord asks that we simply believe that Christ died for our sins. He has done all the work. Our part is to place our faith and confidence in what Jesus did at the cross.

This is why Paul could write, "For the word of the cross is foolishness to those who are perishing, but to us who are being saved it is the power of God" (1 Cor. 1:18), and, "For I determined to know nothing among you except Jesus Christ, and Him crucified . . . so that your faith would not rest on the wisdom of men, but on the power of God" (2:2, 5). And as Paul made it perfectly clear: "For by grace you have been saved through faith; and that not of yourselves, it is the gift of God" (Eph. 2:8).

It is the gospel of the death, burial, and resurrection of Christ that brings salvation. All God asks for is our trust. This is why the apostle could say, "For I am not ashamed of the gospel, for it is the power of God for salvation to everyone who believes, to the Jew first and also to the Greek" (Rom. 1:16).

In salvation, *God* has done it all. And all we do is trust the accomplished finished work. When we believe in the sufficiency of the gospel and believe that Christ died for us personally, we are sealed in Christ by the work of the Holy Spirit.

Scripture Is Sufficient to Interpret Life

Concerning the sufficiency of Scripture for the Christian life, are evangelical churches turning from theology and God's Word toward a secular viewpoint and practice? Unfortunately for many churches and seminaries, the shift seems to be underway.

Ice writes,

Increasingly in evangelical circles, churches are drifting from the sufficiency of Scripture as they equip believers for works of ministry. The pattern is often the same: The Bible does not speak specifically enough in a particular area, so one must dip into the secular pool of wisdom. Areas in which this trend appeared included

1. *Personal living.* Sanctification was replaced by psychology and psychotherapy in an effort to understand the individual rather than God.

2. *Giving.* Fund raising programs became part of marketing strategy.

3. *Evangelism.* Personal witness was replaced by felt-need marketing.

4. *Christian outreach.* Sociology-based church growth sought to understand neighborhood demographics rather than God's view of society.

5. *Missions.* Anthropology became as important in some programs as was theology.

6. *Personal theology.* A redefining of pastor professionalism turned church leaders toward a preoccupation with leadership and management skills.

7. *Theological education.* For working pastors, "how to" training seminars worked on the pragmatic matters that had not been covered in seminary.

Our evangelical heritage is supposed to follow the Reformation principle of *sola scriptura* (Scripture alone). This precept led Protestants to oppose ecclesiastical authority, the natural theology of Romanism, and the authority of human reason. Later biblical Christians used Scripture to oppose the experiential skepticism of liberalism. Evangelicals leave a place for reason and experience, but it is supposed to be subordinate to Scripture. Paul told the wayward Corinthians that he was teaching them "not to exceed what is written" (1 Cor. 4:6). So often evangelicals seem to become caught up in an "experimentalism," as if God has not given us a clear theological framework from which to interpret life.[2]

My Experiences Are Not Sufficient to Interpret Life

Those who believe that their experiences are the key to living for Christ at least imply that the Word of God is not a sufficient guide into a closer relationship with the Lord nor is it enough for developing Christian maturity. This view also restricts the work of the Holy Spirit in illuminating the Word so that true biblical growth may take place. Paul wrote that we have received "the Spirit who is from God, so that we may know the things freely given to us by God" (1 Cor. 2:12). He has already "granted to us everything pertaining to life and godliness, through the true knowledge of Him who called us by His own glory and excellence" (2 Pet. 1:3).

Edgar addresses this and writes,

> Christians often wonder, How can I live the Christian life to its fullest? . . . Is my justification sufficient so that by faith, with the Scriptures and its promises to guide me and motivate me, I can live the Christian life as God intended? Can I be satisfied with that which God has provided for me in Christ?

> For many the answer is, No. A large number of Christians . . . say that we need more. What all believers received when they believed in Jesus Christ is not enough. . . . For these believers the answer to their need is not found in Scripture but in the overt, visible evidence of God's presence.[3]

The stress may be on miraculous experiences that are supposed to strengthen the individual's ministry. But the question is, Has God provided all we need in Christ, or is His work lacking something? Is Christ's work only effective in salvation, and "now the Spirit must provide ongoing evidence for the believer's spiritual life?"[4]

The Bible, however, never says that we are to seek this type of evidence. The gifts of the Holy Spirit come from our being united to Christ's spiritual body by the baptism of the Spirit (1 Cor. 12:13), and the gifts that are bestowed come from a sovereign work of the same Spirit. The Scriptures tell us: "To each one is given the manifestation of the Spirit for the common good" (v. 7), and, "But one and the same Spirit works all these things, distributing to each one individually just as He wills" (v. 11). And finally, "But now God has placed the members, each one of them, in the body, just as He desired" (v. 18).

If anything were to be added to our Christian experience, it would be the spiritual but practical fruit of the Holy Spirit who uses the Word of God to perfect our walk (Gal. 5:22–25). Or it would be certain qualities that evidence themselves in our lives because we are "partakers of the divine nature" (2 Pet. 1:4). These qualities applied to our faith are moral excellence, knowledge, self-control, perseverance, godliness, brotherly kindness, and love (vv. 5–8).

What the Scriptures say about Christian experience should be sufficient.

Scripture Is Our Only Sufficient Guide

Only the Bible, which gives instructions from the Lord who created us and fully understands our makeup, is sufficient for our life and practice. It is God's manual for Christian living and is adequate in itself. It reflects the Creator's evaluation of who we are and explains the devastating problem of sin and the only solution to the problem—Jesus Christ.

The Scriptures tell us, "The heart is more deceitful than all else and is desperately sick; who can understand it? I, the LORD, search the heart, I test the mind, even to give to each man according to his ways, according to the results of his deeds" (Jer. 17:9–10). And, "All souls are Mine; . . . The soul who sins will die" (Ezek. 18:4); "their foolish heart was darkened" (Rom. 1:21); "God gave [men] over to a depraved mind, to do those things which are not proper" (v. 28).

The Father's eternal plan of salvation alone can save us. Christ alone can reconcile us. The Spirit alone can teach us. The Word of God is our only foundation for these truths, our only revelation of God's will, and our only rule for what we should believe about God and practice in our daily lives.

For Further Study

Christian Experience

Lewis, C. S. *Mere Christianity.* Reprint. Grand Rapids: Zondervan, 2001.

Tozer, A. W. *The Pursuit of God.* Reprint. Camp Hill, Penn.: Christian Publications, 1997.

————. *The Pursuit of Man.* Reprint. Camp Hill, Penn.: Christian Publications, 1997.

Yancey, Philip. *What's So Amazing About Grace?* Grand Rapids: Zondervan, 1997.

Theology

Couch, Mal, ed. *The Fundamentals for the Twenty-First Century.* Grand Rapids: Kregel, 2000.

Couch, Mal, ed. *A Pastor's Manual for Doing Church.* Ft. Worth, Tex: Tyndale Seminary, 2002.

Edgar, R. Thomas. *Satisfied by the Promise of the Spirit.* Grand Rapids: Kregel, 1996.

Ryrie, Charles C. *So Great Salvation.* Chicago: Moody, 1997.

Stott, John R. W. *The Authority of the Bible.* Downers Grove, Ill.: InterVarsity, 1999.

Counseling and Psychology

Bulkley, Ed. *Why Christians Can't Trust Psychology.* Eugene, Ore.: Harvest House, 1994.

Crabb, Larry. *Understanding People.* Grand Rapids: Zondervan, 1987.

Endnotes

Preface

1. Edward J. Young, *Thy Word Is Truth* (Grand Rapids: Eerdmans, 1960), 31.

2. Louis Gaussen, *The Inspiration of the Holy Scriptures* (Chicago: Moody, n.d.), 29.

Foreword

1. Benjamin Breckenridge Warfield, *The Inspiration and Authority of the Bible* (Philadelphia: Presbyterian and Reformed, 1948), 173.

Part One: The Inspiration of Scripture

Chapter One

1. Josh McDowell, *The New Evidence That Demands a Verdict* (Nashville: Thomas Nelson, 1999), 3–16.

Chapter Two

1. Paul L Maier, *In the Fullness of Time* (Grand Rapids: Kregel, 1997), xv.

2. John F. Walvoord, *The Nations, Israel and the Church in Prophecy* (Grand Rapids: Zondervan, 1988), 13.

3. Paul N. Benware, *Understanding End Times Prophecy* (Chicago: Moody, 1995), 18.

4. John of Damascus, *Orthodox Faith* 4.17

Chapter Three

1. H. S. Miller, *General Biblical Introduction* (Houghton, N.Y.: Word-Bearer, 1960), 5.

2. Lewis S. Chafer, *Systematic Theology*, 8 vols. (Dallas: Dallas Seminary Press, 1976), 1:21–22.

3. Paul D. Feinberg, "Bible, Inerrancy and Infallibility of," in *The Evangelical Dictionary of Theology*, ed. Walter A. Elwell (Grand Rapids: Baker, 1984), 142.

4. Mal Couch, ed., *An Introduction to Classical Evangelical Hermeneutics* (Grand Rapids: Kregel, 2000), 17.

5. Paul N. Benware, *Understanding End Time Prophecy.* (Chicago: Moody, 1995), 12.

6. F. F. Bruce, *The Canon of Scripture* (Downers Grove, Ill.: InterVarsity, 1988), 77.

7. Everett F. Harrison, *Introduction to the New Testament* (Grand Rapids: Eerdmans, 1982), 97–98.

8. Merrill F. Unger, *Introductory Guide to the Old Testament* (Grand Rapids: Zondervan, 1951), 19.

9. Ibid., 29.

10. Norman L. Geisler and William E. Nix, *A General Introduction to the Bible* (Chicago: Moody, 1971), 263.

11. Sir Frederic G. Kenyon, *Handbook to the Textual Criticism of the New Testament* (Grand Rapids: Eerdmans, 1912), 288.

12. Bruce M. Metzger, *The Text of the New Testament* (reprint, New York: Oxford University Press, 1992), 86.

13. Henry A. Virkler, *Hermeneutics* (Grand Rapids: Baker, 1999), 15.

14. Roy B. Zuck, *Basic Bible Interpretation* (Colorado Springs, Colo.: Victor Books, 1991), 19.

15. Robert H. Stein, *A Basic Guide to Interpreting the Bible* (Grand Rapids: Baker, 1999), 17.

16. Bernard Ramm, *Protestant Biblical Interpretation* (Grand Rapids: Baker, 1982), 10.

17. Miller, *General Biblical Introduction*, 18.

18. Chafer, *Systematic Theology*, 1:110–11.

19. Ibid., 1:111.

20. Horst Balz and Gerhard Schneider, eds., *Exegetical Dictionary of the New Testament*, 3 vols. (Grand Rapids: Eerdmans, 1994), 2:48.

21. Chafer, *Systematic Theology*, 1:111–12.

22. Thomas Charles Edwards, *A Commentary on the First Epistle to the Corinthians* (Minneapolis: Klock and Klock, 1979), 58.

23. Arthur Penrhyn Stanley, *The Epistles of St. Paul to the Corinthians* (Minneapolis: Klock and Klock, 1981), 56.

24. Charles Hodge, *An Exposition of the First Epistle to the Corinthians* (Grand Rapids: Eerdmans, 1956), 39.

25. A.M.S. Gooding, "1–3 John" in vol. 5 of *What the Bible Teaches*, eds. T. Wilson and K. Stapley (Kilmarnock, Scotland: John Ritchie, 1987), 214.

26. Charles C. Ryrie, *Basic Theology* (Chicago: Moody, 1999), 132.

Chapter Four

1. Walter A. Elwell, ed., *Evangelical Dictionary of Theology*. Grand Rapids: Baker, 1997, 946.

2. John Calvin, *Institutes of the Christian Religion*, trans. Henry Beveridge (reprint, Grand Rapids: Eerdmans, 1993), 71.

3. Ibid., 72.

4. Elwell, *Evangelical Dictionary*, 946.

5. Lewis S. Chafer, *Systematic Theology*, 8 vols. (Dallas: Dallas Seminary Press, 1947; Grand Rapids: Kregel, 1993), 1:xxxii.

6. Norman L. Geisler, *Baker Encyclopedia of Christian Apologetics* (Grand Rapids: Baker, 1999), 634.

7. Ibid.

8. Merrill F. Unger, *Unger's Commentary on the Old Testament*. (1981; reprint, Chattanooga, Tenn.: AMG, 2002), 1143.

9. I. W. Slotki, *Isaiah* (London: Soncino, 1972), 6.

10. Elwell, *Evangelical Dictionary*, 947–48.

11. Charles Hodge, *Systematic Theology*, 3 vols. (Grand Rapids: Eerdmans, 1981), 1:50.

12. Chafer, *Systematic Theology*, 1:49.

13. Hodge, *Systematic Theology*, 1:155.

14. Herbert Lockyer, *All the Doctrines of the Bible* (Grand Rapids: Zondervan, 1964), 6.

15. Bernard Ramm, *Protestant Biblical Interpretation* (Grand Rapids: Baker, 1986), 101–03.

16. Chafer, *Systematic Theology*, 1:60.

17. Ibid., 1:48.

18. Ibid.

19. Alexander S. Murray, *Who's Who in Mythology* (New York: Wings Books, 1988), 9.

20. Louis Berkhof, *Systematic Theology* (Grand Rapids: Eerdmans, 1994), 34.

21. Henry C. Thiessen, *Lectures in Systematic Theology* (Grand Rapids: Eerdmans, 1990), 16.

22. Horst Balz and Gerhard Schneider, eds., *Exegetical Dictionary of the New Testament*, 3 vols. (Grand Rapids: Eerdmans, 1994), 3:301.

23. Thiessen, *Lectures in Systematic Theology*, 10.

24. Ibid.

25. Ibid, 29.

26. Harold Lindsell, *The Battle for the Bible* (Grand Rapids: Zondervan, 1976), 29.

27. D. A. Carson, *The Gospel According to John* (Grand Rapids: Eerdmans, 1991), 135.

28. Ibid., 113.

29. H. S. Miller, *General Biblical Introduction* (Houghton, N.Y.: Word-Bearer, 1960), 3. This selection from Miller includes a quote from T. H. Horne, *Introduction to the Critical Study of the Scriptures* (London: Carter, 1872), 1:15.

30. Ibid., 4–5.

31. R. Laird Harris, ed., *Theological Wordbook of the Old Testament*, 2 vols. (Chicago: Moody, 1981), 1:160–61.

32. Benjamin Breckinridge Warfield, *The Inspiration and Authority of the Bible* (Philadelphia: Presbyterian and Reformed, 1960), 100.

33. Chafer, *Systematic Theology*, 7:240.

34. Charles John Ellicott, ed., *Ellicott's Commentary on the Whole Bible*, 8 vols. (Grand Rapids: Zondervan, 1959), 8:194.

35. Augustus Hopkins Strong, *Systematic Theology* (Old Tappan, N.J.: Revell, 1979), 115.

36. Robert P. Lightner, *The God of the Bible and Other Gods* (Grand Rapids: Kregel, 1998), 64.

Chapter Five

1. Edward J. Young, *Thy Word Is Truth* (Grand Rapids: Eerdmans, 1957), 41–42.

2. Louis Gaussen, *The Inspiration of the Holy Scriptures* (Chicago: Moody, n.d.), 34.

3. Everett F. Harrison, *Baker's Dictionary of Theology* (Grand Rapids: Baker, 1960), 286.

4. Frank E. Gaebelein, *Exploring the Bible* (Wheaton, Ill.: Van Kampen, 1950), 28–29.

5. Benjamin Breckenridge Warfield, *The Inspiration and Authority of the Bible* (Philadelphia: Presbyterian and Reformed, 1948), 133. For a helpful discussion on the concept of the "breath" (Spirit) of God in both Testaments, see Walter A. Elwell, ed., *Baker Encyclopedia of the Bible*, vol. 1 (Grand Rapids: Baker, 1988), 307.

6. John Stott, *God's Book for God's People* (Downers Grove, Ill.: InterVarsity, 1982), 51–52.

7. Lewis S. Chafer, *Major Bible Themes* (Grand Rapids: Zondervan, 1975), 23.

8. Stott, *God's Book*, 52.

9. Lewis Sperry Chafer, *Systematic Theology* (Dallas: Dallas Seminary Press, 1947; Grand Rapids: Kregel, 1993), 1:80–81.

10. J. I. Packer, *God Has Spoken: Revelation and the Bible* (Grand Rapids: Baker, 1994), 93.

11. Chafer, *Major Bible Themes*, 22.

12. Stott, *God's Book*, 52.

13. Chafer, *Systematic Theology*, 1:82. For an excellent analysis of 2 Pet. 1:21, see Louis Gaussen, The *Inspiration of the Holy Scripture*, 59–67. For an additional brief but helpful discussion, see Edward J. Young, *Thy Word Is Truth*, 65–82.

14. Stott, *God's Book*, 51.

15. Ibid., 52.

16. H. S. Miller, *General Biblical Introduction* (Houghton, N.Y.: Word-Bearer, 1944), 25.

17. Warfield, *Inspiration and Authority*, 155.

18. Packer, *God Has Spoken*, 94. For excellent material on the individuality of the human authors, see Gaussen, *Inspiration of the Holy Scriptures*, 36–57.

19. Cited in *The Fundamentals for Today*, vol. 1, ed. Charles Feinberg (Kregel, 1958), 127–128.

20. Young, *Thy Word Is Truth*, 35.

21. Ibid. See also: Alan M. Stibbs, "The Witness of Scripture to Its Inspiration" in *Revelation and the Bible*, ed. Carl F. H. Henry (Grand Rapids: Baker, 1958), 107–118.

22. Gaussen, *Inspiration of the Holy Scriptures*, 105. For an extensive and valuable discussion, see Robert P. Lightner, *The Savior and the Scriptures* (Philadelphia: Presbyterian and Reformed, 1970), 58–77.

23. John F. Walvoord, *The Holy Spirit* (Findlay, Ohio: Dunham, 1958), 67.

24. René Pache, *The Inspiration and Authority of Scripture* (Chicago: Moody, 1969), 90.

25. For additional material bearing on the perceptions of the New Testament writers with regard to their writing, see Ibid., 91–96.

26. Young, *Thy Word Is Truth*, 35.

27. Pache, *Inspiration and Authority*, 96.

Chapter Six

1. René Pache, *The Inspiration and Authority of Scripture* (Chicago: Moody, 1969), 119.

2. Gleason L. Archer, *A Survey of Old Testament Introduction* (Chicago: Moody, 1994), 173.

3. Norman L. Geisler and William E. Nix, *A General Introduction to the Bible* (Chicago: Moody, 1971), 98.

4. Merrill F. Unger, *Introductory Guide to the Old Testament* (Grand Rapids: Zondervan, 1951), 78–79.

5. Ibid., 59.

6. Ibid., 66.

7. Ibid.

8. Ibid.

9. Philip Schaff, ed., *The Creeds of Christendom*, 6th ed. (1931; reprint, Grand Rapids: Baker, 1990), 3:602.

10. F. F. Bruce, *The Canon of Scripture* (Downers Grove, Ill.: InterVarsity, 1988), 233.

11. Geisler and Nix, *General Introduction to the Bible,* 181.

12. Ibid., 192.

13. Tractate "Sanhedrin," *Babylonian Talmud*, VII-VIII, 24.

14. Geisler and Nix, *General Introduction to the Bible,* 165.

15. Ibid., 199.

16. Ibid., 202.

17. Westcott, Brooke Foss, and Fenton John Anthony Hort, eds. *The New Testament in the Original Greek* (New York: Macmillan, 1928), II, 2.

18. Wayne Grudem, *Biblical Doctrine* (Grand Rapids: Zondervan, 1999), 45.

Chapter Seven

1. Thomas C. Oden, ed., *Ancient Christian Commentary on Scripture,* 26 vols. (Downers Grove, Ill.: InterVarsity,).

2. John Calvin, *Institutes of the Christian Religion*, trans. Henry Beveridge (reprint Grand Rapids: Eerdmans, 1993), 1:71.

3. Ibid., 1:72.

Chapter Eight

1. Edward J. Young, *Thy Word Is Truth* (Grand Rapids: Eerdmans, 1960), 13.

2. Ibid., 24.

3. Robert L. Thomas and F. David Farnell, *The Jesus Crisis* (Grand Rapids: Kregel, 1998), 94.

4. Ibid., 193.

5. Gleason L. Archer, *A Survey of Old Testament Introduction* (Chicago: Moody, 1994), 173.

6. Ibid.

7. John Elder, *Prophets, Idols and Diggers* (New York: Bobbs Merrill, 1960), 16.

8. Kenneth Hagen, "The History of Scripture in the Church" in *The Bible in the Churches: How Various Christians Interpret the Scriptures,* ed. Kenneth Hagen, Marquette Studies in Theology (Milwaukee, Wis.: Marquette University Press, 1998), 22.

9. Evangelicals hold firmly to the truth that all history is God's history. He is sovereign over every aspect of His universe. He has established the processes as well as the conclusions. His purpose is to rid His creation of the power of sin. He planned from eternity past human redemption by the death of His Son, Jesus Christ. But the material creation will also be transformed and redeemed at the close of time history, as we understand it.

10. Gene Edward Veith Jr., *Postmodern Times* (Wheaton, Ill.: Crossway, 1994), 195.

11. Ibid., 199.

12. Ibid.

13. Thomas and Farnell, *The Jesus Crisis,* 217.

Chapter Nine

1. A clear empirically centered apologetic strategy appears in John Warwick Montgomery, *Where Is History Going?* (Grand Rapids: Zondervan, 1969)

and in his exchange with the presuppositionalism of Cornelius Van Til, "Once Upon An Apriori," in *Jerusalem and Athens*, ed. E. R. Geehan (Nutley, N.J.: Presbyterian and Reformed, 1971).

2. Examples of reference materials would be Josh McDowell's writings, such as his latest work, *The New Evidence That Demands a Verdict* (Nashville: Thomas Nelson, 1999), that provides an extensive bibliography.

3. Classical illustrations of a rationally centered apologetic include the ontological, cosmological, and teleological arguments for the existence of God developed by Thomas Aquinas and others. Mortimer J. Adler has updated this approach in his book *How to Think about God: A Guide for the 20th-Century Pagan* (New York: MacMillan, 1980). A clearly Protestant Reformed and biblically refined example can be seen in the writings of Gordon H. Clark. See, for example, his *A Christian View of Men and Things* (Grand Rapids: Eerdmans, 1952) and his festschrift edited by Ronald H. Nash, *The Philosophy of Gordon H. Clark* (Nutley, N.J.: Presbyterian and Reformed, 1968).

4. For a discussion and defense of classical apologetics, see R.C. Sproul, John Gerstner, and Arthur Lindsley, *Classical Apologetics* (Grand Rapids: Zondervan, 1984). This work critiques presuppositional apologetics to be discussed in this section.

5. Norman L. Geisler, *Baker's Encyclopedia of Christian Apologetics* (Grand Rapids: Baker, 1999), 402.

6. A good introduction to Van Til is his work, *The Defense of the Faith* (Philadelphia: Presbyterian and Reformed, 3rd ed., 1967). His festschrift, cited in endnote 1 above, includes his responses to classical apologists' objections to his presuppositional approach. Popular level expositions of Greg L. Bahnsen and John M. Frame's extensions of Van Til's thought are respectively, *Always Ready*, ed. Robert R. Booth (Texarkana, Ark.: Covenant Media, 1996) and *Apologetics to the Glory of God* (Phillipsburg, N.J.: Presbyterian and Reformed, 1994). Of the two, Bahnsen is the closest to Van Til.

7. See the recent narration of Christianity's role in the rise of modern science in Nancy R. Pearcey and Charles B. Thaxton, *The Soul of Science: Christian Faith and Natural Philosophy* (Wheaton, Ill.: Crossway, 1994).

8. Francis Schaeffer repeatedly used this approach in his ministry, although he did not follow Van Til's presuppositionalism consistently. See his work, *The God Who Is There* (Downer's Grove, Ill.: InterVarsity, 1968).

9. Old Testament history refutes popular ideas such as the belief that a body politic is inherently good (Judges) or that centralized bureaucracy is the key to social justice (Samuel, Kings). Perfect society requires the

ethically perfected people and leaders of the messianic kingdom yet to come. Fascist, Marxist, and Islamic imitations of the messianic kingdom inevitably fail because having wrongly diagnosed the problem, they cannot overcome sin.

10. Unbelief always denies the Creator-creature distinction, so it has to posit a unified reality in which the gods, humans, animals, plants, and matter form a blended spectrum of being that is ultimately impersonal and unintelligible. Documentation of this continuity of being concept from Old Testament times through modern Darwinian evolution may be found in Henry M. Morris, *The Long War Against God* (Grand Rapids, Baker, 1989).

11. Bahnsen insightfully notes that presuppositional apologetics follows the two parts of Proverbs 26:4–5 in critiquing unbelief's failures ("answering a fool according to his folly") and in avoiding compromise with unbelieving ideas ("not answering a fool according to his folly"), *Always Ready*, 61.

12. C. S. Lewis, "On Moving with the Times," *Christianity Today*, (12 March 1971), 537. Early Christians actually accomplished what Lewis suggests so successfully that Julian the Apostate made a decree forbidding Christians to study heathen learning. See John Milton, "Aeropagetica," *Great Books of the Western World* (Chicago: Encyclopedia Britannica, 1952), 32:388.

13. See Josh McDowell, *New Evidence That Demands a Verdict* for an excellent list of materials in every area except the creation-evolution conflict. For those materials, see the Institute for Creation Research and the Creation Research Society, both on the internet. Material for discussing contemporary societal issues within the biblical framework may be found at Chuck Colsen's *Breakpoint* website and on his radio program.

14. Charles Ryrie, *The Holy Spirit* (Chicago: Moody, 1977), 76.

Part Two: The Inerrancy of the Books of Scripture

Chapter Ten

1. See, for example, David S. Dockery, *The Doctrine of the Bible* (Nashville: Convention Press, 1991); Clark H. Pinnock, *A Defense of Biblical Infallibility* (Philadelphia: Presbyterian and Reformed, 1967); Charles C. Ryrie, *What You Should Know about Inerrancy* (Chicago: Moody, 1981); Ned B. Stonehouse and Paul Woolley, eds. *The Infallible Word* (Philadelphia: Presbyterian and Reformed, 1946); B. B. Warfield, *The Inspiration and*

Authority of the Bible (Philadelphia: Presbyterian and Reformed, 1948); Edward J. Young, *Thy Word Is Truth* (Grand Rapids: Eerdmans, 1957).

2. Oswald T. Allis, *The Five Books of Moses* (Philadelphia: Presbyterian and Reformed, 1949); Gleason L. Archer Jr., *A Survey of Old Testament Introduction* (Chicago: Moody, 1974), 83–146; Raymond B. Dillard and Tremper Longman III, *An Introduction to the Old Testament* (Grand Rapids: Zondervan, 1994), 37–106; R. K. Harrison, *An Introduction to the Old Testament* (Grand Rapids: Eerdmans, 1969), 495–662; Herbert Wolf, *An Introduction to the Old Testament Pentateuch* (Chicago: Moody, 1991).

3. Charles Hodge, *Systematic Theology,* 3 vols. (Grand Rapids: Eerdmans, 1995), 1:163.

4. See Norman Geisler and Thomas Howe, *When Critics Ask* (Grand Rapids: Baker, 1992), 15–26, and Charles Ryrie, *Basic Theology* (Wheaton: Ill., Victor Books, 1988), 77–106.

5. Gilbert S. Rosenthal, *The Many Faces of Judaism* (New York: Behrman House, 1978), 46–48; Solomon Nigosian, *Judaism: The Way of Holiness* (Great Britain: Crucible, 1986), 155.

6. Robert P. Lightner, *The Savior and the Scriptures* (Philadelphia: Presbyterian and Reformed, 1970).

7. John D. Hannah, ed., *Inerrancy and the Church* (Chicago: Moody, 1984).

8. The idea is probably that of appearance; Moses was "strong and handsome." In *The Theological Dictionary of the Old Testament,* eds. G. Johannes Botterweck, Helmer Ringgren, and Heinz-Josef Fabry, rev. ed; trans. John T. Willis, 8 vols. (Grand Rapids: Eerdmans, 1977), 5:306.

9. See also Ex 20:4; Deut. 4:12, 15–16, 23, 25; 5:8; Ps 17:15. Timothy R. Ashley, *The Book of Numbers,* vol. 5 of *The New International Commentary on the Old Testament* (Grand Rapids: Eerdmans, 1993), 225–226.

10. Eugene H. Merrill, "Deuteronomy, New Testament Faith, and the Christian Life," in *Integrity of Heart, Skillfulness of Hands,* eds. Charles H. Dyer and Roy B. Zuck (Grand Rapids: Baker, 1994), 27–32.

11. The "decrees and laws" could not be those of the covenant itself, for they were not yet revealed. Most likely these were simply ways of describing a general body of legislation, albeit one revealed by Yahweh. See P. Enns, in the *New International Dictionary of Old Testament Theology and Exegesis,* 5 vols., ed. Willem A. VanGemeren, (Grand Rapids: Zondervan, 1977), 2:250–251.

12. Eugene H. Merrill, *Deuteronomy,* vol. 4 of the *New American Commentary* (Nashville: Broadman and Holman, 1994), 115.

13. Cassuto is correct in suggesting that the use of *Elohim* here rather than *Yahweh* is indicative of divine power behind the act of writing and not the appearance of a literal finger inscribing the text. U. Cassuto, *A Commentary on the Book of Exodus* (Jerusalem: Magnes, 1967), 405–406. Nevertheless, the language here precludes any participation by Moses himself.

14. For a good recent discussion, see Kenneth A. Matthews, *Genesis 1— 11:26,* vol. 1 of the *New American Commentary* (Nashville: Broadman & Holman, 1996), 68–85.

15. John E. Hartley, *Leviticus,* vol. 4 of the *Word Biblical Commentary* (Dallas: Word, 1992), 471. Hartley limits the scope of these summary statements to Leviticus itself, but the present canonical shape of the material which views Leviticus as predicated upon Exodus demands that more than Leviticus should be understood.

16. Budd, like Hartley (see previous note), limits the material to the biblical book itself, in this case Numbers 1:1–35:34. Philip J. Budd, *Numbers,* vol. 5 of the *Word Biblical Commentary* (Waco: Word, 1984), 389. However, as with Leviticus 26:46 and 27:34, which conclude all the post-Sinaitic revelation to that point, Numbers 36:13 provides a summation that adds Numbers to that accumulating corpus of Mosaic writings.

17. Merrill, *Deuteronomy,* 229.

18. Ibid., 266.

19. So, for example, Henry Jackson Flanders Jr., Robert Wilson Crapps, and David Anthony Smith, *People of the Covenant,* 4th ed. (New York: Oxford University Press, 1996), 96–115.

20. Duane Garrett, *Rethinking Genesis* (Grand Rapids: Baker, 1991), 192–197. Garrett rejects the idea proposed largely by P. J. Wiseman and R. K. Harrison that Genesis 2:4 is a colophon referring to the creation account of 1:1–2:3. The view of Matthews that 2:4a forms a bridge between 1:1–2:3 and 2:4b—4:26 has much to commend it *(Genesis 1–11:26,* 183). None of this, however, affects the question of the exclusively divine origination of the cosmos creation account of 1:1–2:3.

21. The following discussion is well aware of contemporary literary criticisms that explain such things as private thoughts and words as narrative devices like authorial "omniscience," point of view, characterization, and the like. See, e.g., Adele Berlin, *Poetics and Interpretation of Biblical Narrative* (Sheffield: Almond, 1983), especially 43–82. Such explanations of divine and even human inner life and its disclosure are hardly

compatible with the Bible's own assertions about the factual reality of these phenomena.

Chapter Eleven

1. David M. Howard Jr., *An Introduction to the Old Testament Historical Books* (Chicago: Moody, 1993), 36.

2. Paul Benware, *Understanding End Times Prophecy* (Chicago: Moody, 1995), 53–57.

3. Charles C. Ryrie, *Basic Theology* (Wheaton, Ill.: Victor Books, 1988; Chicago: Moody, 1999) 83.

4. Leon Wood, *The Distressing Days of the Judges* (Grand Rapids: Zondervan, 1975), 34.

5. John F. Walvoord, *Jesus Christ Our Lord* (Chicago: Moody, 1969), 44–54.

6. Gleason L. Archer, *A Survey of Old Testament Introduction* (Chicago: Moody, 1994), 308.

7. Ibid., 309.

8. Robert L. Hubbard, *The Book of Ruth*, vol. 9 the *New International Commentary on the Old Testament,* ed. R. K. Harrison (Grand Rapids: Eerdmans, 1988), 5.

9. F. B. Huey, "Ruth" in *The Expositor's Bible Commentary, Volume 3: Deuteronomy-2 Samuel*, ed. Frank E. Gaebelein, (Grand Rapids: Zondervan, 1992), 3:514.

10. The prophet Isaiah declared that Hezekiah would die of his illness. But Hezekiah's passionate prayer to God caused an apparent reversal of God's pronouncement, as the Lord granted an extension of his life for fifteen years. Such phenomenon does not indicate that God changes His mind and will or that He is not omniscient and is subject to making errors. "And God's will includes intermediate causes such as human free choice. So God knows what the intermediate causes will choose to do. And God's will is in accord with his unchangeable knowledge. Therefore, God's will never changes, since he wills what he knows will happen." Norman Geisler, *Creating God in the Image of Man?* (Minneapolis: Bethany, 1997), 42–43. "Prayer is not a means by which we get our will done in heaven. Rather, it is a means by which God gets his will done on earth. It is utterly presumptuous for mortal man to believe that his prayer actually changes God. Instead, prayer is a means by which God changes us and others." Ibid., 86–87. God uses various means to accomplish His unchanging will and, in this case, it was the prayer of Hezekiah.

11. John Gill, *Gill's Commentary,* 6 vols. (Grand Rapids: Baker, 1980), 2:533.

12. A. Cohen, ed., *The Five Megilloth* (New York: Soncino, 1974), 180.

13. Merrill F. Unger, *Introductory Guide to the Old Testament* (Grand Rapids: Zondervan, 1981), 404–05.

14. Cohen, *Five Megilloth*, 194.

15. John F. Walvoord and Roy B. Zuck, eds. *The Bible Knowledge Commentary: Old Testament* (Wheaton: Victor Books, 1985), 700–01.

16. Gill, *Gill's Commentary*, 2:579.

17. Unger, *Introductory Guide*, 392–93.

Chapter Twelve

1. Merrill F. Unger, *Introductory Guide to the Old Testament* (Grand Rapids: Zondervan, 1978), 363.

2. Ibid., 366.

3. Ibid., 375.

4. Victor E. Reichert, *Job* (New York: Soncino, 1985), xiv.

5. Elmer B. Smick, "Job" in *The Expositor's Bible Commentary, Volume 4: 1 Kings-Job*, ed. Frank E. Gaebelein (Grand Rapids: Zondervan, 1988), 4:854.

6. Merrill F. Unger, *Unger's Commentary on the Old Testament* (1981; reprint, Chattanooga, Tenn.: AMG, 2002), 704.

7. A. Cohen, *Proverbs* (New York: Soncino, 1985), xi.

8. C. Hassell Bullock, *An Introduction to the Old Testament Poetic Books* (Chicago: Moody, 1988), 148.

9. Ibid., 152.

10. Ibid., 148.

11. Ibid.

12. H. C. Leupold, *Exposition of Ecclesiastes* (Grand Rapids: Baker, 1987), 17.

13. Victor E. Reichert, "Ecclesiastes" in *The Five Megilloth*, ed. A. Cohen, (London: Soncino, 1974), 106.

14. John Gill, *An Exposition of Old and New Testaments*, (Paris, Ark.: Baptist Standard Bearer, 1989), 4:550.

15. Ibid., 632.

16. Benjamin Breckinridge Warfield, *The Inspiration and Authority of the Bible* (Philadelphia: Presbyterian and Reformed, 1948), 245.

17. Louis Gaussen, *The Inspiration of the Holy Scriptures* (Chicago: Moody, n.d.), 67.

Chapter Thirteen

1. Arno C. Gaebelein, "Fulfilled Prophecy a Potent Argument for the Bible" in *The Fundamentals,* ed. R. A. Torrey (reprint, Grand Rapids: Kregel, 1990), 205.

2. Gleason L. Archer, "Alleged Errors and Discrepancies in the Original Manuscripts of the Bible" in *Inerrancy,* ed. Norman L. Geisler (Grand Rapids: Zondervan, 1980), 59.

3. The Old Testament scholar Eugene Merrill is correct when he notes that while this way of arguing has value, it is inadequate for a complete presentation of inerrancy and should not stand alone. See Eugene Merrill, "Internal Evidence for the Inerrancy of the Pentateuch," *The Conservative Theological Journal* 2, June 1998, 102–103.

4. See Paul Helm, "Faith, Evidence, and the Scriptures" in *Scripture and Truth,* ed. D. A. Carson and John D. Woodbridge (Grand Rapids: Zondervan, 1983), 299–320.

5. That is Merrill's main approach in the note cited above. See also the excellent summary given in Wayne Grudem, "Scripture's Self-Attestation and the Problem of Formulating a Doctrine of Scripture," in *Scripture and Truth,* ed. D. A. Carson and John Woodbridge, 19–59.

6. Merrill seems to include the occurrences of prophecies that can be verified as part of Scripture's self-attestation (119–120).

7. See John A. Martin, "Isaiah" in *The Bible Knowledge Commentary: Old Testament,* edited by John F. Walvoord and Roy B. Zuck (Wheaton, Ill.: Victor Books, 1985), 1067–68. This particular rebellion would be an earlier attempt by Babylon to overthrow Assyria and not the final victory of their ascendance in the seventh century. Edward J. Young takes the contrary and more long-term position that relates the passage to the coming of the Medes to destroy Babylon near the end of the Babylonian captivity of the Jews (*The Book of Isaiah,* vol. 2 [reprint, Grand Rapids: Eerdmans, 1996], 61–62).

8. H. C. Leupold, *Exposition of Isaiah,* vol. 2 (reprint, Grand Rapids: Baker, 1971), 52.

9. I am indebted in part for this table to W. A. Criswell, ed., *Criswell Study Bible* (Nashville: Thomas Nelson, 1979), 1504–09.

10. Martin, *Isaiah,* 1059.

11. John T. Willis, "The Meaning of Isaiah 7:14 and Its Application in Matthew 1:23," *Restoration Quarterly* 21 (1978): 1–18.

12. Young, *Isaiah,* 1:283–94. See also J. Gresham Machen, *The Virgin Birth of Christ* (Grand Rapids: Baker, 1930), 287–94.

13. For example, see Gleason L. Archer, *Encyclopedia of Bible Difficulties* (Grand Rapids: Zondervan, 1982), 266–68.

14. W. Arndt, *Does the Bible Contradict Itself?* (reprint, St. Louis: Concordia, 1955), 114.

15. Ibid., 142.

16. Martin, *Isaiah,* 1053.

17. Young, *Isaiah,* 3:199–201.

18. G. W. Grogan, "Isaiah" in *The Expositor's Bible Commentary, Volume 6: Isaiah-Ezekiel,* ed. Frank Gaebelein (Grand Rapids: Zondervan, 1986), 271.

19. Other passages in the Bible could be discussed with respect to this alleged problem. See Arndt, *Does the Bible Contradict Itself?* 120–22.

20. There are some instances when the Book of Isaiah is quoted but not referenced as such. See Rom. 10:15 where the verse itself does not reference Isaiah although the context does.

21. For a concise review of this debate, see Grogan, *Isaiah* 6–11.

22. F. F. Bruce, *The Book of Acts,* vol. 5 of the *New International Commentary on the New Testament* (Grand Rapids: Eerdmans, 1977), 188.

23. Lamentations is not really dealt with in this chapter other than as an appendix to Jeremiah. H. L. Ellison notes that "there is no evidence that the canonicity of Lamentations was ever challenged. If the suggestion about its purpose (a funeral dirge over Judah's past) . . . is correct, Lamentations would have become part of Israel's sacred writings in the same way the Psalms did" ("Lamentations" in *The Expositor's Bible Commentary, Volume 6: Isaiah-Ezekiel,* ed. Frank E. Gaebelein [Grand Rapids: Zondervan, 1986], 699).

24. Charles Feinberg, "Jeremiah" in *The Expositor's Bible Commentary, Volume 6: Isaiah-Ezekiel,* ed. Frank E. Gaebelein (Grand Rapids: Zondervan, 1986), 364.

25. Archer, *Bible Difficulties,* 275.

26. Ibid.

27. Ibid., 272.

28. Ibid.

29. See the discussion by Arndt concerning the use of Zechariah's prophecy in connection with Jeremiah (51–53).

30. The debate over the new covenant is definitely beyond the scope of this book. However, it must be said that the new covenant promised to Israel has not been fulfilled. It awaits fulfillment at the Second Coming and the restoration of all things.

31. Archer, *Bible Difficulties*, 276.

32. See Millard Erickson, *God in Three Persons: A Contemporary Interpretation of the Trinity* (Grand Rapids: Baker, 1995), 163–66.

33. F. Delitzsch and C. F. Keil, vol. 1 of *Commentary on the Old Testament*, (reprint, Grand Rapids: Eerdmans, 1980), 117.

34. Of course, strictly speaking one can only argue logically concerning what is quoted. However, the overall tenor of the Bible and the attitudes among both Jews and Christians about the canon allow the extrapolation.

35. This quotation from Ezekiel highlights the fact that the fourth seal is indeed the wrath of God. This undermines the prewrath view of the rapture and much midtribulationalism since these views argue that Revelation 6 shows the wrath of man, not the wrath of God. On a side note, one can also see images from Ezekiel 1 in Revelation 4 where the throne of God is described.

36. Merrill, "Internal Evidence," 119.

37. This outline is somewhat different than that followed for the previous books. However, the issue of the date of Daniel is so significant that this approach was deemed best.

38. Stephen R. Miller, *Daniel*, vol. 18 of the *New American Commentary*, (Nashville: Broadman and Holman, 1994), 23–24. In general, Miller gives one of the best recent summaries of the higher critical issues with legitimate conservative responses.

39. Ibid., 33. Here Miller refers to (among others) the words of J. E. Goldingay, *Daniel*, vol. 30 of the *Word Biblical Commentary* (Dallas: Word, 1989), 305. Goldingay is an example of many scholars today who claim an evangelical devotion to supernaturalism but still appeal to the late date of Daniel. One wonders if this is because of supposed embarrassment over the issue of supernaturalism. Later discussions will show that any embarrassment is unwarranted.

40. Miller, *Daniel*, 27.

41. Ibid., 28.

42. In actuality, only two words are certain. These words are from the list of musical instruments given in chapter 3. See the classic work by Sir Robert Anderson entitled *The Coming Prince* (reprint, Grand Rapids: Kregel, 1957), xxxiv-xxxv. In this present writer's judgment, the argument about Greek words has not advanced much since Anderson's day.

43. Miller, *Daniel*, 29.

44 Ibid., 30–31.

45. Ibid., 31–32.

46. Harry Bultema, *Commentary on Daniel* (reprint, Grand Rapids: Kregel, 1988), 17–18.

47. Ibid., 17.

48. Miller, *Daniel,* 28.

49. Some New Testament books were recognized and circulated as inspired documents even within the lifetime of the authors. See 2 Peter 3:15–16 and 1 Timothy 5:18.

50. John F. Walvoord, *Daniel: The Key to Prophetic Revelation* (Chicago: Moody, 1971), 21.

51. John C. Whitcomb, *Daniel,* a volume of *Everyman's Bible Commentary* (Chicago: Moody, 1985), 11.

52. Anderson, *Coming Prince,* 119–29.

53. The only other time a person is named *Daniel* other than the character from the Book of Daniel is the second son of David born in Hebron (see 1 Chr. 3:1).

54. See also John Wenham, "Christ's View of Scripture" in *Inerrancy,* ed. Norman Geisler (Grand Rapids: Zondervan, 1980), 3–36.

55. This chapter did not explore this possibility for the Book of Daniel, but the same self-attestation found in the other Major Prophets also exists in Daniel.

Chapter Fourteen

1. Merrill F. Unger, *Introductory Guide to the Old Testament.* (Grand Rapids: Zondervan, 1981), 333.

2. A. Cohen, ed., *The Twelve Prophets.* (London: Soncino, 1970), 1–2.

3. Ibid., 4.

4. Ibid., 59.

5. Ibid., 82.

6. Unger, *Introductory Guide,* 345–46

7. Cohen, *Twelve Prophets,* 137.

8. Unger, *Introductory Guide,* 347.

9. Cited by Merrill F. Unger, *Introductory Guide,* 349.

10. Cohen, *Twelve Prophets,* 192.

11. Unger, *Introductory Guide,* 353

12. Ibid., 354.

13. Cohen, *Twelve Prophets,* 254

14. Ibid., 268.

15. Ibid.

16. Merrill F. Unger, *Zechariah* (Grand Rapids: Zondervan, 1963), 14.

17. David Baron, *Commentary on Zechariah* (Grand Rapids: Kregel, 1988), 17.

18. Unger, *Introductory Guide*, 360.

19. Cohen, *Twelve Prophets,* 336.

20. Gleason L. Archer, *A Survey of Old Testament Introduction* (Chicago: Moody, 1994), 24, 31.

Chapter Fifteen

1. Robert L. Thomas and F. David Farnell, *The Jesus Crisis* (Grand Rapids: Kregel, 1998), 198–232.

2. Ibid., 187.

3. Ibid.

4. Ibid., 190.

5. Ibid.

6. Ibid., 194–195.

7. Ibid., 216.

8. Ibid., 217.

9. Everett F. Harrison, *Introduction to the New Testament* (Grand Rapids: Eerdmans, 1974).

10. Ibid., 153.

11. Ibid., 158.

12. Ibid.

13. Ibid., 159.

14. Ibid.

15. Ibid., 168.

16. Henry Clarence Thiessen, *Introduction to the New Testament* (Grand Rapids: Eerdmans, 1958), 134.

17. Ibid., 135.

18. Charles John Ellicott, "Matthew" in vol. 6 of *Ellicott's Commentary on the Whole Bible*, 8 vols. (Grand Rapids: Zondervan, 1959), 8.

19. Ibid.

20. Ed Glasscock, *Matthew* (Chicago: Moody, 1997), 59.

21. Eusebius' Ecclesiastical History 3.39.15.

22. F.F. Bruce, *The Canon of Scripture* (Downers Grove, Ill.: InterVarsity, 1988), 125.

23. Walter W. Wessel, "Mark" in *The Expositor's Bible Commentary, Volume 8: Matthew, Mark, & Luke*, ed. Frank E. Gaebelein, (Grand Rapids: Zondervan, 1984), 607.

24. Harrison, *Introduction to the New Testament*, 196.

25. Cited by F. F. Bruce, *The Canon of Scripture* (Downers Grove, Ill.: InterVarsity, 1988), 159.

26. Cited by C. Marvin Pate, *Luke* (Chicago: Moody, 1995), 25–26.

27. D.A. Carson, *The Gospel According to John* (Grand Rapids: Eerdmans, 1991), 26.

28. Eusebius, *Against Heresies,* iii.12.

29. Eusebius, *Against Heresies,* vi.14.

30. Carson, *Gospel According to John,* 28

Chapter Sixteen

1. Mal Couch, *A Bible Handbook to the Acts of the Apostles* (Grand Rapids: Kregel, 1999), 103.

2. John Gill, *Gill's Commentary,* 7 vols. (Grand Rapids: Baker, 1980), 7:875.

3. C. H. Lenski, *The Interpretation of 1 and 2 Epistles of Peter* (Minneapolis: Augsburg, 1966).

4. W. Robertson Nicoll, *The Expositor's Greek Testament,* 5 vols. (Grand Rapids: Eerdmans, 1988), 4:106.

5. F.F. Bruce, *The Canon of Scripture* (Downers Grove, Ill.: InterVarsity, 1988), 282.

Chapter Seventeen

1. W. Robertson Nicoll, *The Expositor's Greek Testament*, 5 vols. (Grand Rapids: Eerdmans, 1988), 4:230.

2. Ibid., 4:221.

3. Eusebius, *Against Heresies,* vi.25.

4. Ibid.

5. Charles John Ellicott, *Commentary on the Whole Bible* (Grand Rapids: Zondervan, 1959), 4:278.

6. Henry Clarence Thiessen, *Introduction to the New Testament* (Grand Rapids: Eerdmans, 1958), 301.

Chapter Eighteen

1. Henry Clarence Thiessen, *Introduction to the New Testament* (Grand Rapids: Eerdmans, 1958), 274–275.

2. Ibid., 273.

3. Ibid., 277.

4. A. J. Mason, "The First Epistle of St. Peter" in vol. 8 of *A Commentary on the Whole Bible, 8 vols.,* ed. Charles John Ellicott (Grand Rapids: Zondervan, 1959) 387.

5. Everett F. Harrison, *Introduction to the New Testament* (Grand Rapids: Eerdmans, 1974), 412.

6. F. F. Bruce, *The Canon of Scripture* (Downers Grove, Ill.: InterVarsity, 1988), 259.

7. Thiessen, *Introduction to the New Testament*, 312.

8. Simon J. Kistemaker, *James and 1–3 John* (Grand Rapids: Baker, 1986), 329.

9. Thiessen, *Introduction to the New Testament,* 292.

10. Mal Couch, ed., *An Introduction to Classical Evangelical Hermeneutics* (Grand Rapids: Kregel, 2000), 17.

Chapter Nineteen

1. John F. Walvoord, *The Revelation of Jesus Christ* (Chicago: Moody, 1966), 14–15.

2. Quoted by Walvoord, 15.

3. Clarence Larkin, *The Book of Revelation* (Glenside, Pa.: Clarence Larkin Estate, 1919), 2.

4. Paul N. Benware, *Understanding End Times Prophecy* (Chicago: Moody, 1995), 246.

5. Philip Schaff, *A History of the Christian Church* (Grand Rapids: Eerdmans, 1990), 1:834.

6. Walvoord, *Revelation of Jesus Christ,* 14.

7. A. T. Robertson, *Word Pictures in the New Testament* (Nashville: Broadman, 1933), 6:72–73.

8. Schaff, *A History of the Christian Church*, 2:617–18.

9. Robert L. Thomas, *Revelation 8–22: An Exegetical Commentary* (Chicago: Moody, 1992), 517–18.

10. Tim LaHaye, foreword to *Revelation: Illustrated and Made Plain* (Grand Rapids: Zondervan, 1980).

11. Harold Lindsell, *The Battle for the Bible* (Grand Rapids: Zondervan, 1976), 70.

Appendix

1. Charles C. Ryrie, *So Great Salvation* (Chicago: Moody, 1997), 127.

2. Mal Couch, ed., *The Fundamentals for the Twenty-First Century* (Grand Rapids: Kregel, 2000), 428–29.

3. Thomas R. Edgar, *Satisfied by the Promise of the Spirit* (Grand Rapids: Kregel, 1996), 11.

4. Ibid., 12.

Subject Index

Scripture Index

Mal Couch is founder and president of Tyndale Theological Seminary and Biblical Institute in Fort Worth, Texas. A former news reporter, Dr. Couch has produced over 40 Christian films and documentaries. He has also served as a pastor for 20 years, and has taught Theology and the Biblical Languages for 14 years, including full and/or part time positions at Philadelphia College of the Bible, Moody Bible Institute, and Dallas Theological Seminary. His other publications include The Hope of Christ's Return: A Premillennial Commentary on 1 and 2 Thessalonians, A Bible Handbook to Revelation, and Dictionary of Premillennial Theology. He is also one of the general editors of AMG's Twenty-First Century Biblical Commentary Series.